Ethics Seen Through the Lens
of the
Black American Experience:
How Does It Look?

Sharon T. Freeman, Ph.D.
and
Lisa McClennon, CCEP (Certified Ethics & Compliance Professional)

AASBEA Publishers
Washington, DC
2021

Ethics As Seen Through the Lens of the Black American Experience:
How Does It Look?

Web addresses appearing in this book reflect existing links as of the date of first publication. No endorsement of, or affiliation with, any third-party website should be inferred

For information about special discounts for bulk purchases, please contact:

info@theethicsmovement.org
Website: **www.theethicsmovement.org**

Subjects: Ethics—Compliance—Accountability—Racial Equality—Racial Injustice—Race Relations—Systemic Racism—African American History—Discrimination in Housing, Environment Business, Algorithmic Bias, Privacy—Policing—African American/Black Women/Women of Color

ISBN 978-0-9816885-9-6

Ordering Information:

Direct from Publisher via *PayPal* @ www.theethicsmovement.org/publications/

@ **Amazon** a (search book title name)

AASBEA Publishers
www.AASBEA.MEDIA
1629 K Street, NW, Suite 300
Washington, DC 20006

Cover design and Graphic layout by Gene Hansen

CONTENTS

Community Foreword

The authors, Lisa and Sharon, have created a masterpiece of modern literature in "Ethics Seen Through the Lens of the Black American Experience: How does it Look?" A must read for everyone interested in the fabric of American life, not just through Black eyes, but for all of us that believe in "We the People, In Order to Form a More Perfect Union". The book delivers a powerful, historical perspective that contrasts the *why* of the past, *what* of the present, and the *where* in the future we are going in the eight critical constructs discussed in this book. It brought back memories of my childhood, professional law enforcement career, parenting, and as an educator living the black experience; in many regards privileged, but then again not. Reading this book juxtaposed both critical thinking and emotional awareness like few books do.

While attending the Josephson Institute of Ethics many years ago, I recall ethic's guru Michael Josephson saying that you don't have to be sick to get better. The social experience for Black America may not be completely sick but is clearly broken by real and perceived systemic racial bias. This book was like reading a wonderful blend of conscientiousness that reminded me of the passion of civil rights icon John Lewis, the deliberate constitutional scholarship of former President Barack Obama, and the poetry of former activist/artist Gil Scott Heron, all wrapped in one powerful message. It is nothing short of jazz for the soul!

Philip Newsome, *Professor*
Bowie State University

What is the contribution of ethics to the Black experience in the United States? 250 years of slavery, 90 years of Jim Crow, 60 years of separate but equal as well as the continuing oppression of racist criminal justice, among other burdens, justifies that question. Having endured so much for so long of the antithesis of ethics from official authorities, Black people cannot be blamed for doubting their inclusion in the benefits of government "of the people, by the people, for the people" that Lincoln described.

Yet ethics can be seen to be key to the Black experience in the United States. No group has had to strive harder in the face of pernicious resistance to drive the U.S. to be the "more perfect union" established as the objective of the country in the preamble to the Constitution. Ethics, ethical principles, and ethical justice have been at the core of the case for change that Black people have been making wherever, and however, we could be heard, for generations. Freedom, equality, and justice are ethical values that have not yet been sufficiently realized in the

United States. Black people are still unable to cash, as Martin Luther King Jr. stated, "a check that will give us upon demand the riches of freedom and the security of justice". This book is a welcome exploration of the challenges presented to Black people by unethical policies and practices as well as ways in which ethics can continue to be used as tools for change.

Jay L. Knott
Executive Vice President,
Chief Administrative Officer,
Environmental Defense Fund (EDF)

As a former federal senior executive; a product of a military family; a Christian; and a witness to the Civil Rights movement up close and personal as a little Black girl in Montgomery, Alabama in the 1960s, a discussion on "ethics" in our country, at this time in our nation's history continues to amaze me. I ask myself and others in every walk on my journey through this life, what is so difficult to understand about a concept that simply requires us to do the "right thing?" We all know the difference between right and wrong—and it does not change depending on circumstances. We are forced to understand and to examine why it is so difficult to govern ourselves by this simple notion of doing the "right thing."

The notion and act of doing the "right thing" (ethics), in every culture, language and place on the planet remains constant and must be intentionally and aggressively applied – that is our challenge. We do not need studies to understand or to attempt to intellectualize the reasons why we, as a nation, have failed to do the "right thing" in providing education, health care, fair housing, environmental safety, policing and justice in an ethical manner. As a starting point, many of us recognize that every attempt that we make to address ethics will fail if we do not stop and acknowledge that we are not doing the "right thing" in these important and life-sustaining areas. With the acknowledgement by those in power that there exists blatant unfairness and corruption in every aspect of our lives, caused by the obvious misrepresentation and misinterpretation by those in power of what "the right thing" is, we will continue to fail. The only alternative is to accelerate a shift to a rapid change by the people in power to own and accept responsibility for unethical treatment and immediately employ corrective action. We must all believe this and accept our own responsibility to do the right thing while demanding that others do the "right thing." There is hope.

Connie Matthews Harshaw
President of the Let Freedom Ring Foundation in Williamsburg,
Virginia—charged with protecting and preserving the artifacts
of the Historic First Baptist Church organized in 1776.

The last few years have seen a number of our pre-existing norms fall in this country, and not least in the area of ethics. It seems as if the same time-honored concepts simply don't apply to everyone equally; in fact, it seems that there are no consequences for those who choose to simply ignore the rules. What is clear is that there needs to be a complete rebuilding of the government ethics structure from the ground up, including how to strengthen accountability. At the same time, we have a tremendous opportunity to assure that all voices are heard in this effort. As a host of institutions are grappling with addressing racial injustice, what better time to rethink ethics, not as a lofty academic exercise, but in the nuts-and-bolts application of standard rules applicable to all and inclusive of all life experiences. "Ethics As Seen Through the Lens of the Black American Experience: How Does it Look" calls us to inclusion and action as we reimagine, rethink, and rebuild.

Jim Peters
Former 30-year government ethics expert

There has never been a better or more appropriate time than 2020 to discuss the topic of ethics as seen through the lens of black America. Our nation saw the death of George Floyd as a spark point to highlight the frustrations, injustices, brutality and bias experienced by disenfranchised communities at the hands of the police and the government for centuries. Ethics is needed to ensure constitutional rights, procedural justice, and equality is applied to all Americans. Ethics is defined as the moral principles that govern a person's behavior. It is vital to examine the moral principles society and government uses through police enforcement and actions and laws to fairly and judiciously apply constitutional rights.

I personally know Lisa McClennon. She is a woman of principal, integrity, and faith. As a role model for determination, professionalism, intelligence, both emotional and educational, and living in the law enforcement world, her voice needs to be heard on this topic. She lives her truth and speaks up for what she believes and knows is right. I have always believed the best way to overcome cultural bias, distrust or fear is to break bread and meet people where they are. I see this book as your opportunity to have a seat at the table and hear from a voice of experience and wisdom to learn, grow and recognize the chance to understand and be a part of the change and healing our nation desperately needs.

Bernadette Dipino
Chief of Police
Sarasota Police Department
Sarasota, Florida

The conversation around ethics, and particularly through the lens of the Black American experience is important, relevant, and long overdue because there is a continued struggle between the cost of housing and affordable housing. Most people believe that every person, every child, and every family should have the right to decent housing. In fact, in its Congressional Declaration of National Housing Policy, Congress offered as a goal "a decent home and suitable living environment for every American family." Yet neither the actions nor policies of the federal government or local governments have addressed the disparity in the allocation of resources or the neglect that has overwhelmed housing in the Black community. There are many paths beyond a safe space that must be addressed with housing including health and wealth building. Nonetheless, the black community has struggled to appreciate those paths because the energy required to obtain a safe space is so consuming.

The number of Black people forced to live in low-income deplorable housing is offensive. Our children are growing up victims to environmental injustice before they can talk and walk. Their housing is not only unfit in structure but also in location. No housing development is built anywhere without planning. No housing development is neglected without intention. Whether through planning or intentionality, we must look at our decisions and our policies through the lens that questions the ethics and morality guiding the process.

> **LaRuby Z. May**, *Managing Partner*
> *MayLightfoot, PLLC*
> *Former City Council Member – District of Columbia Ward 8;*
> *Certified General Contractor;*
> *Developer, Roundtree Residences – affordable housing*
> *community*

The subject of ethics is important because it speaks to the standards by which society, in a personal or professional setting, governs interactions with each other. It is a moral measurement of what behaviors are acceptable according to the culture in which they are being applied. Ethics are relevant because they promote fairness, honesty, and integrity in a particular environment. As we prepare to recover as nation, a discussion about ethics is very timely and appropriate in an effort to restore behaviors of common courtesies.

> **Darci Bobo**
> *Former Special Assistant to the National President-National*
> *Organization of Black Law Enforcement Executives (NOBEL)*

Just because it is justified does not make it right! If we are going to make a difference and make the changes necessary to level the playing field so that everyone has the chance to live life and pursue happiness, we must take action now. This book is a call to apply ethics in a way that leads to inclusion, fairness, and equity not only in community service and protection but also in organizational recruitment, hiring, selection, training, promotion, and discipline. Applied ethics allows us to find justice and equality, improve community relations, increase diverse representation, and champion accountability and professionalism our communities so desperately need.

Officer Sean James
Vice President, Ethical Society of Police

With a focus, among others, of this book "Ethics Seen Through the Lens of the Black American Experience: How Does It Look? on algorithms and algorithmic biases is both timely and imperative. Emerging technologies do not discriminate by themselves. It is often the lack of diversity in the humans who are designing the models, along with the lack of understanding of how existing systemic inequalities factor into an algorithm's performance that result in the disparate treatment of vulnerable populations in areas like credit worthiness or employability. Dr. Freeman and Lisa McClennon's work suggests that we must expect these technologies to be just and fair, avoiding the temptations to upend the existing civil and human rights of historically-disadvantaged populations, who have already experienced a massive share of discriminatory and predatory practices in our society.

Nicol Turner Lee, Ph.D., *Senior Fellow*
Governance Studies and Director
Center for Technology Innovation, the Brookings Institution

Ethics and banking are inextricably linked. Bankers have always counted on ethics, integrity, and morality. But just as bankers have to trust their customers, and the customers must trust their bankers, all banks operate within an ecosystem of rules and regulations. The broad topic of ethics pertains equally to the fairness of these rules. In discussing ethics and their application to the treatment of Black people, this book will open eyes, and hopefully hearts, among societal stakeholders to forcefully advocate for fair treatment of all in all circumstances.

Doyle Mitchell
President & CEO, Industrial Bank

Possibly the greatest long-term challenge facing the American way of life is how to manage the existential threat of an evolving capitalist system that has resulted in the loss of a middle class, the lack of opportunity or upward financial mobility for the majority in our country, and the socioeconomic void for our minority communities, all the while, providing an environment for an ever-growing concentration of wealth for a select few. Sadly, this is an issue that was far too evident prior to the COVID-19 devastation but is one that has been ever clearer for all to see in the past 12 months. It is a situation where so many millions of our citizens have needlessly passed away due to a lack of access to adequate healthcare and one in which many more have found themselves dependent on a government lifeline just to keep a roof over their heads and food on their tables. Is this the American Dream? Is the system meant to be a winner-take-all? The ultimate and unavoidable situation we are left facing as a nation is unfortunately moving towards a set of binary choices – Evolution or Revolution? The time is now for an honest, moral, and ethical discussion about reforms that put people on the same level as profits, lifting society as a whole, while providing a visible path forward for those who have been left behind, oppressed by systemic institutional racism.

James Mecca – *Investor*
Former Wall Street analyst; former hedge fund manager

Having spent my career since 1971 researching and analyzing the state of minority-owned businesses, I've witnessed a lot. Some have been able to make amazing progress against great odds, with those employing 20 or more paid employees becoming the fastest-growing segment of the minority-business community. I have also seen that whereas in the past, most Black college graduates focused on preparing themselves to become teachers and spiritual leaders, today, many are taking a new path preparing themselves to be entrepreneurs to make a difference for themselves and for society as a whole. While much has changed, much remains the same. What persists are steep barriers to accessing financing. Though today such barriers take many new and subtle forms—*from bankers requiring more supporting loan documentation from Black applicants, to loan officers refusing to believe in their legitimacy and potential.* Yet, from the smaller businesses to the largest, all Black-owned firms make meaningful contributions to their communities and to the nation. Barriers lessening their ability to do more are not only unethical; they are counterproductive because in our increasingly competitive and challenging world, all who have the internal fortitude and expertise to establish productive enterprises are persons who should be encouraged and supported. Among such people are many diamonds in the rough, not just in Silicon Valley, but throughout every corner in America. When such diamonds are polished, they shine and light a pathway for others.

Within the topic of ethics seen through the lens of the Black American experience explored in this book, we see the possibility for a greater understanding not only of the problems they face but of the potential that such an understanding can promote to lead us to unharnessing ourselves from the thinking and actions that prevent segments of the population from realizing their full potential. After all, every individual business success story is one thread that is woven into the fabric of what makes America great.

Timothy Bates,
Distinguished Professor, Wayne State University

As the President of the Meridien Management Group (MMG) today, a venture capital firm for minority businesses, and as a warrior for over 40 years fighting to empower Black-owned businesses by providing them with capital from public and private resources, I have firsthand knowledge of the struggles facing Black-owned businesses and I know why they have struggled so hard. From redlining, to today's weblining, Black firms must work twice as hard to earn half as much. It is not right, it's not fair, and it's a result of systemic racism. I have known Dr. Freeman for over forty years and know that she is a master "explainer of things". This book not only succeeds in explaining how systemic racism works; it effectively makes the case for why we must all work to bring it down to bring Black people up. When we rise, and when all people are given a chance to rise through their ingenuity, their rise benefits society as a whole and holds the promise of the continued greatness of our nation.

Stanley Tucker
President & CEO
Meridien Management Group (MMG)

Having counseled franchisors and franchisees over the past two decades, I have seen the franchising model become a great equalizer by placing small, independently owned and operated firms on an equal footing.

Outside of the realm of franchising, many Black businesses need an equalizer and the application of ethics is the starting place. That's why the topic of this book is so timely and important; it will help stakeholders understand the dynamic at play and hopefully lead them to create the circumstances under which Black businesses can thrive.

Kendal H. Tyre,
Partner, Co-leader, Franchising & Distribution,
Nixon Peabody

As providers of healthcare throughout the U.S., our Nigerian Diaspora professionals have firsthand knowledge of the healthcare needs of the African American community. Such needs have been longstanding and it's time to make a deeper ethical commitment to addressing them. Such needs existed before COVID-19, but the pandemic has exacerbated them. This book is important because it will shine a light on the darkness in which healthcare disparities live.

> **Dr. Iheanacho Emeruwa,**
> *Founder and Board Member of the African Nigerian Physicians*
> *Association (ANPA)*
> *President & CEO of the Aspen Medical Group, and President,*
> *African Primary Healthcare Foundation*

HBCUs were founded in ethics and science. They were established in the post-Civil War era by faith leaders, for the purpose of teaching the Bible (later the Qur'an, the Torah and other religious texts), the classics, ethics, and science. Today HBCUs remain a significant communal clarion voice; a voice anchored in the ethical constructs and civility taught in religious texts and other texts, well versed in the arts, sciences, technology, engineering, mathematics, humanities, civility, civic engagement, the interconnectivity of humankind, and the art of resistance to hegemonic constructs. They are also taught the worldviews of supremacists that reinforce dominion over black minds, bodies, spirits, and souls—those of other persons of color, persons who have "nooses" around their necks because of their race, color, ethnicity, nationality, immigration status, tribe, religion, gender, age, disability, marital status, affectional or sexual orientation, gender identity and expression, or veteran status.

It is in part, the HBCU "education plus", that well prepares HBCU students to join and some to lead the Black Lives Matters Movement, and other Twenty-first Century movements. HBCU students and alumni are amplifying the voices of those calling for an end to the deliberate dehumanization of some with the intent of limiting their full human expression, potential and ambitions; leading voices in the movements of today to end the bigotry, misogyny, genocide, poverty, social and economic inequality, injustice, and oppression rooted in discrimination.

> **Lezli Baskerville, Ph.D.**
> *President and CEO National Association for Equal Opportunity*
> *in Higher Education (NAFEO)*

Education is designed to create an equal playing field for all. Unfortunately, COVID-19 continues to magnify the inequities of low income and disenfranchised families in our public schools. Prior to COVID-19, many school districts were purposefully developing strategic plans to target equity for *all* students in their districts. As such, those districts began crucial conversations designed to address racial bias and its long-term impact on black and brown students and students from lower socioeconomic backgrounds head-on. While much has been done, more work is needed to bridge the gaps caused by these inequities post-pandemic. Ethics seen through the Lens of the Black American Experience couldn't be more timely.

Ethics, equity, and equality considerations must be at the forefront in education and in all decisionmaking as we recover from this pandemic. All students have been impacted by this crisis. However, black and brown students and families from lower socioeconomic backgrounds have even more odds to overcome. Reimagining public education post-COVID will continue to demand courageous conversations with all stake holders at the table. Exploring consistency in creating equity and equality between all school districts throughout our country must be mandatory. Otherwise, the playing field will always be uneven and biased. This book does not have all the answers, yet it invites everyone to look within, to use their individual and collective voice/s to be the change agents that our society needs during these turbulent times. Our society is only as strong as our most vulnerable members.

K. Feroleto
Retired School Administrator; School Counselor; Classroom Teacher Special Education, K-12

Preface

This book provides snapshots of how ethics play out or fail to play out in the lives of Black Americans. In "seeing" the picture, the lens is focused on a view from the bottom up because ethical failures tend to land on the bottom in spaces inhabited by Black people. Conversely, looking at ethics from the top down, from academic and philosophical vantage points, one "sees" a completely different sight. It's important to see ethics from both vantage points—*what it is doing* and *what it is supposed to do?* The treatment of Black people in America illustrates the cognitive dissonance.

If you were asked you to answer the question, ethics matters because...? How would you answer it?

As you ponder your answer to the question, consider the information about ethics that has been compiled and curated by the BBC in its "Ethics Guide" (bbc.co.uk/ethics/guide/), which is presented below.

What is Ethics? At its simplest, ethics is a system of moral principles. They affect how people make decisions and lead their lives. It is concerned with what is good for individuals and society and is also described as moral philosophy. The term is derived from the Greek word ethos which can mean custom, habit, character, or disposition.

Ethics covers the following dilemmas:

- ✔ How to live a good life?
- ✔ Our rights and responsibilities.
- ✔ The language of right and wrong.
- ✔ Moral decisions – what is good and bad?

Concepts of ethics have been derived from religions, philosophies, and cultures. They infuse debates on topics like abortion, human rights, and professional conduct.

Approaches to Ethics: Today, philosophers tend to divide ethical theories into three areas: metaethics, normative ethics, and applied ethics.

- ✔ **Meta-ethics** deals with the nature of moral judgement. It looks at the origins and meaning of ethical principles.

- ✔ **Normative ethics** is concerned with the content of moral judgements and the criteria for what is right or wrong.

- ✔ **Applied ethics** looks at controversial topics like war, animal rights, and capital punishment.

What Use Is Ethics? If ethical theories are to be useful in practice, they need to affect the way human beings behave. Some philosophers think that ethics does do this. They argue that if a person realizes that it would be morally good to do something then it would be irrational for that person not to do it.

But human beings often behave irrationally - they follow their "gut instinct" even when their head suggests a different course of action. However, ethics does provide good tools for thinking about moral issues.

Ethics Can Provide a Moral Map. Many moral issues cause hot debates - think of abortion and euthanasia, for instance. Because these are such emotional issues, we often let our hearts do the arguing while our brains just go with the flow.

But there's another way of tackling these issues, and that's where philosophers can come in - they offer us ethical rules and principles that enable us to take a cooler view of moral problems.

Ethics provides us with a moral map, a framework that we can use to find our way through difficult issues.

Ethics Can Pinpoint a Disagreement. Using the framework of ethics, two people who are arguing a moral issue can often find that what they disagree about is just one part of the issue, but they can broadly agree on everything else.

That can take a lot of heat out of the argument, and sometimes even hint at a way for them to resolve their problem. But sometimes ethics doesn't provide people with the sort of help that they really want.

Indeed, some people think that for many ethical issues there isn't a single right answer - just a set of principles that can be applied to particular cases to give those involved some clear choices.

Some philosophers go further and say that all ethics can do is eliminate confusion and clarify the issues. After that, it is up to each individual to come to their own conclusions.

Ethics Can Give Several Answers. Many people want there to be a single right answer to ethical questions. They find moral ambiguity hard to live with because they genuinely want to do the "right' thing", and even if they can't work out what that right thing is, they like the idea that "somewhere" there is one right answer.

But often there isn't one right answer - there may be several right answers, or just some least worst answers - and the individual must choose between them.

For others, moral ambiguity is difficult because it forces them to take responsibility for their own choices and actions, rather than falling back on convenient rules and customs.

Ethics and People. Ethics is about the "other". At the heart of ethics is a concern about something or someone other than ourselves and our own desires and self-interest. Ethics is concerned with other people's interests, with the interests of society, with God's interests, with "ultimate goods", and so on.

So, when a person "thinks ethically" they are giving at least some thought to something beyond themselves.

Ethics As Source of Group Strength. One problem with ethics is the way it's often used as a weapon.

If a group believes that a particular activity is "wrong" it can then use morality as the justification for attacking those who practice that activity. When people do this, they often see those who they regard as immoral as in some way less human or less deserving of respect than themselves, sometimes with tragic consequences.

Good People As Well As Good Actions. Ethics is not only about the morality of particular courses of action, but it's also about the goodness of individuals and what it means to live a good life.

Virtue Ethics is particularly concerned with the moral character of human beings.

Searching for the Source of Right and Wrong. At times in the past some people thought that ethical problems could be solved in one of two ways:

✔ By discovering what God wanted people to do.

✔ By thinking rigorously about moral principles and problems.

If a person did this properly, they would be led to the right conclusion.

But now, even philosophers arn't sure that it's possible to devise a satisfactory and complete theory of ethics - at least not one that leads to conclusions.

Modern thinkers often teach that ethics leads people not to conclusions but to "decisions".

In this view, the role of ethics is limited to clarifying "what's at stake" in given ethical problems.

Philosophy can help identify the range of ethical methods, conversations and value systems that can be applied to a particular problem. But after these things have been made clear, each person must make their own individual decision as to what to do, and then react appropriately to the consequences.

Are Ethical Statements Objectively True? Do ethical statements provide information about anything other than human opinions and attitudes?

- ✔ Ethical realists think that human beings discover ethical truths that already have an independent existence.
- ✔ Ethical non-realists think that human beings invent ethical truths.

The problem for ethical realists is that people follow many different ethical codes and moral beliefs. So, if there are real ethical truths out there (wherever) then human beings don't seem to be very good at discovering them.

One form of ethical realism teaches that ethical properties exist independently of human beings, and that ethical statements give knowledge about the objective world.

To put it another way; the ethical properties of the world and the things in it exist and remain the same, regardless of what people think or feel – or whether people think or feel about them at all.

Four Ethical 'isms'. When a person says "murder is bad" what are they doing? That's the sort of question that only a philosopher would ask, but it's actually a very useful way of getting a clear idea of what's going on when people talk about moral issues.

The different 'isms' regard the person uttering the statement as doing different things.

We can show some of the different things I might be doing when I say "murder is bad" by rewriting that statement to show what I really mean:

- ✔ "It is wrong to murder": This is moral realism.
- ✔ "I disapprove of murder": This is subjectivism.
- ✔ "Down with murder": This is emotivism.
- ✔ "Don't murder people": This is prescriptivism.

Moral Realism. Moral realism is based on the idea that there are real objective moral facts or truths in the universe. Moral statements provide factual information about those truths.

Subjectivism. Subjectivism teaches that moral judgments are nothing more than statements of a person's feelings or attitudes, and that ethical statements do not contain factual truths about goodness or badness. In more detail: subjectivists say that moral statements are statements about the feelings, attitudes, and emotions than that particular person or group has about a particular issue.

Emotivism. Emotivism is the view that moral claims are no more than expressions of approval or disapproval.

This sounds like subjectivism, but in emotivism a moral statement doesn't provide information about the speaker's feelings about the topic but expresses those feelings. Some theorists also suggest that in expressing a feeling the person gives an instruction to others about how to act towards the subject matter.

Prescriptivism. Prescriptivists think that ethical statements are instructions or recommendations.

So, if I say something is good, I'm recommending that you to do it, and if I say something is bad, I'm telling you not to do it.

There is almost always a prescriptive element in any real-world ethical statement: any ethical statement can be reworked (with a bit of effort) into a statement with an 'ought' in it. For example: "lying is wrong" can be rewritten as "people ought not to tell lies".

Where Does Ethics Come From? Philosophers have several answers to this question:
- ✔ God and religion.
- ✔ Human conscience and intuition.
- ✔ A rational moral cost-benefit analysis of actions and their effects.
- ✔ The example of good human beings.
- ✔ A desire for the best for people in each unique situation.
- ✔ Political power.

God-based Ethics – Supernaturalism. This point of view makes ethics inseparable from religion. It teaches that the only source of moral rules is God.

So, something is good because God says it is, and the way to lead a good life is to do what God wants.

Intuitionism. Intuitionists think that good and bad are real objective properties that can't be broken down into component parts. Something is good because it's good; its goodness doesn't need justifying or proving.

Intuitionists think that goodness or badness can be detected by adults - they say that human beings have an intuitive moral sense that enables them to detect real moral truths.

They think that basic moral truths of what is good and bad are self-evident to a person who directs their mind towards moral issues.

So good things are the things that a sensible person realizes are good if they spend some time pondering the subject.

Don't get confused. For the intuitionist:

✔ Moral truths are not discovered by rational argument.
✔ Moral truths are not discovered by having a hunch.
✔ Moral truths are not discovered by having a feeling.

It's more a sort of moral 'aha' moment – a realization of the truth.

Consequentialism. This is the ethical theory that most non-religious people think they use every day. It bases morality on the consequences of human actions and not on the actions themselves.

✔ Consequentialism teaches that people should do whatever produces the greatest number of good consequences.

✔ One famous way of putting this is "the greatest good for the greatest number of people".

The most common forms of consequentialism are the various versions of utilitarianism, which favors actions that produce the greatest amount of happiness.

Despite its obvious common-sense appeal, consequentialism turns out to be a complicated theory, and doesn't provide a complete solution to all ethical problems.

Two problems with consequentialism are:

✔ It can lead to the conclusion that some quite dreadful acts are good.
✔ Predicting and evaluating the consequences of actions is often very difficult.

Non-consequentialism or Deontological Ethics. Non-consequentialism is concerned with the actions themselves and not with the consequences.

It's the theory that people are using when they refer to "the principle of the thing".

It teaches that some acts are right or wrong in themselves, whatever the consequences, and people should act accordingly.

Virtue Ethics. Virtue ethics looks at virtue or moral character, rather than at ethical duties and rules, or the consequences of actions – indeed some philosophers of this school deny that there can be such things as universal ethical rules.

Virtue ethics is particularly concerned with the way individuals live their lives, and is less concerned with assessing particular actions.

It develops the idea of good actions by looking at the way virtuous people express their inner goodness in the things that they do.

Simply put, virtue ethics teaches that an action is right if and only if it is an action that a virtuous person would do in the same circumstances, and that a virtuous person is someone who has a particularly good character.

Situation Ethics. Situation ethics rejects prescriptive rules and argues that individual ethical decisions should be made according to the unique situation.

Rather than following rules the decision maker should follow a desire to seek the best for the people involved. There are no moral rules or rights - each case is unique and deserves a unique solution.

Ethics and Ideology. Some philosophers teach that ethics is the codification of political ideology, and that the function of ethics is to state, enforce, and preserve particular political beliefs.

They usually go on to say that ethics is used by the dominant political elite as a tool to control everyone else.

More cynical writers suggest that power elites enforce an ethical code on other people that helps them control those people, but do not apply this code to their own behavior.

Are There Universal Moral Rules? One of the big questions in moral philosophy is whether or not there are unchanging moral rules that apply in all cultures and at all times.

Moral Absolutism. Some people think there are such universal rules that apply to everyone. This sort of thinking is called moral absolutism.

Moral absolutism argues that there are some moral rules that are always true, that these rules can be discovered and that these rules apply to everyone.

- ✔ Immoral acts - acts that break these moral rules - are wrong in themselves, regardless of the circumstances or the consequences of those acts.

- ✔ Absolutism takes a universal view of humanity - there is one set of rules for everyone - which enables the drafting of universal rules - such as the Declaration of Human Rights.

- ✔ Religious views of ethics tend to be absolutist.

Why people disagree with moral absolutism:

- ✔ Many of us feel that the consequences of an act or the circumstances surrounding it are relevant to whether that act is good or bad.

- ✔ Absolutism doesn't fit with respect for diversity and tradition.

Moral Relativism. Moral relativists say that if you look at different cultures or different periods in history, you will find that they have different moral rules.

Therefore, it makes sense to say that "good" refers to the things that a particular group of people approve of.

Moral relativists think that is fine and dispute the idea that there are some objective and discoverable "super-rules" that all cultures ought to obey. They believe that relativism respects the diversity of human societies and responds to the different circumstances surrounding human acts.

Why people disagree with moral relativism:

- ✔ Many feel that moral rules have more to them than the general agreement of a group of people - that morality is more than a super-charged form of etiquette.

- ✔ Many think we can be good without conforming to all the rules of society.

- ✔ Moral relativism has a problem with arguing against the majority view: if most people in a society agree with particular rules, that's the end of the matter. Many of the improvements in the world have come about because people opposed the prevailing ethical view - moral relativists are forced to regard such people as behaving "badly".

- ✔ Any choice of social grouping as the foundation of ethics is bound to be arbitrary.

- ✔ Moral relativism doesn't provide any way to deal with moral differences between societies.

Moral Somewhere-in-Between-ism. Most non-philosophers think that both of the above theories have some good points and think that:

- ✔ There are a few absolute ethical rules.

- ✔ A lot of ethical rules depend on the culture.

The foregoing provides food for thought as readers ponder the answer to the questions of why ethics matter and how *Ethics as Seen Through the Lens of the Black American Experience looks?*

When we look closely at ethics as seen through the lens of the Black American experience, we "see" that ethics are not always applied and when they are not, it is not a pretty sight for those for whom they failed.

In a number of instances throughout this book, it has been stated that "ethics are in the eye of the beholder". But no matter whose eyes are seeing the situation of Black people in America, or which philosophical branch of ethics a person subscribes to, there is no question that Black people have often been treated unfairly and in an unethical manner.

Each chapter of the book illuminates on how systemic racism works and why it is unethical. When we "see" the consequences of systemic racism, we cannot be "unsee" them and the real question becomes: what are we willing to do about it individually and collectively? Who are we, what do we stand for, and what kind of America do we want to reflect us?

About Sharon T. Freeman, Ph.D.

I grew up in Philadelphia as a child of African American parents who had come up from the South–from Atlanta, Georgia–during the migration. They arrived in Philadelphia with their morals, values, and beliefs intact. They were informed by how they lived in the South, where things were structured for Black people in their cordoned-off communities and through the interactions they had with White people. Back then, and there, they better not have put a foot wrong. Their lives were punctuated with "yes, ma'am," "no sir," and "may I, please?"

This is the order they knew and the one that they applied to their new life in Philadelphia. This time, however, they were applying it mostly to their treatment of each other in the Black communities they moved in to. Though they continued to live in a segregated world in the North, it was a world in which they had far more control. They were able to succeed because they followed the rules of how to treat each other, as did many other Black people who had "made it" and thrived there as entrepreneurs. In this world, once again, they didn't have the luxury of putting a foot wrong, because if they did, that was it. They would have nowhere else to go. It was a world that demanded fair treatment, honesty, respect, and holding up one's end of the bargain.

The golden rule was, "do unto others as you would have them do unto you." If someone gave you something or did you a favor, you tried to return it more plentifully through whatever means possible, whether that be in money or deeds. People looked out for each other and mostly tried to do the right thing. When my parents went to their Methodist church every Sunday, with us four girls in tow, they did so to genuinely learn more about how to do the right thing and how to live honorably. While in church, we sang the words of the song "His Eye Is on the Sparrow," and we each knew in our hearts, as the song went, that "He was watching over me."

Ethics, to Black people who had similarly migrated from the South, were no joke; ethics were tools for living. Those people, like my parents, took a big chance on migrating to a new place when they had little money, no backup, and no connections. What they did have was a dream and a set of moral principles that assured them that they knew how to act and operate to realize their dream of a better life. The key was to be a good person and to gain a reputation based on that. This meant being a good neighbor, a decent business partner, and a trustworthy person. Through the consistent application of such ethical principles, they soon became the people who were referred to as "ma'am" and "sir" and to whom people asked, "may I please?"

I witnessed what it meant to have ethics hardwired into one's soul and behavior; I learned how a moral compass is set and where it leads people for whom it was set to "true north". Conversely, I also saw what happens to those who never developed such a compass.

When I took up the position as a Chief Ethics and Compliance Officer, I already knew what "doing the right thing" looked like; it was familiar to me. As a compliance professional, one strives to ensure that pertinent rules and regulations are applied by all who work in an organization. But what becomes apparent is that if ethics are not hardwired into the people who are responsible for taking actions, such rules and regulations become like a finger in a dam trying to hold the water back.

Within the field of ethics and compliance, one sees many things, as I did, as I built and led a compliance department for a large company over many years. I saw how people of all races, ethnicities, and cultures viewed the matter of ethics and compliance. In short, they had different views about it that were informed by their respective backgrounds, just as my moral compass was set by my background. Because ethics are often "in the eye of the beholder," the key is to understand what people are seeing and why. This has never been more important than it is today when all that we do and that we consume often involves chains of people who are not like us. The question is, what can be done to "hardwire" in a moral compass into people that leads everyone in the same direction of true north?

My professional journey has involved working in 120 countries, and wherever I have been, the journey started from the inside out. I am the common denominator in all of it. While I learned from each academic and professional experience, the moral compass I brought along with me allowed me to positively influence those situations as much as they influenced me.

My professional journey has been long, sometimes arduous, and exhilarating. I prepared myself by earning an undergraduate degree in Cognitive Psychology and History from Carnegie Mellon University, followed by a Master of Science in Public Policy and

Management. Finally, I earned a Ph.D. in Applied Management and Decision Sciences from Walden University in 1998.

I started my professional career working at the U.S. General Accounting Office, where I learned how the government worked. Then I worked for Booz Allen Hamilton, where I learned how to help the government work better. Next, I joined the U.S. Government, where I was engaged in helping it be more efficient. Then, I got my wings and relocated to Hong Kong, where I lived for 12 years, having first served in the diplomatic service as the Hong Kong-based Regional Director for Asia of the then Trade Development Program (now the Trade Development Agency). Finally, my career changed direction: I became a trailblazing entrepreneur when I established my first company in Hong Kong. As a serial entrepreneur, I have founded a number of additional companies in the U.S., which today include Gems of Wisdom Consulting (*www.gemsofwisdomconsulting.com*) and the newly established, non-profit, Gemini Ethics Movement (GEM) Foundation (*www.geminiethicsmovement.org*).

As I have learned and experienced things, I have shared my acquired "gems of wisdom" through the 30 books I have written and published to date. Most of them can be found on my website at *www.gemsofwisdomconsulting.com/books*.

Through it all, an important lesson I have learned is that no endeavor can succeed without adhering to ethical principles, and such principles must be embedded in the people, not just on paper.

About Lisa McClennon

Through the sacrifices and support of those around me, I have lived a fulfilled life. I am in a life-long relationship, I have a child and a dog, I am embedded in a supportive community, and have had experiences that exceed the bounds of my imagination. I know I am the beneficiary of the blood, sweat, and tears of those who came before me, who shone a light so bright that I would not have to struggle so hard to see.

Career-wise, I took advantage of any open door that lit a path to a better future, and I gave it my all. I was fortunate enough to join agencies as they were building new programs or starting new initiatives. This gave me training and educational opportunities that most people do not get. Those opportunities, coupled with personal ingenuity, and life-long learning, has ultimately positioned me to become the "wisdom merchant" that I am today.

I am a Certified Fraud Examiner through the Association of Certified Fraud Examiners, Certified Corporate Compliance and Ethics Professional through the Society for Corporate Compliance and Ethics, and a Certified Leading Professional in Ethics and Compliance through the Ethics and Compliance Institute. I hold a BSc in Criminal Justice, an MSc in Human Relations and Business, and completed postgraduate work in Urban Policy and Administration. I am a graduate of two police academies and spent the equivalent of over one year throughout my 30-year career completing several law enforcement training and advanced instruction programs. I am also a graduate of the American University Key Executive Leadership Program (Experienced Leader) and the Federal Executive Institute's Leadership for a Democratic Society residential program.

I began my career in law enforcement as a Reserve Police Officer in the Texas Hill Country. I later became a full-time Police Officer in Dallas, Texas. Three years into my career, I became a federal agent with the Bureau of Alcohol, Tobacco, Firearms, and Explosives and later with the U.S. Immigration and Naturalization Service (now, the U.S. Immigration and Customs Enforcement) and then the Office of Inspector General, U.S. Department of Housing and Urban Development. The last half of my career was in law enforcement management and leadership in the Office of Inspector General at the U.S. Agency for International Development, where I traveled the world leading international investigative teams.

I am from Oakland, California, and am directly descended from domestic servants and farmhands who escaped the oppression of the Louisiana Bayou and the bonds of the banks of Alabama's Coy River. Later in life, going from the progressive Bay Area to living in a military environment, it was necessary to have a supportive tribe. My tribe taught me that I could do anything I put my mind to, and I believed them!

I tried many different things as a young person and conquered many challenges that others warned me not to take on in the first place. Though my paternal great-grandmother did not go to school, my paternal grandmother had a second-grade education, and my father had an eighth-grade education, I knew I could go further. Despite my family's limited resources, they did their best to grease as many skids for me as they could. Through trial and error, I learned which steps were the most slippery, but sometimes I still tripped and fell hard. When I was down, I wasn't out because someone always reached their hand into the ditch I was in to help pull me out. This inspired me to always have hope in humanity.

Holding onto the confidence of ancestral kings and queens that my relatives instilled in me, I have stepped forward to honor their legacy and to pave a path for my children's children. My internal drive to do well made me a potent technician early on. As I grew in my trade, I also developed a cool sense of reason. While the arrogance of my youth made me think I could boil oceans, the humility of maturity gave way to my approach to calming the seas.

Early in my career, I set out to change the world through policing. Clearly, it did not work out that way as life is not linear. As one job led to another, I eventually landed in a place that allowed me to travel the world and truly see what it is about. In those travels, I relearned that those with the least are the ones who gave me the most. In many instances, it was the bartenders, chambermaids, and drivers who taught me to navigate and "read" the landscape in foreign countries, while the policy makers made policies even though they didn't always understand the terrain of the world that existed beneath them.

Although I set out to change the world, the world changed me. The experiences I had on my journey gave me the chance to lead others and make little impacts here and there that will hopefully make a world of positive difference for someone else one day.

Introducing The Gemini Ethics Movement (GEM) Foundation

Who We Are: The Gemini Ethics Movement (**GEM**) Foundation was established as a 501 (c) (3) non profit in Washington, DC in October 2020 by ethics, compliance, and development professionals, Sharon T. Freeman, Ph.D., Lisa McClennon, CCEP, and Lonna Milburn, Ph.D., to shine a light on the ethical dilemmas, failures, and opportunities that respectively disempower or empower marginalized groups in America and to encourage stakeholders to "*do the right thing*" to ensure fair, just, and equal treatment for all in society.

Our Mission: The GEM Foundation will use a "magnifier glass" as a lens through which to see the ethical dilemmas, failures, and opportunities that exist in policies, regulations, systems, machine learning, and in the behavior of people across many domains in the society. Our GEM lens focuses on ethics as they apply to the treatment of people of color, women, and youth, and in respect to institutional practices that disempower or empower our target constituency. The aim is to encourage the minimization of the former and the maximization of the latter.

Our Work: Entails:
- Advocacy, education, and training
- Amplification
- Mobilization, engagement, and promotion
- Research, synthesizing, translating, and disseminating
- Publishing

Our first product, this book, *Ethics As Seen Through the Lens of the Black American Experience: How Does It Look?*, is a demonstration of the depth of our research, synthesis, explanation, and dissemination of information aimed to advocate, educate, and engage stakeholders in staking a claim to lead with ethics.

Contact:

Websites: www.geminiethicsmovementfoundation.org
www.theethicsmovement.org

President, Sharon T. Freeman, Ph.D.   Vice President, Lisa McClennon
Email: Sharon@theethicsmovement.org   **Email:** Lisa@theethicsmovement.org

1629 K Street, NW, Suite 300
Washington, DC 20006

Introduction

Laws, policies, regulations, and money alone do not lead societies to greatness; the heart does. Ethics is the heart that beats the drum for the loftiest goals of mankind—goals and aspirations that strive for equality, justice, fairness, and equal treatment. If the heart is not beating correctly, the whole system fails whether in human beings or in institutions.

Every massive failure in American society has been a failure of the heart, of ethics—from the civil war to today's injustices that are disproportionately experienced by those who lack the power to prevent such injustices from happening to them.

Understanding *how* such injustices happen is one thing; it entails studying the laws, policies, regulations, and institutions that are the pathways through which it happens. But the study of *why* it happens is the study of ethics—of their dilemmas, failures, and opportunities to "do the right thing."

This book focuses on ethics seen through the lens of the Black American experience to understand both the *how* and the *why* – *how* systemic racism works, *what* are its tools, mechanisms, and pathways, and *why* ethics haven't always been applied to the treatment of Black people?

It's latter part, "the *why*", of it all that is the most difficult to understand because it involves matters of the heart, and the heart is where love lives—from the biggest notion of love, for instance, the love of one's fellow man, to smaller individual notions of it that can be applied to defining one's feelings about a person, or even about a cat or a dog. The further one moves away from "my" in being able to articulate love and the closer the notion of love gets to having to define it in terms of "our", the picture becomes increasingly blurry. It is in this haze that Black people are seen or not seen. Seeing them requires an answer to the ethical question, the question of the heart, about why Black people, or any people, matter? The answer is that people only matter when they are not "othered" but rather are seen as "us."

The subject of ethics had been gaining traction steadily and incrementally prior to the pandemic, primarily in the business sector. As experts on ethics and compliance, we, the authors, were called on to imagine how to structure ethics and compliance departments for large companies. By March 2020, as the pandemic grew, we decided to use the time it afforded to write about ethics. Our original intention was to write about ethics for an audience of corporate leaders and government contractors and professionals, but in the process, we made a discovery. As we searched to identify cases to demonstrate ethical dilemmas and failures, we found that if you really want to know what the ethical issues are in a situation, go down to the lowest level of what went wrong and then work your way back up. At the top, you will find edicts, pronouncements, laws, regulations, and guidance, but at the bottom, where the thing actually landed, you will discover what really happened, who it happened to, and why "they" were the ones it happened to.

Little by little, the story of ethics was telling us and not the other way around. Once we changed our direction of how to "see" ethics, switching our orientation from high on the mountain to the valley floor, where ethical problems land, we finally understood that one thing that often goes wrong is the treatment of Black people. It goes wrong because it can.

Ethics, as a philosophy, is a beautiful thing when written about by great philosophers. It is more than beautiful, however, when it is codified in the 14th Amendment to the U.S. Constitution as a promise of citizenship rights and equal protection under the law for all. However, it has been an unkept promise for many Black people.

In the wake of such failures, to borrow a line from a Tennessee Williams' play, *A Streetcar Named Desire,* "[Black people] have always had to rely on the kindness of strangers," in addition to relying on their personal intestinal fortitude.

As we write this, two days after the November 2020 presidential election results were called, we have observed that many are beginning to speak about "finding the soul of America." At the same time, corporations have now declared, through their new purpose statement, that they too have a soul. Well, Black people—who have always had a lot of *soul*—have been lost in the wilderness, and no one was trying to find us.

> *And on that note, I will digress to tell a "funny" personal story. Once, when I was skiing in Mirabelle, France, I was taking lessons with a White man who was a friend of my friend. We were taking beginner lessons together (I already knew how to ski, but I wanted to take a refresher course). The friend followed me down the slopes all day, and at one point, I zoomed past him, and he couldn't find me thereafter. When we met back at the lodge, he said: "You know, it's funny! All of my life, I've been trying not to see Black people, and here I find myself looking for you, a Black woman. Imagine that!"*

I, Sharon Freeman, like so many other Black women, don't have to imagine that. I have lived that all my life—as invisible woman to the many who were not trying to see me.

Ironically, as of the election of President-Elect Biden and Vice President-Elect Kamala Harris, more people are trying to "see" Black people for the first time, when they weren't looking our way previously.

In many ways, we, the authors, also lay a little bit of a claim to being like that man on the ski slope. We weren't really trying to "see" this story through the lens of the Black experience until it became impossible not to see it that way, as all of the breadcrumbs led down that road.

We originally gave this book another title and created a cover image that we tested out with 20 people. No one understood our cover or what the title meant. They consistently inquired about what the book had in store. One after another, they asked: "What is this book about, and who is its audience?" We were then compelled to explain that the book was telling the story of how ethics played out in different areas, as seen through the lens of the Black American experience. They said, "Well then, why don't you call the book that?"

Eureka! We discovered the title of the book. More than discovering the right title, however, we discovered our true purpose in writing this book. It is to raise awareness about the ethical dilemmas and failures that have landed Black people in circumstances, places, and spaces that have caused them to fail because society failed them. Our mission became our desire to shine a light on the many opportunities to make the "right" ethical choices in difficult circumstances.

One thing we have learned in our journey in writing this book is that individuals and the small acts they take to "do the right thing" can make all the difference in the world. We have also learned just how important raising awareness can be. There is perhaps no better story to illustrate this point then the one that recently happened involving a twenty-two year old Black woman, Kennedy Mitchum, and the Merriam-Webster Dictionary definition of "system racism."

On June 10, 2020, a headline *New York Times* article written by Christine Hauser (2020), "Merriam-Webster Revises 'Racism' Entry After Missouri Woman Asks for Changes". The dictionary's editors agreed to revise the definition. In a nutshell, what happened was that the dictionary had three entries to define racism, the first, according to Hauser, defined racism as "a belief that race is the primary determinant of human traits and capacities and that racial differences produce an inherent superiority of a particular race" (para. 2). The second, according to Hauser, "calls it a 'doctrine or political program based on the assumption of racism and designed to execute its principles' and 'a political or social system founded on racism'", and the third section refers to "racial prejudice or discrimination" (para. 3).

Kennedy Mitchum wrote to the editor and explained the following, and here is what happened, according to Hauser (2020):

> Kennedy Mitchum wrote: "Racism is not only prejudice against a certain race due to the color of a person's skin, as it states in your dictionary," she wrote. "It is both prejudice combined with social and institutional power. It is a **system** of advantage based on skin color" (para. 8).
>
> Alex Chambers, an editor at the dictionary wrote: "While our focus will always be on faithfully reflecting the real-world usage of a word, not on promoting any particular viewpoint, we have concluded that omitting any mention of the **systemic aspects of racism** promotes a certain viewpoint in itself," he said. "It also does a disservice to readers of all races" (para. 12).

This story is highlighted to show that one person can make a difference against all odds—by stepping up and stepping in, like David in the biblical story of David and Goliath. This is what ethics is all about; ethics can't just live in someone's heart, it is a verb, it must *do* something. Kennedy Mitchum did something and the editor of the dictionary did something ethical about it; he "did the right thing".

The examples of "system racism" explained throughout this book, align with the new Merriam-Webster definition of its meaning and show, through the lens of the Black American experience, what the **systems and tools of racism** are and how they work, why they are unethical, and why ultimately, they cannot.

We believe that the information provided in the eight chapters of this book will enable all readers to see the situation of Black people in stark relief and that their enhanced awareness will strengthen their resolve and commitment to lead with ethics in their actions—no matter how small the step may seem. Every small step is like throwing a stone in the water, it has a ripple effect.

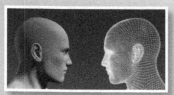

Background About the Eight Chapters in the Book

Eight chapters are included in this book to show how the ecosystems of racism work in each area discussed. While such systems are shown through the lens of the Black experience, the extensive research included in each topic qualifies each chapter to stand as an up-to-the-moment "mini master's class" on the hot issues in each topic area. Leading voices on relevant topics have been corralled, curated, and included in each chapter up to December 2020, rendering a clear and concise snapshot of a moving and dynamic picture.

It is our hope that the information and understanding imparted through this book serves as a clarion call to action by stakeholders, including Black people themselves, to lead with ethics in their actions to make the world a better place. And when we talk about ethics, we are talking about "doing the right thing"—and we know what "the right thing" is because it is enshrined in the 14th Amendment to the U.S. Constitution that promises fairness, protection, and equal justice for all.

At first glance, upon seeing the chapters in the book, the relationship between the topics in the book may not be obvious? For instance, we start out by talking about algorithmic bias; then, we address housing and environmental injustice. What does one have to do with the other? A lot, in fact. When you read one chapter after another, you can't help but come to the same realization that we as authors did—that systemic racism does indeed exist and that all parts of its ecosystems are connected and inextricably linked in perpetuating racism. Even "machines" have now been added to the toolbox of systemic racism.

It may seem counterintuitive to start the book with a chapter on algorithmic bias, but then it becomes clear that what the algorithms are "seeing" through the data that have been fed into them—as they calculate 93 trillion calculations per second—is that Black people are at the bottom of society. Nobody can fool or trick the algorithms. They "see" it as plain as day and faster than anyone can stop them from "seeing" it and from spewing out what they "see." The bias the algorithms reflect is a mirror on the soul of America. The algorithms "see" our income, they know what zip codes we live in, they know our education levels, and they know all knowable data points about us. They then chime in to suggest that we are ineligible, a risk, or that we should be denied things of value.

And why are Black people always at the bottom? It is because systems of racism designed it that way. Ta-Nehisi Coates identified the key numbers that explain the reasons why:

250 years of slavery, **90** years of Jim Crow, **60** years of separate but equal, and **36** years of racist housing policies.

And so, each chapter of this book sheds light on what came next.

Chapter Four, which focuses on the example of the Harlem Children's Zone®, shows what it takes to overcome dire circumstances. It reveals how Black people have endeavored to empower themselves, against all the odds. When Geoffrey Canada, the founder of the Harlem Children's Zone® marched, he didn't just march on the streets; he marched directly into the homes and hearts of people in neighborhoods in Harlem in the 1970s with a new dream and plan of education and community empowerment. He persuaded the people to believe in and adopt it. It worked and is still working! This story is a very important one because it demonstrates that there is always hope and that we all must take action to create the change we seek. It also emphasizes that the work must also be done in Black neighborhoods from the inside out and not just from the outside in.

Today, we have an opportunity to create the change we want to see in our neighborhoods and society. But it starts in our hearts, and our hearts and actions can be joined in unity, as we plant the seeds of hope and nourish them as they grow.

One thing we know for sure: To be ethical is to "do the right thing," as ethical principles implore us to do. In fact, one could say that ethics is the heart and soul of everything. While we in society are currently and collectively engaged in trying to find our souls, this book is intended to shine a light on the way forward. Ethics, after all, does not live in darkness—it thrives in the light and switches on the light in our hearts and souls.

Brief Description of the Book's Eight Chapters

As authors, we view ourselves as archeologists unearthing the facts and truth of matters. Our aim is to shed light, if only in snapshots, on how ethics plays out and fails to play out in eight different areas. We are doing this because we believe that, as Ken Burns expressed, "storytelling is liberating because it frees us from the tyranny of ignorance."

Each of the eight topics in this book is a piece of a gigantic puzzle, just as an archeologist finding one tooth of a dinosaur might be, but it is a starting point. We view the pieces we have found in our search through the lens of the Black experience in order to amplify what ethics means—or doesn't mean—in the lives of Black people. At the end of each chapter, in the "Road to Progress" section, we find hope in the actions stakeholders have taken in the public and private sectors to demonstrate that Black lives really do matter after all.

It is our hope that readers can find new information, the latest information, and nuanced perspectives in each chapter that can serve as a foundation for further conversation, but we are well aware that these are fast-moving, top-of-mind topics we have chosen. We know that by the time this book comes out in January 2021, there will be more information on all the areas discussed. In such case, we hope that readers will take what we have written, build on and discuss it, and make it better in what they write thereafter. For our part, we will do the same and hopefully add updates and other chapters in the future.

A brief glimpse of our approach to telling the story of each chapter is given below.

Chapter One: **Algorithm Bias, Data Privacy, and Ethics**

The first chapter in this book is like starting at the end and then going back to the beginning in the chapters that follow. Algorithms have come into the picture fairly recently, long after many of the ills of society have been experienced by Black people. But the algorithms "see" it all through what they have been trained to see, what they extrapolate from the data, and from the biases their programmers have programmed in. In many ways, algorithms are a mirror on the soul of America as it pertains to the history of Black people in the nation. What algorithms see is not a pretty sight.

Chapter Two: **Unfair Housing, Environmental Injustice, COVID-19, and Ethics**

Our thesis for telling this part of the story is that Racial = Spatial. We invite readers to consider the following: What do housing segregation, environmental injustice, and COVID-19 have in common? The answer is the containment of races to specified spaces (i.e., segregation). The negative impact of forced segregation has led to the ill health of many Black people because they have lacked the power to prevent polluters from invading their neighborhoods. It has also led to the inability of Black people to accumulate wealth over many decades due to redlining (and now in part due to "weblining"). Many of these outcomes have contributed to positioning Black people as the most susceptible to the impact of COVID-19. These factors explain why Black people are at the bottom of society and why the algorithms, "seeing" that many Black people are there, are now exacerbating and amplifying the situation.

Chapter Three: **Policing and Ethics**

Policing is one of the most difficult topics to be addressed today. Many are tackling the burning questions about policing that have been raised, and they are doing so in blogs, books, workshops, zooms calls, corporate boardrooms, and in the halls of Congress. As these conversations continue, it is our hope that by focusing on three aspects of a very complex problem—the militarization of the police, qualified immunity, and "defunding," which we view as meaning "reforming" the police, we can shed a little additional light on the darkness and mystery surrounding these topics.

Chapter Four: Switching the Light On: The Ethical Example of the Harlem Children's Zone® (HCZ®)

In this chapter, we point out that it takes power to fight back. Specifically, it takes utilizing the levers of power—the 3Ps of purse, policies, and persuasion—wisely to bring about desired changes. In helping Harlem fight its way back to a better place after a dark period, the Harlem Children Zone ® (HCZ ®) was envisioned in the 1970s not only to switch the light on but also to "turn off the dark".

To flip the switch, the Harlem Children Zone ® (HCZ ®) started by leveraging one of the most important levers of power: **persuasion**. Geoffrey Canada, HCZ®'s founder, marched right into the homes and neighborhoods in Harlem not with signs and slogans but with tangible programs and strategies for changing the status quo, in the process creating a new pathway for moving out of the darkness and into the light.

Chapter 5: Ethical Environmental, SOCIAL, and Governance (ESG) Investing

The Environmental, Social, and Governance (ESG) movement, though relatively new, is impactful and also hopeful. This chapter focuses on what is referred to as "S-factors"— social factors— including the responsibility of big corporations to help address needs in the community. As the case is made throughout the book, no community is in greater need than the Black community. The ESG movement is moving steadily in the direction of "seeing" and addressing some of these needs.

Chapter 6: Imperiled Black-Owned Businesses, COVID-19, and Ethics

This chapter illuminates why COVID-19 is the end of the line for many of the nation's two million Black-owned firms. Previously, when at the end of their ropes, they would tie a knot and hang on, but in the face of COVID-19, the rope won't hold.

The story of Black-owned businesses makes it clear that being in a capitalist nation without capital is a curse and a vicious cycle: Black company owners can't get bank loans because they never got bank loans. As a result, of the two million Black-owned firms, only 124,000 employ workers. For the others, the owners and their families are the workers. Either way, it's a zero-sum game for society because when their dreams die, they are replaced by nightmares, both for themselves and for society as a whole.

Chapter 7: The Ethics of Empowering and Protecting Women in the Time of COVID-19

COVID-19 has colored everything and has revealed the true colors of what has been happening in American society for a very long time. COVID-19 has also had a disproportionally negative impact on women of color, and especially on Black women. Little fissures everywhere have become craters swallowing up Black women. It has become clear that the most challenging, pre-existing condition for Black women is existing as Black women.

A five-alarm fire is going off in all categories of life for Black women in the time of COVID-19, and kindling is everywhere because of their pre-existing conditions. As with all raging fires, if they are not extinguished, the damage spreads quickly.

Chapter 8: Ethics, Compliance, and Accountability

If it can be asserted that the genius of management rests on how well it articulates and facilitates the interconnections of one function to another and that its merits can only be determined when it interacts with other systems, then wouldn't the same hold true for ethics?

Accordingly, ethics only matters when it applies to something and influences that to which it applies. However, as can be summarized from all that is written in this book, ethics has always been easier said than done. This chapter focuses on how ethics are being done and/or undone in private and public institutions, and on how *doing* ethics creates more opportunity for everyone.

———

In conclusion, there is no conclusion—there is only a journey. At the end of each chapter, we provide glimmers of hope about the road of progress in the long journey ahead.

CHAPTER ONE

Algorithm Bias, Data Privacy, and Ethics

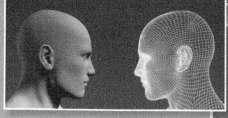

About Chapter One: **Algorithm Bias, Data Privacy, and Ethics**

A s the first chapter in this book, it is like starting at the end then going back to the beginning in the chapters that come next. Algorithms have come into the picture fairly recently, long after many of the ills of society have been experienced by Black people. However, training the algorithms involves the collection and analysis of enormous quantities of historical data that is used to inform decisionmaking and optimization; therefore, any historical biases embedded in the data can be absorbed and reproduced in the algorithm—and that's the problem.

Algorithms are a mirror on the soul of America as it pertains to the history of Black people in the nation. The biases that are embedded in the algorithms are a function of two things: The biases of their programmers and the biases that are deeply embedded within the society.

With the capacity to calculate 93 trillion calculations per second, algorithms can see things that we thought were invisible. They see the underbelly of America when it comes to Black people, which has led them, for instance, to send the results of gorillas photos when the search sought photos of Black people, or to send the results of pornographic photos when the search was seeking photos of Black girls.

These are among the unintended consequences and legacy of systemic racism in America. It's not surprising therefore that many things associated with Black people are negative in the algorithmic world—but how did it get that way? This is where the subsequent chapters are the beginning of the story. Black people have been undervalued because they were not permitted to have things of value, to live in places that were valued, or to build wealth—and as a result, many Black people are poor. Within the context of the algorithmic world, poor is bad; poor means that one is more likely to do bad things and less likely to be eligible for things that are good.

This chapter tells the story of the role that algorithms and a lack of data privacy are now playing as the newest latest tools in the toolkit of systemic racism.

And while more ethical algorithms are encouraged, it is acknowledged that correcting flawed feedback loops is only one step in addressing the larger problem of racism. Technology alone cannot solve difficult social issues; remedying entrenched social biases and defining concepts such as fairness and privacy sit firmly within the human domain including carefully balancing accuracy and fairness within algorithms.

This chapter aims to show the Black experience through the lens of artificial intelligence, while underscoring that the reality of the racism that Blacks experience is everywhere, even in the machines. The only escape from it is to place a greater emphasis on an ethical framework that prioritizes the respect, dignity, and equal opportunity for all and the protection of those in need of protection.

Algorithm Bias, Data Privacy, and Ethics

A lgorithms: they know you, but you do not know them. While we are searching on the Internet, the Internet is searching us; "it" knows us and our search results are curated just for us. If you do not believe it, try a little experiment. Ask three people in different zip codes to perform the same Google search for the same thing using the exact same words. The search results will be different based on each searcher's profile.

Machine Learning (ML) algorithms are designed to capture, analyze, inform, predict, and mimic the rhythms of our lives—those that are random, regular, alternating, flowing, and progressive alike. With every move we make we are building algorithmic computations into our everyday experience and into our profiles that are used to persuade us to take actions that maximize someone else's gains.

D ata privacy: it is a secret even to you, and it is your data (that you do not own). In 2016, Cambridge Analytica said that it possessed at least 5,000 data points on everybody in the U.S.—that was then; imagine how many data points are possessed by various entities on every individual today. Your data, which is a secret to you, are not a secret to the many users  of them to whom it is sold. Yet, the control and usage of data has serious ramifications for personhood and safety.

Most Americans are concerned about algorithmic bias and data privacy, but Black Americans are more concerned about it than others because there is no other group more disproportionately negatively impacted by it.

It turns out that everything that is challenging in American society is exponentially more challenging for Black people because they lack the power to demand that their concerns be addressed in a timely manner. Their concerns are about the impact of COVID-19, the impact of climate change, the impact of a slowing economy, the need for police

reform, the need for more affordable housing, and the need for protection from algorithmic bias and protection of their data. But, historically and presently, the needs of Black people are the last to be considered—literally at the end of the day—when it is no longer possible to ignore the consequential discrimination that they endure.

The end of the day is today. The demands for social justice have sped up time. We now see and can no longer ignore one part of the systemic racism equation, which is algorithmic bias and a lack of data protection that have been added to the toolbox of systemic racism. Previously, the worry was about racist people, racist policies, and institutional frameworks; now, all of that has been transferred to machines as well.

Algorithms do what they are taught. Inadvertently, they are capable of being taught prejudices and unethical biases by patterns hidden in the data, but once they learn them, they exploit them.

Algorithm Bias: How It Works Against Black People

Consider this: compare what human beings see in the photo of former President Obama and what the algorithm "sees." Herein lies the problem.

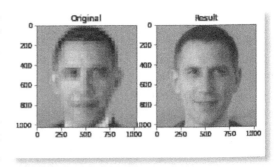

Praharaj's (2020) article, "Bias in AI Algorithms" explained what happened in creating this image and what the dangers are with bias in AI:

> Machine Learning (ML) algorithmic systems are biased when data are biased. The face unsampling makes everyone look White because the network was pretrained on FlickFaceHQ, which mainly contains pictures of White people. Train the 'exact' same system on a dataset from Senegal and everyone will look African (para. 7).

Can algorithms be biased against certain demographic cohorts—especially Black people? Yes, and they can be biased in different ways. For instance, according to Panch et. al. (2019), in their article "Artificial Intelligence and Algorithmic Bias: Implications for Health Systems," in a health context, it can be defined as follows:

Algorithmic bias in the context of Artificial Intelligence (AI) I and health systems is defined as: the instances when the application of an algorithm compounds existing inequities in socioeconomic status, race, ethnic background, religion, gender, disability or sexual orientation to amplify them and adversely impact inequities in health systems (para. 3).

However, bias against Black people does not only exist in the context of health—it exists in multiple realms, and when it does exist, it is compounding and/or amplifying existing inequities. A few examples show how bias happens and underscore that closer attention should be paid to the ethical failures they represent.

Bias Against Black Girls: Google Ad Portal Equated Black Girls with Porn

Yin et al. (2020), in their article, "Bias Against Black Girls: Google Ad Portal Equated 'Black Girls' with Porn," said that the referenced Google search returned hundreds of terms leading to adult content. The authors explained that Google's *Keywords Planner*, which helps advertisers choose which search terms to associate with their ads, offered keyword suggestions related to Black, Asian, and Latina girls that were mostly pornographic. At the time, searches in the *Keywords Planner* for "boys" of those same ethnicities also primarily returned suggestions related to pornography. Searches for "White girls" and "White boys," however, returned no suggested terms at all.

There you have it: bias in action.

What you also have in this example is a demonstration of disparate impact and how societal bias creeps in through AI learning from the data it analyzes. Google did not know that its algorithm "learned" the equation minorities=sexual objects, but it somehow learned it and applied it.

Yin et al. (2020) explain the situation, which clearly underscores that Google's systems contained a racial bias that equated people of color with objectified sexualization while exempting White people from any associations whatsoever. In addition, they state, "by not offering a significant number of non-pornographic suggestions, this system made it more difficult for marketers attempting to reach young Black, Latinx, and Asian people with products and services relating to other aspects of their lives" (para. 4).

Algorithms are holding up a mirror on the soul of America. With their powerful computing power algorithms can "see" everything that's hidden underneath, "they see" the reality of systemic racism and are factoring it in faster than the eye can see into a new reality for Black people who continue to be valued less.

Notably, according to Yin et al. (2020), eight years ago, Google was publicly shamed for more or less the same problem—but, that time, it was associating minorities with pornography. UCLA professor Safiya Noble wrote an article for a magazine in 2015 describing how searches for "Black girls" regularly brought up porn sites in the top results. While this problem has now been fixed, others continue to emerge.

Black people as gorillas. Back in 2015, there was a notorious case against Google because its photo service labeled Black people as gorillas. Again, Google was unaware of what its ML had learned, and it fixed the problem, but the problem resurfaced three years later. The interim fix was to block the labeling of anything—or anyone—as a gorilla, including gorillas; now, that too has been fixed. But you see the problem.

Google Cloud's AI Recognition Code Biased Against Black People

Another problem with Google's labeling technology is discussed by Quach (2020) in the article "Google Cloud's AI Recognition Code Biased Against Black People." In the example cited, the bias is more nefarious and portends more serious consequences. According to Quach (2020), the following happened:

Algorithm Watch fed an image of someone with dark skin holding a temperature gun into its vision recognition model the API, and the object was labelled as a "gun." But when a photo of someone with fair skin holding the same object was fed into the cloud service, the temperature gun was recognized as an "electronic device" (para. 2).

One wonders what the algorithm was "thinking" and what data had it been fed would lead it to conclude that the object being held by the Black person was a gun and that the same object held by the White person was an electronic device? The algorithm was not "thinking"—it was "doing" what it was designed to do by taking all of the available information, analyzing it, and producing a result. The result was, in fact, a result of years of societal biases that was baked into the algorithm.

There is a Racial Divide in Speech Recognition Systems, Researchers Say

Technology from Amazon, Apple, Google, IBM, and Microsoft misidentified 35% of words from people who were Black. White people fared much better, however. Metz (2020) explained the situation in his article "There is a Racial Divide in Speech-Recognition Systems, Researchers Say":

The systems misidentified words about 19 percent of the time with White people. With Black people, mistakes jumped to 35 percent. About 2 percent of audio snippets from White people were considered unreadable by these systems, according to the study, which was conducted by researchers at Stanford University. That rose to 20 percent with Black people (para. 3).

As facial recognition systems move into police departments and other government agencies, they can also be far less accurate when trying to identify women and people of color. Separate tests have also uncovered sexist and racist behavior in "chatbots," translation services, and other systems designed to process and mimic written and spoken language.

There is Also a Racial Divide in Facial Recognition Systems

In his article "Wrongfully Accused by an Algorithm," Hill (2020) explains what may be the first known case of a faulty recognition match that led to a Michigan man's arrest for a crime he did not commit.

As Hill (2020) explains, "facial recognition systems have been used by police forces for more than two decades, but recent studies by M.I.T. and the National Institute of Standards and Technology, have found that while the technology works relatively well on White men, the results are less accurate for other demographics, in part because of a lack of diversity in the images used to develop the underlying databases" (para. 12).

It turns out that not all algorithms are created equal; some are good, and some are bad. When police departments use the bad ones, it often has bad consequences for Black people. Hill (2020) cites Clare Garvie (2020), a lawyer at Georgetown University's Center on Privacy and Technology, who states, "Low-quality search images such as a still image from a grainy surveillance video should be banned, and the systems currently in use should be tested rigorously for accuracy and bias" (para. 15).

Causes of Algorithmic Bias

In an article, "Embedding Fairness into Algorithmic Decision-making", Lisa Balboa (2019) explains that "bias in algorithms is often endemic due to the datasets used and/or the way the algorithm operates" (para. 2). She also suggests how such biases can be redressed, as follows:

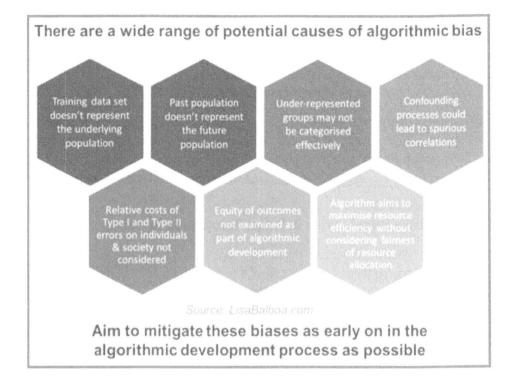

Big Data Platforms Enable Racial Profiling

Take the case of Amazon delivery services, which Turner-Lee and Resnick (2019) describe in their article, "Algorithmic Bias Detection and Mitigation: Best Practices and Policies to Reduce Consumer Harms," giving an example of how bias plays out to the disadvantage of minorities:

> For example, Amazon made a corporate decision to exclude certain neighborhoods from its same-day Prime delivery system. Their decision relied upon the following factors: whether a particular zip code had a sufficient number of Prime members, was near a warehouse, and had sufficient people willing to deliver to that zip code. While these factors corresponded with the company's profitability model, they resulted in the exclusion of poor, predominantly African American neighborhoods, transforming these data points into proxies for racial classification. The results, even when unintended, discriminated against racial and ethnic minorities who were not included (para. 31).

Once upon a time, we imagined that the Internet would usher in a promising new era where shoppers that were invisible on the web could not be judged based on their race or otherwise discriminated against. Today, however, online behavioral targeting combines a home address and a few more characteristics to create an almost perfect proxy for race. Once one's race and socioeconomic status are identified, the algorithms do the rest to accomplish its missions in accordance with its work instructions. The results are often discriminatory, and have led to the new practice of "weblining."

Weblining

Redlining in real estate practices is old news—that is, dog bites man. Today, the news is: "man bites dog" in the form of "weblining." One example of how it works can be gleaned from an example from Wells Fargo. In orchestrating the listing of houses for sale, it collected zip codes of online browsers and directed those buyers toward neighborhoods of similar racial makeup. This is modern-day redlining, in effect.

> **Enabling Weblining**: A user's browsing history, their location and IP information, combined with information available from Google's public data explore (including US census, education, population, STD stats, and state financial data) are a mere sampling of information that could be folded into the personalized search algorithm to surmise a lot more than one's race. In essence, if it's out there, it can be included "in there"—into the personalized algorithm.

In an article, "Managing The Ethics of Algorithms", the *Forbes Insight* team suggested one way to audit and manage algorithms.

> Rigorous auditing of algorithms has emerged as one method of dealing with this, and in many cases, this is an effective way to detect bias. As an example, say we have an insurance claims processing algorithm that decides if a claim should be approved or not. The AI may be looking at income, gender, demographics, age, location, credit history, claims history, and more to determine whether a claim is likely to be valid. If a claim is approved, we can take that transaction and *change one variable*, asking the model what if it was a female instead of a male. If the claim is then denied, then you know the model is biased (para. 12).

Where there is a will, there is a way. But, standing in the way is the fact that by addressing biases, companies are admitting that they exist, and they do not want to do that because they could be sued. This becomes a compounded ethical problem: first creating the bias and then denying that the bias exists.

Algorithms as Workhorses

Algorithms are workhorses that are galloping at 93,000 trillion operations per second to accomplish specific missions. But what are those missions? Their mission is to accomplish a specific goal based on their work instructions. But who is giving them their work instructions? The short answer is that work instructions are given by anybody who is using algorithms to accomplish something—a company, a government agency, a prison system, or a police force. Algorithms are ubiquitous and encircle our lives. The biggest companies in the world have access to trillions of digital assets of our data that they harvest, collect, model, and monetize with the help of the algorithmic workhorses.

> **The algorithmic workhorses have been let out of the barn** and are galloping so fast we can't perceive their speed as they take us to places that we didn't know existed, and when we arrive "there", we don't know where we are.

But who are "we," exactly? As individuals, we are the calculable sum of everything about ourselves that can be *validated, perceived, inferred,* or *assumed* through our *proxies* or *actions.*

When we search for something on Google, for instance, that act of searching becomes part of the story of who we are; when we "like" or share something on Facebook, that becomes another part, and so on.

When what we do is mixed together with who we are by the proxies of our race, gender, age, economic status, zip codes, etc., a basis is formed for the *algorithmic workhorses* to calculate the probability of what we might do, how persuadable we might be, and how likely it is that we already did something or that we will do something. In this, we have the equations of our lives, *past, present,* and *future,* as calculated and assumed by algorithms.

Algorithmic Bias and Fairness

To be clear, what exactly is algorithmic bias and why does it matter? Lia Newman (2020) summarized an important discussion on this topic that was held at Brookings Institution in September 2020. The discussion was called "The Ethical Algorithm: A Conversation with Authors Michael Kearns and Aaron Roth." As reported by Newman (2020), the authors explained that **"bias occurs when errors are disproportionately concentrated in one**

group, such as an algorithm that rejects employment applications from a minority group at a higher rate than background groups."

> **The ethical question is one of fairness**. It is not fair that bias tends to occur disproportionately in regard to Black people and other people of color, and it is also not fair to reduce people down to their "clicks" or to the probabilities of what they are or might do based on their characteristics of race, age, gender, earnings, or other factors? What about a person's intentions, beliefs, and feelings—how are they factored into the equation of a person's life?

The reality is that the intangibles cannot be factored in by the algorithms without specific work instructions and proxies that tell the *workhorses* to run in that direction.

It is important to bear in mind that regardless of the context in which they are used, algorithms are essentially problem solvers—their purpose is to solve and often automate a solution to a particular problem. They are fundamentally a set of steps to accomplish a task—no mystery there, but the mystery is sometimes what comes out on the other end.

As *workhorses*, algorithms are at the center of modern life as we know it. They are at the heart of search engines, social media, video games, credit cards, and anything that requires an online interface with something or somebody. In *The Ethical Algorithm: The Science of Socially Aware Algorithm Design*, Kearns et al. (2019) note that over the course of a generation, algorithms have gone from mathematical abstractions to powerful mediators of daily life. In the process, according to the authors, algorithms have made our lives more efficient, more entertaining, and, sometimes better informed. They have also increasingly violated the basic rights of individual citizens.

Kearns and Roth (2020), in their article "To Improve Algorithms, Embed Human Principles Into Code," address the issue of moral character and make a very interesting point that reminds us that 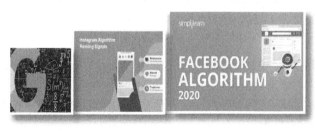 bias is not the fault of the algorithms; it is the fault of the humans that program them:

> **Don't blame the hammer**. One is excused for some skepticism about imparting moral character to an algorithm. An algorithm, after all, is just a human artifact or tool, like a hammer, and who would entertain the idea of an ethical hammer? Of course, a hammer might be put to an unethical use—as an instrument of violence, for example—but this can't be said to be the hammer's fault.

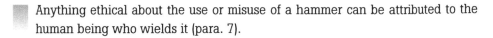

Anything ethical about the use or misuse of a hammer can be attributed to the human being who wields it (para. 7).

Praharaj (2020), author of "Bias in AI Algorithms," underscores a similar point, noting that "we are flawed creatures and every decision we make involves a certain kind of bias. Unfortunately, algorithms haven't proven to be much better" (para. 4).

Tellado (2020) also addresses the issue of bias and fairness and adds the following insights in her article "Biased Big Tech Algorithms Limit Our Lives and Choices. Stop the Online Discrimination":

In the years ahead, algorithms are poised to influence an ever larger share of what we pay, receive, see, learn and decide between — from the cost of goods and services to the headlines and search results that do and do not make it into our personal feeds. As their influence rises, the question becomes more critical: How can we guard against algorithmic biases and hold our tech giants accountable for maintaining fairness in the digital marketplace? (para. 13)

Algorithm bias, data privacy, data usage, and data ownership concerns are essentially concerns about **rights**—what is right and who has the right to do what by virtue of what? It is important to consider the answers to these questions.

Algorithm Bias: What is Right and What is Wrong?

Why should anyone be concerned about algorithm bias? It is simple:

Unintended Consequences. When algorithms do the job of amplifying racial, social and gender inequality, instead of alleviating it; it becomes necessary to take stock of the ethical ramifications and potential malevolence of the technology.

Hao and Stray (2019) in their article for the *MIT Review*, "Can You Make AI Fairer Than a Judge? Play Our Courtroom Algorithm Game", readers are reminded about what fairness means to ordinary citizens and about the difficult task being given to algorithms to be the judge of it.

As a child, you develop a sense of what "fairness" means. It's a concept that you learn early on as you come to terms with the world around you. Something either feels fair or it doesn't. But increasingly, algorithms have begun to arbitrate fairness for us. They decide who sees housing ads, who gets hired or fired, and even who gets sent to jail. Consequently, the people who create them—software engineers—are being asked to articulate what it means to be fair in their code.

This is why regulators around the world are now grappling with a question: How can you mathematically quantify fairness? (para. 2)

In the context of decisionmaking, fairness is the *absence* of any prejudice or favoritism toward an individual or a group based on their inherent or acquired characteristics. An unfair algorithm is skewed toward a particular point of view and outcome.

However, prejudice is not absent in developing the work instructions for algorithms, and it is not *absent* because it is *present* in its human programmers.

In the article "Bias and Algorithmic Fairness," author Jan Teichmann (2019) explained, "the reality is that any data point generated or derived from human behavior is intrinsically tainted by the seemingly endless list of our human biases" (para. 2). Examples of sources of bias, according to Teichmann (2019), include:

In-group favoritism and out-group negativity: A preference for people in the group versus a bias to punish or place burdens upon an out-group.

Fundamental attribution error: Attributing someone's behavior to an intrinsic quality of their character rather than the situational context.

Negativity bias: Emphasizing negative experiences over positive ones, which has important impacts on social judgments and impression formation.

Stereotyping: Expecting a member of a group to have certain characteristics without having actual information about that person.

Bandwagon effect: Believing things because many other people do so.

Bias blind spot: Our tendency not to see our own personal biases (para. 12).

In "Fairness in Algorithmic Decisionmaking," an article published by the Brookings Institution's Artificial Intelligence and Emerging Technology (AIET) Initiative as a part of its "AI and Bias" series, MacCarthy (2019) explains the negative consequences of bias, noting:

Fulfilling the Promise? Undetected and unaddressed, potential biases might prevent machine learning systems from fulfilling their promise of significantly improving the accuracy and fairness of automated decision systems (para. 4).

What Does Society Stand to Lose When Bias Exists?

The short answer is a lot because algorithms are doing a lot. One important aspect of what they are doing that greatly impacts society is making decisions by using data and statistical analyses to classify people for the purpose of assessing their eligibility for a benefit or penalty.

Think about that. Determining one's eligibility for a benefit or a penalty—this is the reason "**fairness bias**" or "**societal bias**" matters and why it's an ethical issue.

For instance, as MacCarthy (2019) notes, "such [algorithmic] systems are traditionally used for credit decisions, employment screening, insurance eligibility, and marketing" (para. 1). In the public sector, the stakes are even higher, as algorithms are used to determine eligibility for the delivery of government services; in criminal justice, they influence sentencing and probation decisions.

In such circumstances, as MacCarthy (2019) explained, "they will often find new, unexpected connections that might not be obvious to analysts or follow from a common sense or theoretic understanding of the subject matter" (para. 6). When they do what they are doing, they are effectively operating behind a curtain of wizardry to a certain extent.

When everything is working according to expectations, algorithms can help discover new factors that *improve* the accuracy of eligibility predictions and the decisions that are based on them. In many cases, they can also improve the fairness of these decisions by, for instance, expanding the pool of qualified job applicants to improve the diversity of a company's workforce. That is the good news, but, unfortunately, the news is not always good, and when it is not, it becomes an ethical concern. MacCarthy (2019) explains why it is so difficult to understand and address algorithmic bias:

Factoring in Bias. A significant challenge with machine learning systems is ascertaining when and how they introduce bias into the decision-making process. Several technical features of these systems might produce discriminatory decisions that are artifacts of the models themselves, or the input data used to train the systems could underrepresent members of protected classes or be infected by past discriminatory practices. Consequently, the data could inadvertently reproduce or magnify historical patterns of bias (para. 8).

Further definitions are needed to explain the nuances and scope of the problems with algorithms and to distinguish between different concepts and practices such as bias, prejudice, discrimination, and racism, as they mean different things under the law and are, therefore, addressed differently in a legal context.

Bias: a preference for or against something. This can be positive, negative, or neutral.

Prejudice: a strong bias—usually negative.

Discrimination: the actions taken based on a prejudice. Discrimination is when you put your thoughts or feelings about a specific person or group of people into action. Someone who just feels uneasy around Black people is prejudiced. Someone who will not hire them is practicing discrimination.

Racism refers to prejudice or discrimination against individuals or groups based on beliefs about one's own racial superiority or the belief that race reflects inherent differences in attributes and capabilities. Racism is the basis for social stratification and differential treatment that advantage the dominant group.

Algorithm Bias and the Law of Unintended Consequences

Whether intentional or unintentional, when bias is programmed in, the law may step in to reddress it.

To understand the circumstances that might trigger the law to step in, it is necessary to define yet another term: disparate impact.

Disparate Impact Defined. It is often referred to as unintentional discrimination, whereas disparate treatment is intentional. It occurs when policies, practices, rules, or other systems that appear to be neutral result in a disproportionate impact on a protected group.

How is a protected group defined? A protected group or protected class is a group of people qualified for special protections by a law, policy, or a similar authority.

How is a protected class protected under the law if they are indeed protected? MacCarthy (2019) explains that a range of U.S. laws forbid discrimination against protected classes in a variety of contexts, such as employment, credit, housing, public accommodations, public education, jury selection, use of genetic information, and health care and health insurance.

> **Title VII of the Civil Rights Act of 1964**, as amended, protects classes that include racial, ethnic, religious, and national minorities, women, seniors, and people with genetic vulnerabilities, disabilities, or pre-existing medical conditions.

Are algorithms covered by the law that protects the protected classes? The short answer is yes. According to MacCarthy (2019), anti-discrimination laws cover the use of automated decision systems whether they are based on traditional statistical techniques or machine learning algorithms. The legal risk in using these systems arises less from the possibility of intentional discrimination and more from exposure to claims of disparate impact. But it gets tricky to make the case, as MacCarthy (2019) explains:

> **Proving Disparate Impact**: When evaluating legal complaints for disparate impact, a three-stage burden–shifting framework typically applies. The plaintiff must show that a decision procedure causes a disproportionate harmful effect on a protected class. Then the burden shifts to the defendant, who is required to show that the decision procedure serves a legitimate business purpose. Then the burden shifts back to the plaintiff who must produce evidence of an available alternative that would achieve the purpose with a less harmful impact on the protected class (para. 10).

Who needs protection the most and who is protected the least? One group is Black people. The "protected class" is protected for a reason: it is because they are in need of protection from many things, including from algorithmic biases.

Discovering and Removing Bias

Discovering bias is easier said than done, but it will never be done unless society demands that it be done.

Presently, many algorithmic systems are woefully biased, but, as Metz (2019) stated, this means that building ethical artificial intelligence is an enormously complex task, but it gets even harder when stakeholders realize that ethics are in the eye of the beholder.

But what should the absence of bias look like?

There are concrete answers to the question of what it should look like. It should look like the results are fair and that no one in the protected class is being treated unfairly. It is possible to play around with the variables—add some in, take some out, and see if there are hidden biases. One thing is for sure: prioritizing finding biases is the first step toward eliminating them.

In McKinsey's Global Institute's report, "Tackling Bias in Artificial Intelligence (and in Humans)," Silberg et al. (2019) state that "AI can play a role in identifying and reducing the effect of human biases, thereby addressing some of the biases that its creators introduced and the processes that its creators employed" (para. 21). They explain how it could be accomplished:

> Running algorithms alongside human decision makers, comparing results, and examining possible explanations for differences are a step in the process of reducing human biases. Similarly, if an organization realizes an algorithm trained on its human decisions (or data based on prior human decisions) shows bias, it should not simply cease using the algorithm but should consider how the underlying human behaviors need to change (para. 22).

However, that is only part of what needs to happen to address bias. Silberg et al. (2019) recommend six ways to maximize fairness and minimize bias from AI, which are as follows:

1. Be aware of the contexts in which AI can help correct for bias as well as where there is a high risk that AI could exacerbate bias.

2. Establish processes and practices to test for and mitigate bias in AI systems.

3. Engage in fact-based conversations about potential biases in human decisions.

4. Fully explore how humans and machines can work best together.

5. Invest more in bias research, make more data available for research (while respecting privacy), and adopt a multidisciplinary approach.

6. Invest more in diversifying the AI field itself (para. 25).

Are There Black People in the Artificial Intelligence Field?

Alake (2020) asked the question in the article, "Are There Black People in AI?". He answered the question by stating "we remain one of the least represented races in AI...[and that] diversity is being invited to the party, but inclusion is being asked to dance" (para. 1).

But there are some Blacks in the AI field and they are dancing all of the way to the bank.

In an article, "What Atlanta Can Teach Tech About Cultivating Black Talent", by Latoya Petersen and Stephanie Dinkins. (2020), twin Black brothers are profiled as two success stories that show what is possible when Black people acquire the right set of skills.

> **The Nunnally "Tech Twins" brothers in Atlanta, Georgia.** After discovering a love of engineering by building soapbox derby racing cars as kids, the brothers launched a few different companies in Atlanta. Holding two master's and a doctorate from Georgia Tech between them, the twins are cofounders of Brain Rain Solutions, which builds augmented-reality, IoT (Internet-of-Things), and technology-based products for companies. Their most recent product, FaceMD+, uses dermatologist databases and machine learning to create a customized skin-care tracker—with algorithms providing customized data for each skin tone and type.
>
>
>
> The Nunnally brothers specialize in applying machine learning to a variety of problems, and their growing business means that they spend a lot of time hiring employees and contractors.

But as two black men on the forefront of the machine-learning revolution, they are also concerned about the readiness of black tech talent: Machine learning requires knowledge of Python coding, algorithmic optimization techniques, and advanced math like calculus. 'The first step into the pipeline is a developer,' Troy says. 'Once you have that base, you can add on the skill set. In the African American community, the funnel gets narrow. The Nunnallys represent a rarity in tech, much less AI. 'When I graduated in 2014, there were less than 100 black men in the whole nation with a PhD in machine learning,' Troy says. "We get scared because we don't see anybody like us. We do see people at the top in entertainment, in sports, but we don't see people at the top of technology."

What would it take to make more tech twins? And how can technology become more diverse and welcoming to underrepresented groups?

Source: Petersen, L. & Dinkins, S. (2020). What Atlanta Can Teach Tech About Cultivating Black Talent? Retrieved from https://www.wired.com/

Data Privacy, Usage, and Ownership

In some ways, people feel worse off today than before the Internet was in common use because of the fear that machine learning algorithms are secretly doing things to them that they do not understand. For instance, while many consumers love their "Alexas," "Google Homes," and "Echos," these gadgets are nevertheless scary and intrusive. Yet, they have been invited into our homes and into our lives without being properly introduced  and without a full understanding of what they will do once they are in our homes.

Data and what is being done with it is a major concern for several reasons. One reason is that the pace of technological change is happening faster than the development of our human capacity to fully comprehend it.

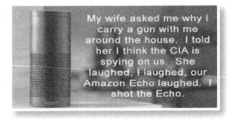
My wife asked me why I carry a gun with me around the house. I told her I think the CIA is spying on us. She laughed, I laughed, our Amazon Echo laughed. I shot the Echo.

The world has become mysterious. As compared to olden times when the masses lacked information, today the problem is reversed: we have too much information. As a result, our modern day and olden times predicaments have landed us in a similar place—in a wilderness wondering around without an understanding of what's surrounding us.

If Elon Musk is scared of AI, it is no wonder that average American citizens are scared of it.

In an article, "Elon Musk Has a Complex Relationship with the A.I. Community," Sam Shead (2020) explains the apparent contradictions in Musk's views. On one hand, he is a major investor in AI companies, and on the other, he warns about the possible dangers of AI in the future. Musk has a company that is looking to push the boundaries of AI. Founded in 2016, Neuralink wants to merge people's brains and AI with the help of a Bluetooth-enabled processor that sits in the skull and talks to a person's phone. Last July, the company said that human trials would begin in 2020.

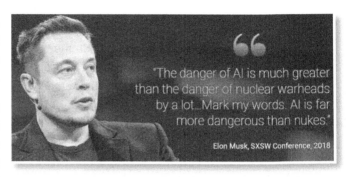

"The danger of AI is much greater than the danger of nuclear warheads by a lot...Mark my words. AI is far more dangerous than nukes."

Elon Musk, SXSW Conference, 2018

„AI doesn't have to be evil to destroy Humanity."

Yet, some of the specific concerns Musk has raised about AI over the years, which Snead (2020) listed in his article (para. 15), reflect his fears of the consequences of AI:

- In September 2017, Musk said on Twitter that AI could be the most likely cause of a third world war. His comment was in response to Russian President Vladimir Putin who said that the first global leader in AI would "become the ruler of the world."

- In July 2017, Musk warned that robots will become better than each and every human at everything and that this will lead to widespread job disruption.

- Transport will be one of the first to go fully autonomous. But when I say everything—the robots will be able to do everything, bar nothing."

Exactly what AI is capable of today is one question and what it might be capable of tomorrow is another. Those who have deep knowledge of the capabilities of AI, like Elon Musk, have concerns about its future, whereas average Americans are more concerned about what is happening now and specifically about what is happening with their data.

> On the one hand, Americans understand that they are getting something free when using certain Internet platforms, but on the other they understand that they know that there is no free lunch. The cost of the lunch may be too high, however, as it stands, the full price is not known.

How Much is Our Personal Data Worth?

In the article, "Big Data Market Size Revenue Forecast Worldwide from 2011 to 2027", Holst (2020) provided data to estimate the value of data. He stated, "the global big data market is forecasted to grow to $103 billion dollars by 2027, more than double its expected market size in 2018. With a share of 45 percent, the software segment would become the largest big data market segment in 2027" (para. 3). The author further explains that the combined global big data and business analytics market was valued at $169 billion in 2018 and is expected to grow to $274 billion in 2022.

Jamison (2020) in an article, "How Much Our Personal Data Is Worth?", could not precisely answer the question. However, he presented some information about a new regulation in the State of California that hints at its value.

The regulations proposed in California on June 1, 2020, which implement the recently enacted California Consumer Privacy Act (CCPA), state that consumers will now have the right to know what personal information businesses collect, use, share or sell, the right to delete personal information, the right to opt out of the sale of personal information, and the right to direct a business to stop selling that information.

Jamison (2020) also explains that the CCPA applies to companies that have gross annual revenues in excess of $25 million, and that buy, receive, or sell the personal information of 50,000 or more consumers, households, or devices, or derive 50% or more of annual revenues from selling consumers' personal information. Under the proposed regulations, businesses must also disclose financial incentives offered in exchange for the retention or sale of a consumer's personal information and how they were calculated. The CCPA aims to protect over $12 billion worth of personal information annually.

But why does your data have value? In simplistic terms, it has value because it can be used to influence "your" behavior. This is a discipline called "persuasive technology."

Persuading You Through Persuasive Technology

Remember, the workhorse algorithms are on a mission, and their work instructions lead those horses to the water. Persuasive technology makes you drink it.

> **Persuasive technology** is broadly defined as technology that is designed to change attitudes or behaviors of the users through persuasion and social influence, but not through coercion.

But There is a Thin Line Between Persuasion and Manipulation

Persuasion and manipulation—we are scared of it, we know it is happening, but we do not know what it exactly is nor what we can do about.

The difference between persuasion and manipulation lies in:

1) The intent behind your desire to persuade that person,
2) The truthfulness and transparency of the process,
3) The net benefit or impact on that person.

Manipulation implies persuasion with the intent to fool, control, or contrive the person on the other side of the conversation into doing something, believing something, or buying into something that leaves them either harmed or without benefit.

The thing about having so much data on people is that the algorithms "know" how to use it in order to *manipulate* you into taking certain actions—the ones "they" want you to take.

The film *The Social Dilemma highlights* the dangers of social media. It underscores that "they" (the algorithms) want you to do is something that makes money for "them" (their masters). But who are they? They are the big tech companies like Amazon, Google, Facebook, Twitter, politicians, national governments, and others. The algorithms they put to work use your data to build a profile of you to predict whether you are persuadable and how they can manipulate you. This is why your kids are addicted to *Fortnite* and other video games, and it is the reason why many programmers do not allow their kids to play those games. The quotes above from *The Social Dilemma* film highlight the problem.

> Social media isn't a tool that's just waiting to be used. It has its own goals, and it has its own means of pursuing them.

> Social media starts to dig deeper and deeper down into the brain stem and take over kids' sense of self-worth and identity.

While parents were worried about their children playing *Fortnite* and other games, the kids were also on TikTok, along with millions of others.

TikTok Deal and the Value of Algorithms and Data

The importance of algorithms, data privacy, usage, and ownership is at the forefront of the ongoing negotiations to buy or buy into TikTok.

On September 14, 2020, Oracle confirmed that it was chosen to serve as a U.S. technology partner for TikTok, whose Chinese parent company, ByteDance, has faced pressure from the Trump administration to sell off the popular video-sharing app over national security concerns. The structure of the deal is not yet known, and the deal has not been finalized. The reason for the deal was the Trump administration's concerns that the app could give the Chinese government access to sensitive data.

The concerns about TikTok and the disposition of the data it collects on Americans has been a concern for a while. In 2019, the U.S. Federal Trade Commission (FTC) fined TikTok $5.7 million after determining the personal information that the app collected from children broke U.S. privacy laws. And it is the subject of a further investigation by the FTC and the U.S. Department of Justice over allegations that it did not clean up its act. On May 15, 2019, President Trump signed Executive Order (EO) 13873 to counter the "national security, foreign policy, and economy of the United States" posed by TikTok. The executive order states, in part:

TikTok, a video-sharing mobile application owned by the Chinese company ByteDance Ltd., has reportedly been downloaded over 175 million times in the United States and over one billion times globally. TikTok automatically captures vast swaths of information from its users, including Internet and other network activity information such as location data and browsing and search histories. This data collection threatens to allow the Chinese Communist Party access to Americans' personal and proprietary information — potentially allowing China to track the locations of Federal employees and contractors, build dossiers of personal information for blackmail, and conduct corporate espionage.

The threat that TikTok poses, according to the EO, spans multiple concerns, including the capacity of TikTok to spread debunked conspiracy theories (deep fakes). Despite these concerns, as it stands in the deal negotiating process, it appears that TikTok will not transfer ownership of its valuable recommendation algorithm (its workhorse) to Oracle.

National Security Concerns

Congress is concerned about "deep fakes." It refers to a term that first emerged in 2017 to describe realistic photos, audio, videos, and other forgeries generated by AI technologies. It is believed that they could present a variety of national security challenges in the years to come. According to the Congressional Research Service (CRS), this is how it works:

Deep Fakes. Though definitions vary, deep fakes are most commonly described as forgeries created using techniques in machine learning (ML)—a subfield of AI—especially generative adversarial networks (GANs). In the GAN process, two ML systems called neural networks are trained in competition with each other. The first network, or the generator, is tasked with creating counterfeit data—such as photos, audio recordings, or video footage—that replicate the properties of the original data set. The second network, or the discriminator, is tasked with identifying the counterfeit data. Based on the results of each iteration, the generator network adjusts to create increasingly realistic data. The networks continue to compete—often for thousands or millions of iterations—until the generator improves its performance such that the discriminator can no longer distinguish between real and counterfeit data.

Source: Congressional Research Service (2020). Deep Fakes and National Security. Washington, DC.

The concern that CRS (2020) expresses about deep fakes is explained as follows:

> Deep fakes could also be used to embarrass, or blackmail elected officials or individuals with access to classified information. Already there is evidence that foreign intelligence operatives have used deep fake photos to create fake social media accounts from which they have attempted to recruit Western sources. Some analysts have suggested that deep fakes could similarly be used to generate inflammatory content—such as convincing video of U.S. military personnel engaged in war crimes—intended to radicalize populations, recruit terrorists, or incite violence (para. 5).

In short, the battle between man and machine is a battle *within* humans. Humans must decide what is important to society and give "work instructions" to the "workhorse" algorithms to carry them out. Our common mission in society is to 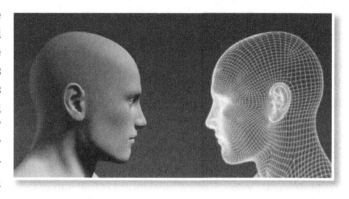 live in accordance with our ethical principles and be guided by our moral compasses in all that we do. In the end, it is our humanity that makes us more intelligent than machines.

Algorithms and Section 230

Tucked inside the Communications Decency Act (CDA) of 1996 is one of the most valuable tools for protecting freedom of expression and innovation on the Internet: Section 230. It says that "no provider or user of an interactive computer service shall be treated as the publisher or speaker of any information provided by another information content provider." In other words, online intermediaries that host or republish speech are protected against a range of laws that might otherwise be used to hold them legally responsible for what others say and do.

There have been a number of congressional hearings on the matter. There are two things at the heart of the concern. First, there is fear that another Cambridge Analytica situation, which happened in 2016, might happen again during the November 2020 elections. Secondly, there is a general concern about the power of social media and what it can do with that power—especially when it unleashes the full might of the algorithmic workhorses. As discussed above, those workhorses are galloping so fast that no one can catch them, and no one fully understands where they are going and what tracks they are running on. The big social media giants are essentially unchecked, and the legislators feel left out of the biggest game in town.

Big Tech and Anti-Trust

The concerns of Congress are similar to those that are at the heart of Section 230: very big things are happening, and the legislators are left out of the loop. Yet, they are not sure of what problem they are trying to solve, other than wanting a role to play. The fact is, understanding big tech is no small task—neither is fully understanding where it is going.

Tellado (2020) in an article for *USAToday* perhaps stated the case best in, "Biased Big Tech Algorithms Limit Our Lives and Choices. Stop the Online Discrimination." She noted the following:

> The abuse of trust by the platform-based companies we rely on most has largely flown under the radar as a global pandemic heightens and highlights fissures in our society. But our data and our choices continue to be manipulated in problematic ways – often by algorithms that subtly introduce bias into the prices we pay, and the information and options made available to us. It is essential that we hold our digital gatekeepers accountable (para. 2).

Legislators are indeed endeavoring to hold the gatekeepers accountable, but how is the question.

The concerns of Congress in many ways mirror those of average citizens. We are scared of what is behind the curtain and the power of the wizard.

Data Privacy and Transparency

In the article, "Is Data Privacy a Privilege? The Racial Implications of Technology Based Tools in Government," Foucek (2020) puts the issue of data privacy into the context of our present situation, as we are struggling with systemic racism. She stated the following:

As our country currently addresses the decades of systematic racism inherent in our political and societal systems, privacy must be included in the conversation and reform. I believe that data privacy today is regarded as a privilege rather than a right, and this privilege is often reserved for white, middle, and upper-class citizens. The complex, confusing and lengthy nature of privacy policies not only requires some familiarity with data privacy and what the government and companies do with data, but also the time, energy and resources to read through the entirety of the document (para. 10).

As noted, there is even a built-in bias against Black people who do not have the time or wherewithal to read the privacy statements they receive because, at this moment, they are busy homeschooling while working and trying to outrun the virus, as many of them are essential workers.

There is seemingly nowhere to turn to catch a break.

And yet, many turn to social media for some sense of connection and community in this time of isolation without realizing that they may not be using social media as much as social media is using them.

Social Media and Privacy

In "100 Data Privacy and Data Security Statistics for 2020," *The Data Manager* (2020), a highly ranked privacy management software company, listed hot-button issues. Social media policy was high on the list, especially in light of the Netflix docudrama *The Social Dilemma*, which explores the damages done to consumers by the advertising that fuels the industry.

Data presented in the report shows the broad concerns that consumers have about data-related issues overall. The report cites statistics from DuckDuckGo that indicate, for instance, that 79% of people have adjusted privacy-related settings on their social media accounts or reduced their social media usage. It also cites other pertinent data from a broad range of sources that raise privacy and security concerns, including the following:

- Facebook owns **80%** of the market share of social media platforms, and Google owns **90%** of the market share of search engines.

- **80%** of social media users are concerned about advertisers and businesses accessing the data they share on social media platforms.

Facebook: The True Costs of Connection

In 2019, Facebook had to pay a record $5 billion fine to the U.S. Federal Trade Commission (FTC) to settle privacy concerns. It is the biggest fine ever imposed on any company for violating consumers' privacy.

The FTC required the social network to establish an independent privacy committee that Facebook's chief executive, Mark Zuckerberg, will not have control over. The FTC had been probing allegations that political consultancy firm Cambridge Analytica improperly obtained data of up to 87 million Facebook users. The probe then widened to include other issues, such as facial recognition. "Despite repeated promises to its billions of users worldwide that they could control how their personal information is shared, Facebook undermined consumers' choices," said FTC chairman Joe Simons.

Here is how the Cambridge Analytica breech happened. In 2014, a quiz on Facebook invited users to find out their personality types. It was designed to harvest not only the user data of the person taking part in the quiz, but also their friends' data. Christopher Wylie, who worked with Cambridge Analytica, alleges that because 270,000 people took the quiz, the data of some 50 million users, mainly in the U.S., was harvested without their explicit consent via their friend networks.

According to Kleinman (2018), the data was gathered using Facebook's infrastructure at that time, but the data was not authorized for them to share with others, as explained in "Cambridge Analytica: The Story So Far." The other key point, according to Kleinman (2018), "is that even the people directly taking part in the personality quiz would have had no idea that they would be sharing their data with Trump's 2016 election campaign" (para. 17).

As reported in "100 Data Privacy and Data Security Statistics for 2020":

> Cambridge Analytics scandal made more than **73%** of U.S. users concerned about how their information is used on the internet. **26%** stated they are extremely concerned, **22%** stated they are very concerned, and **25%** stated they were somewhat concerned (para. 54).

Data contained in "100 Data Privacy and Data Security Statistics for 2020," which draws on multiple research reports, shows how scared we are and why we should be scared.

- **63%** of Americans say they understand very little or nothing at all about the laws and regulations that are currently in place to protect their data privacy.

- **97%** of Americans say they are ever asked to approve privacy policies, yet only about one-in-five adults overall say they always (**9%**) or often (**13%**) read a company's privacy policy before agreeing to it. Some **38%** of all adults maintain they sometimes read such policies, but **36%** say they never read a company's privacy policy before agreeing to it.

When companies are forced to act to remediate their unethical handling of data, it costs them. A few statistics quantify some of the business costs associated with redressing the problem (note that PII refers to Personally Identifiable Information). (Kleinman, 2018, para. 71).

A few additional statistics from "100 Data Privacy and Data Security Statistics for 2020", convey the extent to which data are being breached. The report compiled data, which is shown below, from various sources that are cited alongside each statistic in the report.

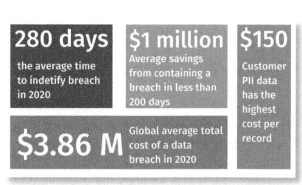

- From May 25, 2018 to January 27, 2020 there have been a total of **160,921** personal data breaches notified by organizations to data protection supervisory authorities within the EEA.

- A hacker attack occurs every **39 seconds**.

- Only **2%** of firms that have reported a breach to a supervisory authority have been fined.

- **$3.86 million** is the average total cost of a data breach.

- It costs **$150** per lost PII record.

- The average time to identify a breach in 2019 was 206 days, and the average time to contain a breach was 73 days, for a total of **279 days** (**4.9% increase from 2018**). In 2020, the average time to identify a breach was **280 days**.

- Breaches with a lifecycle longer than 200 days were on average **$1.12 million more** costly than breaches with a lifecycle of less than 200 days ($4.33 million for 200-plus days versus $3.21 million for less than 200 days).

■ For the period from May 25, 2018 to January 27, 2019, there were, on average, **247 breach notifications per day** in the E.U. For the period from January 28, 2019 to January 27, 2020, there were on average **278 breach notifications per day** (a **12.6%** increase), so the current trend for breach notifications is upwards.

■ **58%** of the total breaches in 2019 were the result of hacking incidents, which impacted **36.9** million patient records.

Is the U.S. Government Protecting Our Data?

Our concerns about what happens to our data are not just limited to their commercial use by private sector entities; we are also concerned about what the government does with our data. Foucek (2020) explains that data breaches have happened on a massive scale involving local government data, school data, and other data breaches and warns society to be on the lookout:

> There is a real threat that algorithms do not achieve the intended goals of objectivity and fairness, but further perpetuate the inequalities and biases that already exist within our societies. Artificial intelligence has enabled governments to cultivate big data and thus, have added another tool to their arsenals of surveillance technology. Advances in computational science have created the ability to capture, collect, and combine everyone's digital trails and analyze them in ever finer detail. Through the weaponization of big data, governments can even more easily identify, control, and oppress marginalized groups of people within a society—when its job is to protect people, especially the "protected class" (para. 4).

In short, no matter which way they turn, Black people just cannot catch a break—not from people and their biases, not from machines that replicate them, nor from institutions that employ "weaponized" data to exploit them.

Road to Progress

In undertaking research for this chapter, I was reminded of my early days as a student of cognitive psychology at Carnegie-Mellon University under the tutelage of Nobel Prize Laureate Dr. Herbert Simon.

Back then, I was learning something that had not previously existed as a discipline, and I did not understand how the bits and pieces of things I was being taught fit together. One day, I would learn about the eye vision of frogs, the next day, I would take a course on psycholinguistics, and the next day, we would play a game so that our strategic movements could be studied by Dr. Simon, and so on. There was only one person who knew how the pieces fit together, and that was Dr. Simon; however, he was seeing "it" clearly like a workhorse algorithm. He could see beneath the surface of things, understand how things were connected, and then know where to go next in the learning and discovery process.

But how could a little Black girl from Philadelphia possibly understand cognitive psychology—a field that had no past and whose future was unclear? When I was invited to continue on in the Ph.D. course in cognitive psychology, I declined the invitation because the vision of what it could mean had not been shared with me, and I lacked the background to imagine it on my own.

Today, collectively as it relates to AI and all of its usages, we are all in the position of that little Black girl from Philly in the 1970s: we know that there are many pieces to the puzzle, but we cannot see the picture.

When I was at university, I gave up on cognitive psychology and the early AI disciplines I was being taught because I could not perceive the vision; instead, I opted to study something else at the graduate level, management, which was a well-established discipline.

We do not have a choice today; we must embrace AI, but we should do so wisely.

Each one in society has to take responsibility for learning more about the things that scare us. As consumers, we have to refrain from clicking until we know what we are clicking on. As government legislators, we must utilize our considerable resources to run alongside the algorithmic horses to understand the track they are on. As businesses, we must take the time and effort to truly protect the "protected classes" and all of society from the ills of bias and manipulation.

In the end, we do not need to be saved from the algorithms; we need to be saved from ourselves by being better, doing better, and by giving the algorithmic workhorses work instructions that factor in and prioritize our shared ethical values.

There are many experts, practitioners, and scholars who have studied the issues that are raised in this chapter, and many have advice on how to address them. While it is not possible to review the many recommendations that have been put forward, we have chosen to highlight a few that specifically address and acknowledge that ethical frameworks matter in reducing bias and protecting privacy.

An Ethical Framework to Reduce AI Bias

Brookings Institution scholars Nichol Turner-Lee and Paul Resnick (2019) developed what they refer to as a "template for a bias impact statement." It is presented in Table 1 in their article "Algorithmic Bias Detection and Mitigation: Best Practices and Policies to Reduce Consumer Harms." The template presented in the Turner-Lee, Resnick (2019) article is as follows:

What will the automated decision do?

- Who is the audience for the algorithm and who will be most affected by it?
- Do we have training data to make the correct predictions about the decision?
- Is the training data sufficiently diverse and reliable?
- What is the data lifecycle of the algorithm?
- Which groups are we worried about when it comes to training data errors, disparate treatment, and impact?

How will potential bias be detected?

- How and when will the algorithm be tested? Who will be the targets for testing?
- What will be the threshold for measuring and correcting for bias in the algorithm, especially as it relates to protected groups?

What are the operator incentives?

- What will we gain in the development of the algorithm?
- What are the potential bad outcomes and how will we know?
- How open (e.g., in code or intent) will we make the design process of the algorithm to internal partners, clients, and customers?
- What intervention will be taken if we predict that there might be bad outcomes associated with the development or deployment of the algorithm?

How are other stakeholders being engaged?

- What's the feedback loop for the algorithm for developers, internal partners and customers?
- Is there a role for civil society organizations in the design of the algorithm?

Has diversity been considered in the design and execution?

- Will the algorithm have implications for cultural groups and play out differently in cultural contexts?
- Is the design team representative enough to capture these nuances and predict the application of the algorithm within different cultural contexts?
- If not, what steps are being taken to make these scenarios more salient and understandable to designers?
- Given the algorithm's purpose, is the training data sufficiently diverse?
- Are there statutory guardrails that companies should be reviewing to ensure that the algorithm is both legal and ethical?

Considerations for Protecting Privacy

In July 2018, Cameron Kerry wrote an article that was published by the Brookings Institution, which was titled "Why Protecting Privacy is a Losing Game Today—And How to Change the Game." It was a little ahead of its time, but it was spot on in highlighting that "more and more data about each of us is being generated faster and faster from more and more devices, and we can't keep up. It's a losing game both for individuals and for our legal system" (para. 2).

Two years later, the warning is increasingly being heeded by the federal government and state governments that are proposing and passing legislation to protect consumers. But COVID-19 has presented a conundrum:

> The World Health Organization (WHO) says AI and big data are an important part of the pandemic solution. Data from smartphones, mobile apps, fitness trackers, and other sources can be fed into predictive AI models to help public health officials evaluate the risks and potential impact of efforts to contain the virus or build up defenses for the next wave.

In addition to the complications that COVID-19 has introduced, there are also questions about what the best approaches are for protecting consumers in ways that limit the inhibition of big tech's innovation and growth. In searching for the right approach, legislators have looked to the legislation of the E.U. called the "General Data Protection Regulation or GDPR."

> The General Data Protection Regulation or GDPR, focuses on ensuring that users know, understand, and consent to the data collected about them... The law protects individuals in the 28 member countries of the European Union, even if the data is processed elsewhere.

The GDPR has been an inspiration and a guiding framework for states and the federal government to craft their own legislation. In reviewing the GDPR legislation, Kerry (2018) highlights the most important areas it protects, which include the following:

- Privacy rights for individuals.
- Consumer access to modify or delete data.
- Data minimization to prevent collection of personally identifiable information.
- More Federal Trade Commission enforcement powers.
- Algorithmic bias studies.
- Rules for how businesses collect and use personal data.

The Importance of Prioritizing Ethics in Artificial Intelligence

In an article on December 4, 2020, "Google widely criticized after parting ways with a leading voice in AI ethics", Metz (2020) revealed that "many Google employees and others in the tech and academic communities are furious over the sudden exit from Google of a pioneer in the study of ethics in artificial intelligence—a departure they see as a failure by an industry titan to foster an environment supportive of diversity" (para 1). Metz explained the back story, as follows:

Timnit Gebru is known for her research into bias and inequality in AI, and in particular, for a 2018 paper she coauthored with Joy Buolamwini that highlighted how poorly commercial facial-recognition software fared when attempting to classify women and people of color. Their work sparked widespread awareness of issues common in AI today, particularly when the technology is tasked with identifying anything about human beings.

At Google, Gebru was the co-leader of the company's ethical AI team, and one of very few Black employees at the company overall (3.7% of Google's employees are Black according to the company's 2020 annual diversity report)— let alone in its AI division. The research scientist is also cofounder of the group Black in AI.

In her own words, according to Metz (2020), Gebru wrote that she felt "constantly dehumanized at Google and expressed dismay over the ongoing lack of diversity at the company" (para. 5). Gebru explained that her treatment was "because there is zero accountability…and no incentive to hire 39% women" (para. 6). Adding further insights into the problem, Gebru, as reported in the Metz (2020) article, explained: "your life gets worse when you start advocating for underrepresented people, you start making the other leaders upset when they don't want to give you good ratings during calibration. There is no way more documents or more conversations will achieve anything" (para. 7).

As can be seen from the foregoing, Google has veered off the "road to progress", but clearly needs to get back on it. Hopefully, they will make the right turn.

Clearly, the issues discussed in this book are important, and all eyes are on them. But we are in the "Wild, Wild West" in the world of artificial intelligence. We tamed the Wild West before, and we must tame it anew—along with the horses it is riding in on.

Source: Metz, C. (2020). There is a Racial Divide in Speech-Recognition Systems, Researchers Say. Retrieved from https://www.nytimes.com

CHAPTER TWO

Unfair Housing, Environmental Injustice, COVID-19, and Ethics?

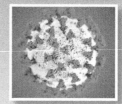

About Chapter Two: **Unfair Housing, Environmental Injustice, COVID-19, and Ethics**

his chapter explains a simple equation: **Racial = Spatial**.

Though seemingly simple, there's a formula behind it. **Isolate, target and destroy.**

Once Black people were relocated into "othered" *redlined* spaces, the ills of society could be contained to them in those isolated spaces and places.

How are housing, environmental injustice, and COVID-19 connected? They are connected by the tools and instruments of **systemic racism.**

First came housing segregation, which **isolated** the Black population and denied them the opportunity to accumulate wealth. Next, came environmental injustice that was perpetrated on Black people because it was possible to **target** them in their isolated spaces, as they lacked the power to protest "NIMBY" (not in my backyard) against the placement of industrial pollution their communities. Then, came the disproportionately negative impact of COVID-19 that is **destroying** Black people who were already sick.

This chapter explains how systemic racism works and how it has segregated Black people into spaces where they were/are denied the opportunity to experience the American dream. Specifically, it shows what the systems of systemic racism are and how they were codified during the New Deal when the Federal Housing Authority's (FHA) Underwriting Manual demanded the physical segregation of Black and White neighborhoods. **Racial = spatial**.

This chapter also shows how change can only happen when power is used to force it to happen and that power in our society is wielded through the "3Ps"—the **Purse, Policies**, and **Persuasion**.

The hope for changing and improving the situation of Black people depends on how the **3Ps** are leveraged to force change, and on everyone acting ethically.

The current Black Lives Matter movement is scaring those who don't want change. Opponents of it are stoking the fears of stakeholders who have vested interests in the status quo by blaring dog whistles proclaiming, **"they"** are coming to **"your"** beautiful suburbs and will destroy "your" beautiful way of life. But who are "they" and who is "your"?

This chapter makes the answer clear and encourages readers to ponder the ethical and moral case for all Americans, including Black Americans, to have an equal opportunity to experience the American dream.

Unfair Housing, Environmental Injustice, COVID-19, and Ethics?

When I was growing up in West Philadelphia in the mid-1950s and early 1960s, I thought Philadelphia was the center of the world and that Black people were at the center of it. With so many Black people around me in my direct line of sight, I had no conception of being a "minority." When I first heard that Blacks were a minority, I thought it was a lie, a misunderstanding. How could that be? I could walk miles in any direction without seeing a single White person—that is, unless I went into a store that sold anything other than food.

While I never saw White people walking around the neighborhoods, they were always nearby in the pharmacies, hospitals, cleaners, movie theaters, clothing stores… and in all places of business that weren't corner groceries or selling food. The power structure was clear: Whites owned the businesses, and Blacks worked in them.

I grew up in a bifurcated world with Blacks at the bottom of society and Whites at the top. It was just the way it was. Through my childhood eyes, it appeared that all was just singing along, but I didn't understand the tune that was playing.

I didn't understand the meaning of Blacks always being on the bottom and Whites always being on top. I did notice that all of my teachers were White yet all of the students were Black, but frankly, that didn't register in my childish mind as being a problem. It was simply the way it was.

When we went to church on Sundays and witnessed the old Black ladies wailing, crying, and fainting, I didn't realize it was because of the trouble many of them were experiencing in their lives or that when they uttered the term Hallelujah, it meant that they were expressing gratitude for being able to have lived to see another Sunday under their dire circumstances.

The frenetic activity of the Black street vendors on the storied 52nd Street in West Philadelphia in my neighborhood, the loud music blaring on street corners, the busy hair salons and barbershops, and the frequent smell of Black soul food cooking combined to create a false sense of acceptance in my childhood mind of an order of life that was, in fact, out of order.

Being brought up in a large home on Chestnut Street, not far from the University of Pennsylvania, blinded me to the reality of the poor neighborhoods in other parts of Philadelphia where most Black people lived. Had I visited those neighborhoods with my eyes wide open, I might have seen the rows  after rows of dilapidated houses; I might have noticed the sewage billowing over into the streets and the poor state of the infrastructure; and I might have asked questions. But as it was, I was purposefully shielded from those areas by my parents, who worked day and night to make sure that we didn't wind up there. That was no easy feat on their part, but I didn't understand that at the time.

Having been shielded from many of the realities of Black life in Philadelphia, when I entered Carnegie Mellon University (CMU) in the 1970s, I did so as a socially ignorant person. And though I obtained a degree in history while at CMU, it did not lessen my social ignorance of the reality of Black life in America because what I learned studying history had nothing to do with the history of Black folks or their circumstances. It would take many years to awaken my senses to the broader world beyond myself and the circumstances of Blacks in America.

The overall circumstances in which most Blacks lived in Philadelphia was not a mystery to most, however. Black neighborhoods were nearby many other neighborhoods; they even surrounded the University of Pennsylvania, so to learn more about them, the university commissioned W. E. B. Du Bois to undertake a study about them. Du Bois's findings were presented in *The Philadelphia Negro* in 1899 as the first sociological case study of a Black community in the United States.

On the one hand, his research revealed a community of diversity and advancement and, on the other hand, one that was riddled by poverty, crime, and illiteracy. Addressing this contradiction, Du Bois posited that Black members of the community possessed their own internal class structure and, therefore, should not be judged solely by the "submerged tenth," the 10 percent beneath the surface of socioeconomic viability.

Du Bois also explained that "the 'Negro problem' was ostensibly not one problem but rather a plexus of social problems that had less correlation to a Black 'social pathology' than to Whites' enforcement of racial discrimination and a provision of unequal opportunity".

> Du Bois emphasized that socio-economic and historical causes of the "Negro problem", "were notably the result of the exclusion of blacks from the city's premier industrial jobs, prevalence of black single-family homes, and the continued legacy of slavery and unequal race relations." Such biased provision was evident in housing. He found that Blacks had to pay 'abnormally' high rents for the poorest accommodations, and race-prejudice accentuates this difficulty, out of which many evils grow." (Stanford Encyclopedia of Philosophy, W. E. B. Du Bois, 2017, Section 2).

It's important to understand that the prevailing moral sentiment held during those times, and still today, was "manifest destiny." It was the moral compass and the basis for ethical judgments. The problem is that the compass pointed in a direction that only served the White establishment.

> **Manifest Destiny Defined**. In 1845, the term "manifest destiny" emerged to describe the commonly held belief that White settlement and expansion across North America was inevitable and even divinely ordained. But long before then, this ideology provided the justification for ethnic cleansing and systematic displacement.

In many ways, this sentiment and belief continues to inform policymaking to this day and to undergird commonly held ethical and moral beliefs among the majority population.

As a result, the current state of Black American communities bears many likenesses to that of the past.

Solomon et al. (2019) explained in the report, "Systemic Inequality: Displacement, Exclusion, and Segregation: How America's Housing System Undermines Wealth Building in Communities of Color", that the United States (U.S.) government played a key role in disadvantaging Blacks by denying them a fair opportunity to access land and housing in areas that would have enabled them to have wealth-building opportunities through homeownership:

American lawmakers have long sought to secure land for, reduce barriers to, and expand the wealth-building capacity of property ownership and affordable rental housing. But these efforts have almost exclusively benefited White households; often, they have removed people of color from their homes, denied them access to wealth-building opportunities, and relocated them to isolated communities. Across the country, historic and ongoing displacement, exclusion, and segregation continue to prevent people of color from obtaining and retaining their own homes and accessing safe, affordable housing (para. 12).

Exactly how Blacks were relocated was often a tricky thing. For instance, Solomon et al. (2019) pointed to examples of how it was done by using public policies under the guise of creating new public spaces to combat urban blight or to bolster economic development. The authors gave two specific examples:

In the early 1850s, New York City lawmakers used eminent domain to destroy a thriving predominantly Black community in Manhattan, displacing thousands of residents to create the public space known today as Central Park. And just 30 years ago, Atlanta lawmakers demolished the United States' oldest federally subsidized affordable housing project, displacing more than 30,000 predominantly Black families to create Centennial Olympic Park. These are just two examples of the countless policies that have displaced Black communities for the so-called benefit of the greater population. But there is scant evidence that Black Americans see long-term benefits from these revitalization efforts (para. 8).

The examples of New York and Atlanta joined many more across the U.S. at the time.

The case of Detroit's "Black Bottom" is one such example that underscores how the destruction of one Black neighborhood forced Blacks into locations that were worse. As Weber-Davis et al. (2015) told the story in their article, "How A 1900s Black Detroit Community Was Razed For A Freeway," an entire Black Detroit neighborhood was vanished for a freeway that took away the freedom of its residents.

In explaining how this section of Detroit came to be a predominantly Black neighborhood, Weber-Davis et al. (2015) quoted a woman interviewed in 1975 who recounted the history of the area:

Detroit is a melting pot, and African Americans come primarily from the south... everybody was from the South at that time. The woman went on to explain that men and women went north for jobs in manufacturing... especially at Ford Motor Company because it was offering $5-a-day. However, the sad part was that they packed families into one room and charged them about $50 in rent, which was exorbitant at that time because they were only making $5 a day. They were packing families into Black Bottom homes because there were limited options and Black families were rarely allowed to purchase homes (para. 5).

The aptly named "Black Bottom" was indeed at the bottom of society where Blacks lived. They didn't live there by choice, however; it was one of the few places they were allowed to live.

Weber-Davis et al. (2015) cited Ken Coleman, a Detroit-based historian and author who provided further insight into the history of Black Bottom and how it came to be that so many Black people lived there. According to Coleman:

[R]estricted covenants and deeds restricted you from living in most of the city, and really, outside of a couple of small enclaves in Detroit, Black Bottom was the only place you could live. Perhaps as much as 80% of deeds in Detroit prevented Black homeownership. So African American families were forced to live in Black neighborhoods. By some estimates there were 350 black-owned businesses in Black Bottom – doctors, lawyers, restaurants, pharmacies, general stores, and entertainment venues (para. 9).

Though there was frenetic social and economic activity that sustained the lives of the people who lived in the Black Bottom and adjoining areas for decades, years of a lack of investment in the physical infrastructure in those areas took its final toll. In the early 1960s, the City of Detroit declared it a slum, and under its urban renewal program to combat "Urban Blight," the entire Black Bottom district was razed and replaced with Chrysler Freeway and Lafayette Park.
Many of the residents were relocated to large public housing projects such as the Brewster-Douglass Housing Projects Homes and Jeffries Homes.

The combined Brewster-Douglass Project was five city blocks long, and three city blocks wide, and housed anywhere between 8,000 and 10,000 residents, at its peak capacity. Though the Detroit Housing Commission initially required an employed parent for each family before establishing tenancy, the Commission became less selective and crime became a problem. The buildings were demolished in 2014.

The "where to locate the Black people problem" persisted as a reoccurring one over the years, and the solutions contrived to solve it were never good. Being forced into high-rise buildings was a particularly bad idea because they were merely places to lay one's head but not places with land and access to resources to enable Blacks to use their heads to start businesses or to fill their hearts with the joys of community life. High-rise *living* was high-rise *dying* of the soul.

The Brewster-Douglas projects of the world weren't located in neighborhoods or communities; they were strictly containment centers. As such, they came to contain the ills of society.

By hook and by crook, and by federal, state, and local policies during much of the twentieth century, Blacks were displaced to subsidize the development of prosperous White suburbs in metropolitan areas across the country. Solomon et al. (2019) explained that "they also constructed new highway systems—often through communities of color—to ensure access to job opportunities in urban centers for primarily White commuters". All the while, Solomon et al. (2019) noted, "many appear to [have] drawn heavily from the ideology of '**manifest destiny**'—that White settlement and expansion are inevitable" (para. 8).

Racial = Spatial

What do housing segregation, environmental injustice, and COVID-19 have in common? The **containment of races to specified spaces** (i.e., segregation), and when that happens, all manner of bad things follow.

Decades of scholarship point to three main reasons for persistent segregation: money, preferences, and discrimination. As a result, the majority, almost 60 percent, of the Black population is now contained with 10 states, as shown on the U.S. Census Bureau, State and County Maps 2017.

As of 2017, there were 41.4 million Blacks, representing 12.2 percent of the U.S. population. Almost 60 percent of the population was located in 10 states in rank order of: Texas, Georgia, Florida, New York, North Carolina, California, Illinois, Maryland, Virginia, Louisiana.

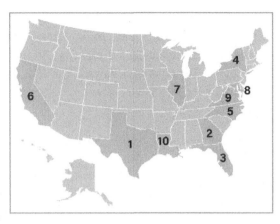

Though by 2018, according to the U.S. Census Bureau State and County Maps (2018) estimates, there was a slight reordering of the rankings of the top 10 states, with a few states dropping into the top 10 while a few dropped out, nevertheless, the overall picture of the circumstances of Blacks in those states and in others has not substantially changed.

The fact remains that wherever Blacks are located, they have historically and continuously experienced **unfair housing practices, environmental injustice, and disproportionately negative impacts of COVID-19**.

To understand what happened to locate Blacks in the disadvantaged spaces they have inhabited throughout their lives in America and why, it's important to acknowledge that the engine of change is **power**. But how is power obtained?

Arguably, the levers of power within our society are the **3Ps: purse, policies,** and **persuasion**. Therefore, unfair housing, environmental injustice, and the disproportionate impact of COVID-19 on Blacks warrant being examined through the lens of the **3Ps**.

Blacks, Unfair Housing, and the 3Ps

"A Snapshot of Race & Home Buying in America", compiled by the research group of the National Association of Realtors (NAR) led by Yun et al. (2020), presented the latest data on the homeownership rate among the races in 2018 using the U.S. Census Bureau's American Community Survey data by state. The report also examined the change in the homeownership rate among African Americans from 2008 to 2018 using American Community Survey data. Finally, using the Profile of Home Buyers and Sellers data from 2019, the report examined the characteristics of who purchases homes, why they purchase, what they purchase, and the financial background of the buyers based on race.

The data showed that the highest percentage of homeownership of Blacks in 2018 was 50 percent in the state of Alabama. By contrast, the comparable figure for Whites was 74 percent in West Virginia, and it exceeded or approached over 70 percent in most other states, except California and Hawaii. The NAR data for the homeownership of African Americans by state is shown below:

While the ownership data vary across racial groups, there is one constant: People want to own their own home; it's part of the American dream.

The likelihood of being able to purchase a home, however, is the factor that varies between the races. According to Yun et al. (2020), **62 percent** of Blacks were denied home loans due to their debt to income ratio, whereas the denial rate for Whites was half that amount.

> **The American Dream Denied:** For African Americans who have faced a history of housing segregation, owning a home is all but an impossible dream for an increasing number of poor families. More likely, finding safe and affordable housing is an aspiration and costly struggle of making daily ends meet rather than a joyous reflection of belonging to a community.

There is an impact on human beings who are denied the opportunity to experience belonging, community, and happiness. It hurts from the inside out as well as from the outside in.

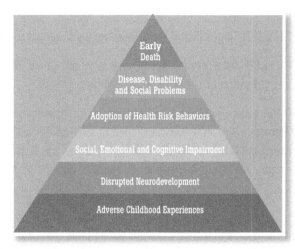

The Power of the PURSE: The Inability of Blacks to Acquire Wealth

Considering the aspect of the purse, it's important to note that housing is a big business. There's a lot of money and vested interests involved. Those who have wealth wield it to lobby for their interests, and those who lack it rely on the pendulum to swing slowly in their favor over time.

According to Manhertz (2020), in a *Zillow Research* article titled, "Recovery Riches: The U.S. Housing Market Gained $11 trillion in value in the 2010s", the combined value of every residential home in the U.S. is a staggering $33.6 trillion—almost equal to the combined 2018 GDP of the U.S. (~$20.5 trillion) and China (~$13.6 trillion), by far the world's two largest national economies. "If all the 2,200+ billionaires in the world (as of 2018) were to pool their assets, their paltry $9.1 trillion in wealth couldn't even buy a third of the nation's homes" (para. 1).

> Over the past year, between the end of 2018 and the end of 2019, the total value of every residential property in the country grew by 3.4%, or approximately $1.1 trillion – a sum higher than the entire 2018 GDP of all but 15 nations. But the real story, according to Zillow, may be in measuring the difference a decade can make: Between 2010 and the end of 2019, the total value of all U.S. homes grew 51%, or $11.3 trillion (para 1.).

And what group has been largely left out of the opportunity to acquire wealth in this story? Black people. Yet they, like most Americans, seek to own property, to have high incomes, to have interesting and safe jobs, to enjoy the finest in travel and leisure, and to live long and healthy lives. However, all of these "values" are unequally distributed, and all may be utilized as power indicators.

Black people lack wealth, and their "purses" have been mostly empty for a long time. Ta-Nehisi Coates (2014) identified the key numbers that explain the reasons why:

> **250** years of slavery, **90** years of Jim Crow, **60** years of separate but equal, and **35** years of racist housing policies.

In an article published by the Center for American Progress, "Systemic Inequality: How America's Structural Racism Helped Create the Black-White Wealth Gap", Hanks et al. (2018) explained how the system works in practice and how it has led to the inability of Blacks to accumulate wealth, pointing to a number of persistent factors, such as:

- A well-documented history of mortgage market discrimination means that blacks are significantly less likely to be homeowners than whites, which means they have less access to the savings and tax benefits that come with owning a home.

- Persistent labor market discrimination and segregation also force blacks into fewer and less advantageous employment opportunities than their white counterparts. Thus, African Americans have less access to stable jobs, good wages, and retirement benefits at work– all key drivers by which American families gain access to savings.

- Black households have far less access to tax-advantaged forms of savings, due in part to a long history of employment discrimination and other discriminatory practices.

- Under the current tax code, families with higher incomes receive increased tax incentives associated with both housing and retirement savings. Because African Americans tend to have lower incomes, they inevitably receive fewer tax benefits– even if they are homeowners or have retirement savings accounts. The bottom line is that persistent housing and labor market discrimination and segregation worsen the damaging cycle of wealth inequality (para. 5).

Lerner's (2020) article in the *Washington Post*, "One Home, a Lifetime of Impact," puts a human face to the story of what homeownership means to families and the role it can play in helping Blacks to accumulate wealth.

Lerner shared the story of Tai Christensen's great-grandmother, who, as a housekeeper and widow in North Carolina with four sons, saved up $500 and bought a house at age 35. "That decision, which changed the trajectory of her family's finances for generations to come, wasn't easy for a Black woman facing racist housing policies, especially as her and her late husband's parents had been enslaved," Christensen explained in Lerner's article (para. 1).

"The decision to buy a house changed the entire trajectory of the family," according to Christensen; as a result, she said, "My father and my uncle own multiple properties and pretty much everyone in my family owns a home and has gone to college because of her decision" (Lerner, 2020, para. 1).

In *The Color of Money: Black Banks and the Racial Wealth Gap*, Baradaran (2017) presented a startling fact. When the Emancipation Proclamation was signed in 1863, the Black community owned less than one percent of the total wealth in the U.S., and more than 150 years later that percentage has barely budged.

Discriminatory policies throughout the twentieth century, according to Brookings, including the Jim Crow Era's **"Black Codes"** limiting opportunity in many Southern states, the G.I. Bill, the New Deal's Fair Labor Standards Act's exemption of domestic agricultural and service occupations, and redlining, collectively prevented Blacks from accumulating and growing wealth.

This history matters for contemporary inequality because its legacy is passed down generation-to-generation through unequal monetary inheritances which make up a great deal of current wealth. In 2020, Americans are projected to inherit about $765 billion in gifts and bequests, excluding wealth transfers to spouses and transfers that support minor children. Inheritances account for roughly 4 percent of annual household income, much of which goes untaxed by the U.S. Government (Baradaran, 2017, p. 46).

Ironically, after over a half a century of being denied housing loans, suddenly in the 2000s, like a miracle, Blacks could magically access them. But it was a trick: It was **"reverse redlining"** targeted for subprime loans. Finally, it appeared that Blacks would be able to experience the American dream. Who wouldn't want to purchase the best house with the best grounds on seemingly the best terms?

Redlining happened because once a line was drawn around people and their neighborhoods, they could be easily targeted, and there was no spillover into White neighborhoods or into society at large—or so "they" (the entire financial industry) thought.

In fact, after a lot of money was made through subprime lending when the bubble burst in 2008 and a national financial crisis ensued, everybody lost more than they had gained.

The Impact of Subprime Lending on Minority Borrowers

Imagine from the perspective of minority borrowers that all of a sudden, the road was paved for their inclusion. The paved roads in newly built developments led to beautiful homes—in fact, to what appeared to be "mini-mansions" in some cases, especially in Prince George's County, Maryland, where Blacks had the highest incomes. After a lifetime of denial in most spheres of life, suddenly there was easy acceptance. But it was a trick.

The trick was adjustable-rate mortgages (ARMs). Offering an initial teaser of low interest rates together with other seemingly attractive terms, such as low-down payments and the ability to overcome unattractive credit scores, and the borrowers' uncertainty of being able to repay the loan, who wouldn't take such an offer? After all, by the time the new variable exorbitantly high interest rates were scheduled to kick in, you could simply sell the house and make a lot of money because the asset would have appreciated greatly, as the house was so beautiful and desirable, right?

It turned out that the **red lines around the areas still existed**. The houses did not appreciate. When it was time to pay the high interest rates, owners defaulted at alarming rates. Who wanted to go into those all-minority neighborhoods and pay high prices for their homes, even if the homes were beautiful? Not the Whites, that's for sure. Then who, other than Black people? Nobody!

Everybody was stuck: the lenders, such as Wells Fargo, that had set up entire Black subprime lending units staffed by Blacks who marketed the loans through the social structures of the Black community; and through the insurers; and the whole financial ecosystem, which is why there was the financial sector crisis of 2008.

Why didn't the Black borrowers know better? Why did they agree to the ARMs? The short answer is they had never been in the game and didn't understand how it was played. Knowledge acquisition happens in mainstream society through multiple channels, from family and friends and through, in this case, the actual contract documents. With little experience with such contracts, the borrowers did not easily understand them. When the agents, often Black people specifically hired by the perpetrators of the lending schemes who were promoting the loans said, "my sister or my brother, don't pay attention to any of that boilerplate", you didn't. It was the new carpetbagging scheme of the twenty-first century.

Today, Black *Purses* Remain Largely Empty

For argument's sake, let's assume that the three key levers of power: The purse, politics, and persuasion were equal with each lever representing one-third weight. By the measure then of the "purse", Blacks are already essentially one-third less powerful compared to the White population and housing has everything to do with the gap. Tendayi Kapfidze, Vice President, Chief Economist at *LendingTree* explains the situation.

Kapfidze's (2020) article, "*LendingTree* Study: Black Homebuyers More Likely to Be Denied Mortgages Than Other Homebuyers", highlights one of the biggest hurdles that disproportionately impacts Black homebuyers: being denied for a mortgage. Specifically, LendingTree's study looks at the spread in mortgage denial rates between Black Americans and the overall population in each of the nation's 50 largest metropolitan areas. For both purchase and refinance mortgages, LendingTree found that Black Americans are more likely to be denied a home loan than the overall population of homebuyers. Key study findings are presented below.

Key Findings

✔ The mortgage purchase denial rate for Black homebuyers is higher than the denial rate for the overall population of homebuyers in each of the nation's 50 largest metros. On average, Black homebuyers are denied mortgages 12.64% of the time. This is 6.49 percentage points higher than the overall denial rate of 6.15%.

✔ Milwaukee, St. Louis and Cleveland, are the metros with the largest spread between the denial rate for Black homebuyers and the overall denial rate for mortgage purchase loans, while Sacramento, Calif., Seattle, and San Diego are the metros with the smallest spread. The average spread in the metros with the widest gap in denial rates is 10.96%, compared to 3.45% in the three metros with the narrowest gap.

✔ As was the case for mortgage purchase loans, mortgage refinance loans are also denied at a higher rate for Black homeowners in each of the nation's 50 largest metros. Black refinance borrowers are denied mortgage refinance loans, on average, 30.22% of the time. That's 13.15 percentage points higher than the overall denial rate of 17.07%.

✔ Phoenix, Philadelphia and Denver are the metros where the spread between the denial rate for Black homebuyers and the overall denial rate for mortgage refinance loans is the largest. Dallas, Minneapolis and Miami are the metros where the refinance denial rate spread is the smallest. The average spread is 21.93% in the metros with the largest gap, and 4.44% in the metros with the smallest gap.

✔ Racial disparities in denial rates for purchase and refinance loans can be even more extreme on the county level. In some counties, even those with relatively high black populations, the denial rate for Black homebuyers and refinance borrowers alike can be as high as 100%. This can result in the spread between the overall denial rate and the denial rate for Black homeowners and buyers being over 90%.

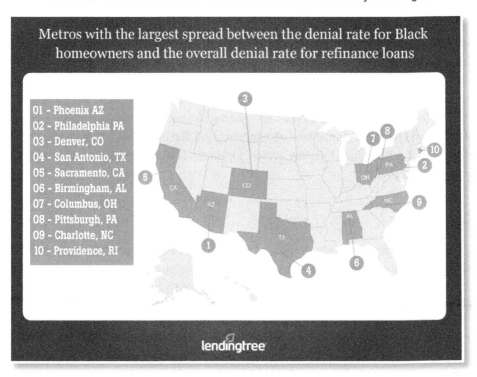

Metros with the largest spread between the denial rate for Black homeowners and the overall denial rate for refinance loans

01 - Phoenix AZ
02 - Philadelphia PA
03 - Denver, CO
04 - San Antonio, TX
05 - Sacramento, CA
06 - Birmingham, AL
07 - Columbus, OH
08 - Pittsburgh, PA
09 - Charlotte, NC
10 - Providence, RI

lendingtree

That being said, there are some counties where the denial rate for Black homeowners and buyers is lower than the denial rate for the overall population.

✔ Even in majority Black counties, the denial rate is disproportionately high for both Black homeowners and homebuyers. Black homebuyers in 83 of the 95 counties with majority black populations looked at in LendingTree's study face a higher denial rate than the overall population in those areas. Denial rates for Black refinance borrowers are equal to or lower than those of the overall population in only 9 counties para(s). 4-9).

Black Homeowners Pay Higher Real Estate Taxes

In the ongoing saga of Blacks just can't catch a break, unfair property assessments lead to widespread over-taxation of Black Americans' homes.

Andrew Van Dam (2020), in his article for the *Washington Post*, "Black families pay significantly higher property taxes than white families, new analysis shows", tells the story. The bottom line is, according to Van Dam, state by state, neighborhood by neighborhood, black families pay 13 percent more in property taxes each year than a white family would in the same situation, a massive new data analysis shows. "Black-owned homes are consistently assessed at higher values, relative to their actual sale price, than white homes, according to a new working paper by economists Troup Howard of the University of Utah and Carlos Avenancio-León of Indiana University" (para. 2).

It's not just that the real estate taxes are taxing, its that all of life as a Black person is taxing. It is referred to as a "black tax". A person, named Charles, interviewed in the Van Dam article, put it this way:

> "It's almost like it's in the soil," he said. "It stretches all across the board. It's not just real estate. It's not just housing. It's not just food deserts. It's not just racism on the street. It's not just that you can't get a cab at night. It's everything." (para. 10).

With the cards stacked against them, today, even the algorithms have joined in to make an assessment that many Black people are disqualified, ineligible, a risk, and the most likely to do something bad. This assessment comes at the end of a dirt road where Black people have historically been placed where bad things were done to them. Over time, such things placed them in the disadvantaged positions observed by the algorithms. One of the worse things that has happened to Blacks is having been denied a fair opportunity to purchase homes in places that had a reasonable chance to appreciate in value and that were fairly taxed. As explained in Van Dam's (2020) article:

Inequities in tax assessment are among many factors weighing on black homeownership rates nationwide. Facing the accumulated disadvantages of centuries of repression and systemic racism, black Americans are likely to earn less than similar white workers in lower-paying service jobs, a dynamic that makes it more difficult to buy a home. Now, by hitting those jobs first and hardest, the coronavirus pandemic has made a bad situation worse. One in five black households have reported missing a mortgage payment since mid-March, compared with about 1 in 20 white ones (para. 9).

The history of overtaxing Black-owned properties goes back to the Jim Crow era when local White officials routinely manipulated property tax assessments to overburden and punish Black populations and as a hidden tax break to landowning white gentry. (Van Dam, 2020, para.12). It was also explained in the article that many county assessors intentionally overvalued black properties, sometimes in direct retaliation for black political action. In other words, if Blacks "acted up" and tried to leverage one of the other 3Ps, namely, the power of persuasion, they would pay for it by being charged higher real estate taxes.

The Hidden Value of Property Value Assessments

Here is where it gets tricky. Let's assume that Black properties in certain areas do not appreciate in value at the same rate that White-owned properties do in nearby areas— because of self-imposed segregation. Then assume that an assessor assumes a Black-owned home gains value as quickly as a White-owned home, the assessed value of the black-owned home will quickly outstrip its market value. Every year, the Black family pays more in property taxes, even though the sales price of its home is not increasing as quickly. Nearby white families benefit from the opposite trend: Their homes increase in value more rapidly than their assessments, giving them an ever-growing tax break.

It's a catch 22 scenario for many Black homeowners and yet another example of how hard it is to catch a break: if it's not one thing, it's another.

The Power of POLITICS: Segregation Policies and Unfair Housing

The roots of formal and sanctioned housing segregation were firmly planted during the Great Depression of the 1930s. It was the time when President Franklin D. Roosevelt's New Deal response was to create the nation's first public housing for civilians.

From the beginning, race determined the program's design, and central to that design was the exclusion of Blacks from all developments—yet, arguably, nobody needed public housing more than Blacks.

To understand what happened to Blacks in the housing sector, it's important to understand the concept and practices of systemic racism.

Systemic Racism Defined. "Systemic racism", or "institutional racism", refers to how ideas of white superiority are captured in everyday thinking at a systems level, taking into account the big picture of how society operates, rather than looking at one-on-one interactions.

By any definition or measure, what the New Deal did to Blacks in formally establishing the roots of housing segregation was a function of systemic racism. There were many systems, policies, and sentiments involved in segregated housing—including laws, regulations, education, hiring practices, and access restrictions.

Blacks were systematically excluded from New Deal programs such as the Tennessee Valley Authority (TVA) and the Civilian Conservation Corps (CCC). Both institutions constructed homes for their workers, but Blacks were excluded both from living in the temporary worker housing and from owning the permanent housing that was constructed. The TVA officials were reported to have stated that "Negroes did not to fit into the program." Blacks did not fare any better with the CCC, which established work camps for jobless youths and adults, because various governors wouldn't allow camps for Black members within their boundaries due to what they claimed

Public Works Administration (PWA)

America Builds

> PWA granted 45% of labor/material costs; remainder paid by localities/states

> PWA also granted $$ to other fed. gov't agencies

> Over $6 billion granted for 34,000 projects nationally

> Over $100 million for 922 projects in Texas

would be "local resentment." As Rothstein (2017) wrote in "The Color of Law: A Forgotten History of How the U.S. Segregated America", the Black crew had to travel many miles away, as there was no room at the inn for them (p.19).

One policy on top of another built an impenetrable system of segregation that excluded Blacks from publicly funded or financially backed housing. The Secretary of the Interior, for instance, directed that housing efforts establish *neighborhood composition rules* that required federal housing projects to reflect the previous racial composition of their neighborhoods. This in turn led cities to zone areas for Black residents only and, eventually, to remove the entire "colored" population from areas that were zoned for Whites.

Brick by brick, the foundations of segregation were built in cities across America. From the federal government, to the state government, to local governments and local institutions, to boards of supervisors, housing authorities, civic associations, and real estate agents—all had a role to play in solidifying housing segregation.

Arguably, the most consequential role was played by the federal government in leading the way in enforcing housing discrimination. A perfect example is that although Congress ended the Public Works Administration's (PWA) role in the direct construction of public housing in 1937, it required localities to establish their own agencies to build public housing directly with subsidies provided by the newly created U.S. Housing Authority (USHA) to adhere to the segregationist policies the federal government had laid down. According to Rothstein (2017):

> The USHA continued the policy of 'respecting the make-up of the existing neighborhood's racial characteristics' and went one step further by issuing a manual that expressly stated that "it was undesirable to have project for White families in areas now occupied by Negroes...and that the aim of local housing authority should be the preservation rather than the disruption of the community social structures" (Rothstein, 2017, p. 23).

In other words, to qualify for the USHA subsidies, local housing agencies were required by the federal government to continue the practice of housing segregation.

The lines were drawn, and they were red for Black neighborhoods. The real estate agents, the bankers, the insurers, and all within the ecosystem of residential housing didn't cross the red lines.

Redlining. The term refers to the presumed practice of mortgage lenders of drawing red lines around portions of a map to indicate areas or neighborhoods in which they do not want to make loans. Redlining on a racial basis has been held by the courts to be an illegal practice.

World War II, Urban Housing, and Ghettos

The New Deal got the discrimination ball rolling in housing, but once the ball started rolling downhill, it picked up momentum. As the nation prepared for war in 1940, Congress adopted the Lanham Act to finance housing for workers in the defense industries. Its projects played a major role in segregating urban areas. By the war's end, the Lanham Act had helped to solidify residential racial segregation in every metropolitan area it touched.

After the war ended and veterans returned home, the housing shortage once again become a major crisis, as Rothstein (2017) explains:

> One year into Harry Truman's term in 1948 as an elected president, he proposed a new public housing effort to address the crisis, but there was opposition to it in Congress. Whereas the Lanham Act had been authorized as a presumed "one-off" wartime measure, further government involvement in the private sector housing was opposed by Conservative Republicans so they sought to kill the bill. They knew exactly how to do that, which was saddle the bill with a requirement to oppose segregation. They knew that southern Democrats wanted public housing for their White constituents and would vote for Truman's bill as long as it did not require desegregation. (Rothstein, 2017, p. 25).

Faced with a classic ethical dilemma of having a bill that provided segregated housing or having no housing bill at all, liberals such as Humbert Humphrey were backed into a corner and opted to have a bill that continued the practice of segregation in public housing.

What is an Ethical Dilemma? It is a situation in which a difficult choice has to be made between two courses of action, either of which entails transgressing a moral principle.

The choice was made. Segregation held.

The most potent glue that cemented segregation was the Federal Housing Administration **FHA Underwriting Manual** that explicitly laid out the segregationist policies to which to adhere. Rothstein (2017) explains the practice as follows:

> Its *Underwriting Manual* stated that "incompatible racial groups should not be permitted to live in the same communities." Meaning that loans to African Americans could not be insured. In one development ... in Detroit ... the FHA would not go ahead, during World War II, with this development unless the developer built a 6-foot-high wall, cement wall, separating his development from a nearby African-American neighborhood to make sure that no African-Americans could even walk into that neighborhood. The Manual also recommended that highways would be a good way to separate African American from white neighborhoods, which according to Rothstein was 'a de jure unconstitutional expression of government policy as something written in law.' (Rothstein, 2017, p. 48)

Levittown Was Built in Accordance With the Terms and Conditions of the Manual

And according to the *Underwriting Manual,* no Blacks were allowed.

Levittown in Long Island, New York, one of the biggest housing developments of the late 1940s consisting of 17,500 homes, was built with the FHA's pre-approval. Such pre-approvals were highly coveted, as they meant that banks could subsequently issue mortgages to buyers without further appraisal. The FHA's pre-approvals were granted for the Levittown development on the strict condition that neighborhoods be zoned to permanently exclude Black peolple.

> To ensure that Whites lived in areas far removed from Blacks, the federal government spurred the development of the suburbs by guaranteeing bank loans to mass production builders who created all-White subdivisions. When today, eighty years later the term, "your beautiful suburbs" is Tweeted by the President, it paints a clear picture of who is "your" and why are they so "beautiful"? Clearly, "your" means White, and "beautiful" means no Blacks.

Levittown was not just about model homes; the development also modeled how to leverage U.S. Federal Government funding by perpetuating segregation.

Impact on Black Wealth Accumulation

Families started moving into the new homes on October 1, 1947. While the original homes sold for just $7,990 in 1949, the median price of a Levitt home today is $400,000, according to the Multiple Listing Service of Long Island (Rothstein, 2017, p.70).

Imagine the positive impact on generational wealth that an inheritance of a property with an appreciating value has for any group in society. Then, understand that such inheritances have historically been denied to Black people over many generations.

The exclusion of Blacks from Levittown, and from being able to purchase properties in other federally funded developments, involved many stakeholders including:

▶ Insurers: Insurance companies helped solidify housing segregation by recommending that zoning laws be supplemented by deed restrictions to prevent incompatible ownership occupancy.

▶ State and Local Governments: Both used every tool in the book to ensure segregation. They increased the fees of sewer lines for projects that proposed integrated housing; they denied drainage; they changed zoning, created zoning, and rezoned areas. They changed school districts and offered many excuses, such as reserving areas for parks, as reasons why an integrated housing project could not be developed in the areas. They required expensive engineering drawings and engaged in slum clearance to move Blacks out of areas.

▶ Real Estate Brokers and Agents: The National Association of Real Estate Boards adopted ethics rules prohibiting agents from selling homes to Blacks in White neighborhoods, and vice versa. They also engaged in blockbusting tactics to scare Whites out of a neighborhood and to purchase their homes at a discount and then sell them to Blacks for more than they were worth.

▶ Neighborhood Associations, Commissions, Boards, and Others: All played their roles in protesting, petitioning, engaging in scare tactics, and using all available tools to ensure their areas remained segregated.

Were these actions ethical? Were they consistent with the moral and ethical intent of the Fourteenth Amendment? No.

Were they consistent with the long-held view of **manifest destiny,** however? The answer is yes. Were such actions consistent with and part of systemic racism? Again, the answer is yes.

Over the years, systemic racism has been perfected with the many tools in the toolbox that have been used to solidify segregation. Such tools have historically and presently included, for instance:

- State constitutional **amendments** in the 1950s that required a local **referendum** before building low-income public housing projects.

- **Interpretations** of the Housing and Home Finance Agency (HHFA) that the Supreme Court's 1954 decision invalidating "separate but equal" public education did not apply to housing.

- **Abolishing** Truman's 1952 adopted **policy** on a "racial equity formula" to build separate projects to house low-income Blacks in proportion to their need.

- Local housing authorities **evicting** Whites from integrated projects to create all-Black complexes.

- Ward aldermen **vetoing** proposed low-income housing for Blacks.

- Cities **blocking** efforts by the Department of Housing (HUD) to comply with **consent decrees.**

- **Limiting** how and where Blacks could use **vouchers** in the community for rentals of apartments.

- Restrictive **covenants** and **deeds prohibiting** rentals and sales of property to Blacks.

- **Zoning** rules **decreeing** separate living areas for Black and White families.

- **Zoning** areas from residential to industrial to render Blacks ineligible for FHA banked loans because their properties were deemed risky because they were near industrial establishments.

- **Spot rezoning** for commercial and industrial facilities to locate them in Black neighborhoods.

- **Exclusionary ordinances** to prevent low-income families from residing in White areas.

- Granting **variances** for the classification of housing from one category to another to prevent the inclusion of Black families.

- Citizen **petitions** against the inclusion of Blacks in housing developments.

- **Codes of ethics** adopted by real estate boards to require that real estate agents would not sell properties to Blacks.

- **Industrial and toxic waste zoning** to permit toxic waste facilities in Black neighborhoods.

More Tools in the Toolbox of Systemic Racism

In addition to the foregoing sanctioned tools of systemic racism, there were also a lot of underhanded, under the table shenanigans going on to the detriment of Black people and their ability to own homes. One of the notable tactics was a practice called "blockbusting." Solomon et al. (2017) explain what it means in their article, "Systemic Inequality: Displacement, Exclusion, and Segregation":

> In the decades preceding the Fair Housing Act, government policies led many white Americans to believe that residents of color were a threat to local property values. For example, real estate professionals across the country who sought to maximize profits by leveraging this fear convinced white homeowners that Black families were moving in nearby and offered to buy their homes at a discount. These "blockbusters" would then sell the properties to Black families—who had limited access to FHA loans or GI Bill benefits—at marked-up prices and interest rates. Moreover, these homes were often purchased on contracts, rather than traditional mortgages, allowing real estate professionals to evict Black families if they missed even one payment and then repeat the process with other

Black families. During this period, in Chicago alone, more than 8 in 10 Black homes were purchased on contract rather than a standard mortgage, resulting in cumulative losses of up to $4 billion. Blockbusting and contract buying were just two of several discriminatory wealth-stripping practices that lawmakers permitted in the U.S. housing system (para. 19).

There have been so many cards stacked against Black people, they are hardly in the game.

The Power of PERSUASION: Fighting Back

No matter how bad the hands are that they have been dealt, no matter how marginalized they are, Black people must stay in the game, they have nowhere to go and can never give up.

Relegated to relying on the power and promise of democracy to deliver the change they seek has been a disappointing experience for Black people.

But Black people understand that power must be wrestled away from those who possess it, and in wrestling, one has to go to the mat. It takes power to get power, and while Blacks have lacked financial power, they have used their powers of persuasion to organize and to convince stakeholders that to deny them housing opportunities would cost them more than they would gain from the denial.

Protesting works on two levels: It works on the hearts and souls of ethical people, and it works on creating inconvenience for unethical people. In both cases, it takes time to cause change because it takes time to realize that not changing is more costly than changing.

What is the Ethical Problem?

To deny Blacks the right to property was unconstitutional and, thereby, inconsistent with the moral principles and presumed shared ethical beliefs of society. Such flagrant disregard of the Fourteenth Amendment to the Constitution that guaranteed that no citizen would be deprived of property meant that the Black population was not considered to be part of society nor treated as citizens. Section 1 of the Fourteenth Amendment states:

> The following Constitutional amendment was approved by Congress on June 13, 1866 and ratified on July 9, 1868.
>
> **Section 1.** All persons born or naturalized in the United States, and subject to the jurisdiction thereof, are citizens of the United States and of the State wherein they reside. No State shall make or enforce any law which shall abridge the privileges or immunities of citizens of the United States; nor shall any State deprive any person of life, liberty, or property, without due process of law; nor deny to any person within its jurisdiction the equal protection of the laws.

From this lofty, high perch and aspiration, the reality of life for the Black population was at the bottom of the society.

The Ghetto

Elvis Presley's "In the Ghetto" peaked at No. 3 on the American singles chart when it was released in 1969. The song tells the story of a Chicago family beset by poverty, crime, and violence. A verse halfway through portrays "a hungry little boy with a runny nose" who "plays in the street as the cold wind blows / In the ghetto / In the ghetto" —an unusual Top 10 hit.

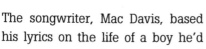

The songwriter, Mac Davis, based his lyrics on the life of a boy he'd grown up with in Lubbock, Texas— "a black kid" whose home was in "a dirt-street ghetto."

Davis had originally called his song "The Vicious Circle"; not until the '60s, he said, did the word "ghetto" cease to recall "Jewish ghettos in Poland." During the civil-rights era, the word evolved "to describe the parts of urban areas where poor people were living and couldn't get out," Davis explained. "They were stuck there, and everybody took off to the suburbs." His song makes no reference to the hungry little boy's race but arriving as it did in 1969—even refracted through Elvis—its allusions were clear. The ghetto was poor, black, urban, and difficult to escape. The ghetto was a problem, a riot waiting to happen, an object of pity and fear.

Source: Kim, T. (2016). Stuck in the Ghetto. Retrieved from https://www.thenation.com

Since it was established in 1909, the NAACP has endeavored to use the power of persuasion to change hearts and minds. Sometimes, it has been joined by labor unions, and sometimes, it has been opposed by the unions. Sometimes, the courts have sided with it and sometimes not. But through it all, and still today, the NAACP keeps fighting because discrimination persists.

The NAACP often brought housing cases to court, citing that segregated housing violated the Fourteenth Amendment. Sometimes, it won various court judgments, but they were hollow victories because often, by the time the NAACP won, a "workaround" was found for the particular contested development and different segregated developments were constructed in its stead.

Arguments such as "the law didn't say this"; "the law actually meant that"; "the law didn't apply to…" gradually worked their way into the pattern of segregation that went around the laws with the ease of water flowing downhill.

When winning is not winning, that's a problem.

In 1945, a Black family by the name of **Shelley** purchased a house in St. Louis, Missouri, but was unaware that there was a restrictive covenant placed on the property in 1911.

The restrictive covenant prevented "people of the Negro or Mongolian Race" from occupying the property. Louis **Kraemer**, who lived ten blocks away, sued to prevent the Shelleys from gaining possession of the property.

The Supreme Court of Missouri held that the covenant was enforceable against the purchasers because the covenant was a purely private agreement between its original parties. As such, it ran with the land and was enforceable against subsequent owners. Moreover, since it ran in favor of an estate rather than merely a person, it could be enforced against a third party.

> ## Restrictive Covenants and the United States Supreme Court
>
> - *Shelley v. Kraemer*, 334 U.S. 1 (1948)
>   - The federal guaranty of due process extends to state action through its judicial as well as through its legislative, executive or administrative branch of government. . . . We hold that, in granting judicial enforcement of the restrictive agreements in these cases, the States have denied petitioners the equal protection of the laws, and that, therefore, the action of the state courts cannot stand.

In a majority opinion that was joined by the other five participating justices, U.S. Supreme Court Chief Justice Fred Vinson struck down the covenant, holding that the Fourteenth Amendment's Equal Protection Clause prohibits racially restrictive housing covenants from being enforced. Vinson held that private parties could abide by the terms of a racially restrictive covenant but that a judicial enforcement of the covenant qualified as a state action and was thus prohibited by the Equal Protection Clause.

And yet, the 1949 Housing Act permitted local authorities to continue to design separate public housing for Blacks and Whites, ceding the high moral ground.

On this slippery moral slope, Blacks slid down further to the bottom of society. They were packed into high-rise ghettos where community life was impossible, where access to jobs was difficult, and where the provision of services was negligible.

Again, the NAACP fought against such segregation and sometimes won battles but never the war. Courts interpreted the intent of Congress as promoting segregation.

The 1960s: A Golden Age of Enlightenment About the "Negro Problem"

No light comes on by itself unless it's the sun; there has to be a switch.

The switch that turned on the light in the mid-1960s was strategically organized civil unrest. Led most famously by Dr. Martin Luther King, it was also supported by powerful and everyday ethical White supporters. The protests and riots made it clear that *doing nothing was not an option*. These acts finally made it "inconvenient" and costly to ignore the rights of Blacks.

> Blacks didn't have their own money to fight their fights; their fights cost the White establishment money so in a sense they used OPM (other people's money).

In rapid succession—*once the lights were switched on*—in 1964, the Civil Rights Act was passed; in 1965, the Voters Rights Act was passed; and in 1968, the Fair Housing Act was passed.

President Lyndon B. Johnson is shown below signing the Civil Rights Act and the Voters Rights Act.

The Fair Housing Act of 1968 Came Next as the Wheels of Justice Slowly Turned

There have always been those in leadership positions who have acted ethically and who have advocated on behalf of Blacks to improve their circumstances. Black advocates, and their allies and fellow protestors and supporters, have won and lost battles. One big win, in principle, was the Fair Housing Act of 1968.

Title VIII of the Civil Rights Act of 1968 (Fair Housing Act) prohibits discrimination in the sale, rental, and financing of dwellings based on race, color, religion, sex, or national origin. Title VIII was amended in 1988 (effective March 12, 1989) by the Fair Housing Amendments Act that expanded the coverage of the Fair Housing Act to, among other things, create new administrative enforcement mechanisms, with HUD attorneys bringing actions before administrative law judges on behalf of victims of housing discrimination.

Despite the role that the federal government originally played in creating and supporting housing segregation and discrimination, it is nevertheless relied on as the best hope to regulate issues that affect the wellbeing of all Americans, especially when private companies—in this case landlords, realtors, and developers—can't always be trusted to self-regulate.

But, as seen throughout U.S. history, one tool can conflict with another, and one person's moral compass is different from another's. We have also seen that concepts and beliefs about ethics and morals change over time or fail to change over time. It is not surprising, therefore, that fair housing has not been achieved. What is clear is that promulgating laws is only a starting place in bringing about change—real change happens when the law is enforced.

In an ideal world, the Fair Housing Act would mean that people of color, women, people with disabilities, and people of different religions would all be given a fair chance to buy or rent housing the same as any White male. Fair housing claims are still regularly filed, and racist slumlords still prevent people from accessing the housing they want.

Past as Prologue: The Pendulum Swings Back

On July 1, 2020, over 50 years after the passage of the Fair Housing Act, during the "golden age of enlightenment" that supported Black people being treated according to the principles set forth in the Fourteenth Amendment, a headline read: "Trump threatens to scrap 'devastating' fair housing rule."

Specifically, Trump was referring to the 2015 Affirmatively Furthering Fair Housing (AFFH) rule, casting it as a thinly veiled warning to the **"great Americans who live in the suburbs"** that Democratic presidential nominee Joe Biden would bring chaos to their neighborhoods. Sound familiar? The familiar tactics are "us" versus "them" and segregation: "You don't want to be around them, do you?"

LOOK At These Homes NOW!
An entire block ruined by negro invasion. Every house marked "X" now occupied by negroes. ACTUAL PHOTOGRAPH OF 4300 WEST BELLE PLACE.
SAVE YOUR HOME! VOTE FOR SEGREGATION!

Rescinding a sweeping Obama-era fair housing rule, the 2015 Affirmatively Furthering Fair Housing (AFFH) rule is stepping up the administration's efforts to gut anti-discrimination laws and to go back in time—a time in the "beautiful 1950s" before the Civil Rights Act, before the Voters Rights Act, and before the Fair Housing Act—to a time when blatant discrimination and segregation not only went unchallenged but were sanctioned and required.

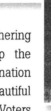

President Donald Trump argues that home prices are going to increase now that his administration has rescinded an Obama-era housing regulation.

On July 22, 2020, President Trump took to Twitter to say he had rescinded the Affirmatively Furthering Fair Housing (AFFH) rule, established by the Department of Housing and Urban Development under the Obama administration in 2015.

Trump claimed that people in the suburbs would "no longer be bothered or financially hurt by having low-income housing built in your neighborhood."

"Your housing prices will go up based on the market, and crime will go down," Trump said in his tweets.

Property developers and real estate agents, in particular, have used such words to influence the residential housing market for a hundred years. Such words are classic "dog whistles."

What is the AFFH Rule? "Affirmatively" is the operative word, and as is the case of all verbs, it means actually doing something, not just stating or proclaiming something—and herein lies the problem.

Through the AFFH rule, HUD provides HUD program participants with an approach to **affirmatively** further the purposes and policies of the Fair Housing Act of 1968. The AFFH Rule not only prohibits discrimination but also directs HUD program participants to **take significant actions** to overcome historic patterns of segregation, **achieve truly balanced and integrated living patterns**, promote fair housing choice, and foster inclusive communities that are free from discrimination.

How the AFFH Is Supposed to Work

Through the rule, HUD commits to provide states, local governments, public housing agencies (PHAs), the communities they serve, and the general public, to the fullest extent possible, with local and regional data on integrated and segregated living patterns, racially or ethnically concentrated areas of poverty, the location of certain publicly supported housing, access to opportunity afforded by key community assets, and disproportionate housing needs based on classes protected by the Fair Housing Act. Through the availability of such data and available local data and knowledge, the approach provided by this rule is intended to make program participants better able to evaluate their present environment to assess fair housing issues such as segregation, conditions that restrict fair housing choice, and disparities in access to housing and opportunity, identify the factors that primarily contribute to the creation or perpetuation of fair housing issues, and establish fair housing priorities and goals.

Source: Federal Register. (2015). Affirmatively Furthering Housing. Retrieved from https://www.federalregister.gov

In January 2020, HUD Secretary Ben Carson, who had already effectively delayed enforcement of the AFFH rule, unveiled a proposal to water it down by **redefining** the way jurisdictions are required to promote fair housing and scrapping a key assessment tool used to map patterns of segregation.

Trump claims decision to repeal fair housing rule will boost home prices, lower crime

On July 26, 2020, Trump claimed that his recent decision to replace an Obama administration rule targeting racial housing discrimination would boost suburban housing prices and reduce crime.

In a pair of tweets, Trump asserted that his efforts to prevent low-income housing from being built in affluent areas would prevent suburbanites from being **"bothered or financially hurt"** by a rule intended to expand access to housing for minorities.

"I am happy to inform all of the people living their **Suburban Lifestyle Dream that you will no longer be bothered or financially hurt by having low income housing built in your neighborhood,"** Trump tweeted.

The Fair Housing Act made discrimination in housing lending decisions illegal. Wallace (2020) explained its importance in her article, "Addressing Racial Inequality by Investigating Mortgage Denials." She underscored the following:

> Historically, the real estate industry kept Black families and other racial and ethnic minorities from securing home mortgages through "redlining," or deeming certain neighborhoods as "hazardous" and denying mortgages there as a matter of policy, regardless of the applicant's means. In Atlanta, for example, neighborhoods that were deemed "hazardous" or "definitely declining" were majority Black, whereas those tagged "still desirable" or "best" were majority White. We can see these historic designations from the 1930s using risk maps from the Home Owner's Loan Corporation (para. 2).

The Housing Crisis Today

Albert Camus's 1942 novel *The Myth of Sisyphus* comes to mind in trying to describe the plethora barriers put in the way of Blacks and home ownership. Even when they believe that have gotten to the top of the hill, they inevitably come rolling back down again. But few ever ascend to the top of the hill; most are at the bottom and at the bottom is where the rain falls.

COVID-19 has made it worse, of course, especially for those living in poor public housing.

In an article, "Pandemic Enhances 'Deplorable Conditions' in Public Housing", Tobi Raji (2020) explains just how bad it is. Raji gives a number examples of what some of the residents in public housing in Washington, DC are experiencing. One example, reported is:

> On any given day, residents at Greenleaf Gardens' 493-unit public housing complex in Southwest Washington deal with rodent-infestation, lead, mold, and flooding from clogged sewer lines. Last week, a resident said she saw a neighbor clearing buckets of sewage water with feces and urine from her home. Other residents complain about rats "bigger than your feet" that creep out at night and leave large, gaping holes in their walls. One resident blames the stress from dealing with the rodent-infestation, holes in her unit, and the pandemic for her recent stroke (para. 7).

Raji (2020) explained that since the pandemic, living conditions at Greenleaf have deteriorated and the maintenance crews only respond to dire emergencies.

It seems that the entirety of the lives being lived by the residents in such public housing throughout the nation is one multifaceted emergency, however, but no one responds to their calls.

Blacks, Environmental Injustice, and the 3Ps

Housing and neighborhood segregation landed Blacks "here." To get "here," they traveled on roads that were unpaved, that were dead ends situated on lands where landfills and hazardous waste were located. They were in locations that highways passed by, where their living quarters were dilapidated and later painted with lead paint, where the air and water were polluted, and where their zip codes and zoning put them into the Twilight Zone. "Here," in the Black ghettos of America, are places where environmental injustice was bred and where it continues to thrive today.

Location, location, location! Racial=Spatial

Location means one of two things in real estate: It's either somewhere you want to *run to* or some place you want to *run from*. Historically, Blacks have been forced live in places that they and everybody else want to run from. The worst among them are places with high concentrations of polluting industrial plants that would not be allowed in any other place in America other than those inhabited by Black people. One of the worse is St. Gabriel, Louisiana, known as "Cancer Alley."

The headline of an article authored by Baurick (2019) and published by the *Times Picayune* and *The Advocate* reads "Welcome to Cancer Alley Where the Toxic Air is About to Get Worse." The story is a personal one for Hazel Schexnayder, who, at 88, "saw this riverside hamlet transformed from a collection of old plantations, tin-roofed shacks and verdant cornfields into an industrial juggernaut" (para.1).

"Over a fifty year period," Schexnayder, according to Baurick (2019), "witnessed increasing numbers of towering chemical plants with 'mysterious white plumes', roadside ditches oozing with blue fluid, air that smelled of rotten eggs and nail-polish remover, and neighbors suffering miscarriages and dying of cancer" (para. 2).

"The industrial polluting plants took over, as if they were the living things; they stole the air, the water, the vegetation, the land, and the lives of many" (para. 2).

The Eastman plant looms behind St. Gabriel apartments. (Sophia Germer/The *Times-Picayune* and *The Advocate*)

By 1993, Baurick (2019) reported, Schexnayder and others began fighting back against the many injustices they endured. They voted to turn their corner of the then-unincorporated Iberville Parish into the city of St. Gabriel. "They wanted sidewalks and other amenities, but more than that they wanted some say over the chemical plants popping up in their backyards," Schexnayder said (para. 3).

However, while the newly created city was able to keep new plants out, the petrochemical pileup continued unabated beyond St. Gabriel's borders, according to Baurick (2019).

Despite their gallant efforts, Schexnayder said, "I bet you money there are 20 plants right now just around St. Gabriel." But she was wrong, said Baurick (2019); "there are now 30 large petrochemical plants within 10 miles of her house, most of them outside the city limits. Thirteen are within a 3-mile radius of her home. The nearest facility, only a mile away, is the world's largest manufacturer of polystyrene, commonly known as Styrofoam." (para. 6). As Baurick (2019) reported:

> "[S]tories of fed-up Louisianans like Schexnayder fighting back against corporate polluters have gotten worldwide media attention," especially since 2018, "as a raft of enormous new petrochemical facilities takes shape along the Mississippi River corridor." Much of the focus, Baurick (2019) explained, "has been on the potential hazards posed by specific plants, including the $9.4 billion plastics factory that Formosa plans to build in St. James Parish and the long-standing Denka neoprene facility in St. John Parish, whose dangerous emissions were highlighted in an Environmental Protection Agency (EPA) model that estimates cancer risk around chemical plants." The stretch of the Mississippi River between New Orleans and Baton Rouge is nicknamed "Cancer Alley" because of its concentration of petrochemical facilities (para. 8).

Baurick (2019) explained the meaning of the term Cancer Alley: The "Cancer Alley" moniker was well earned. In 1969, Baurick said, DuPont opened a plant to manufacture the chemical chloroprene, the main ingredient in neoprene (synthetic rubber). The area immediately adjacent to the Denka/Dupont neoprene plant in St. John the Baptist Parish has been recognized by the EPA as having **the likelihood of getting cancer from air pollution over 700 times the national average**.

St. Gabriel is not just an alley; it is modern day living proof of what Du Bois observed in 1899 in Philadelphia, noting that many evils grow out of racial discrimination. There is no NIMBY for the people of St. Gabriel, nor is there any opportunity for them to leverage any of the **3Ps** levers of power to better their situations. They are just plain old poor, and they aren't even benefitting monetarily from the plants located in their backyards. According to Baurick (2019):

> Whether or not plant managers are hiring people from the surrounding community, it's clear that the profusion of plants has never translated into prosperity for St. Gabriel. Today, the town's annual per-capita income is $15,000 — nearly a third below the state average, and about half the national average. The poverty rate, 29%, far exceeds the state rate of 20% (para. 43).

"St. Gabriel has long been a place to tuck away undesirables. A leper colony, once the largest on the continent, operated here for more than a century. The state stuck a prison in St. Gabriel in 1961, a second one in 1979, and added a military-style boot camp for at-risk teens in 1999." According to Baurick, in 2005, "the bodies of hundreds of Hurricane Katrina victims were trucked to a hastily built morgue here". He describes St. Gabriel further in bleak terms.

> ...St. Gabriel has no downtown, no commercial center. Within its city limits is a discordant patchwork of large steel petrochemical complexes, farm fields and small neighborhoods. About two-thirds of St. Gabriel's 7,300 residents are black. Many families have been rooted here for centuries, brought as slaves and forced to cut and process sugar cane on the vast plantations that once dominated the river parishes. After the Civil War, many stayed on as sharecroppers, free but still beholden to white landlords. (Baurick, 2019, para. 15)

As for Schexnayer, her memories of the cornfields blowing in the wind and of believing that she wasn't poor when she was growing up are of a past gone by. As she reported in Baurick's (2019) article, "we ate every day, and didn't eat just anything, we had good meals." Combined with other memories of the past, such as of the gravel roads that kept the traffic slow, the quiet nights unmarred by the blight of industry, and the absence of fumes and bad smells, she longed for the past when "it was just night air and clean" (para. 33).

The Power of Wealth: Who in Society Bears the Pollution Burden of Industrial Development?

Quite simply, Black people bear the burden associated with living in polluted areas because they have nowhere else to go and cannot leverage any of the 3Ps of power to avoid bearing the burden.

Location matters more than many understood. One can imagine the meetings in many town halls in America when the discussion came up about where to locate
the newly proposed polluting industrial plants. The decision was often to locate them in the places where Blacks lived, far away from White neighborhoods.

The creation of segregation turned into a discipline involving both art and science. The art was often trickery, but the science leveraged all available tools including our founding documents, the amendments to them, and the interpretations of them. It involved all branches of government, governance at every level, the private sector, civil society, religious institutions, and other institutions of power. Collectively, these instruments and tools of power were used to create the separation of the races that was required as a precursor for being able to locate harmful environmental practices in the segments of society that lacked the power to prevent it.

This is applied "systemic racism."

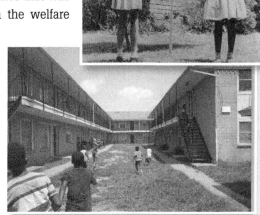

There are few issues in our society where all of these assets, tools, and institutions have been brought to bear in a more coordinated, impactful, and lasting way than in regard to residential areas.

Segregation caused separation, and once that was accomplished, resources to maintain the welfare of members of society could be concentrated in areas where the people whose welfare mattered were located, namely in the White suburbs. It meant that those whose welfare was not prioritized (Black people) could be forcibly located in areas to bear the brunt of industrial pollution and an underinvestment in the things that are needed to secure the well-being of humans.

Location, location, location! It matters. Racial = Spatial.

Environmental injustice is a byproduct of racial segregation. Suffering from the overall negative situation they found themselves in, Blacks lacked the strength and wherewithal to strongly advocate for themselves. Having neither a front nor backyard, they lacked the muscle to protest against locating harmful materials and industrial plants in their neighborhoods. The lacked the voice to cry out "not in my backyard" (**NIMBY**).

Industrial development is not always pretty, and some segment of society has to shoulder the ugly parts. When the population can be divided into the "desirables" and the "undesirables," it follows that projects with the greatest potential to cause environmental harm are located in areas populated by the "undesirables." The bifurcated segregated world that was created wherein Blacks were physically distanced from Whites served many purposes for segregationist stakeholders, industrialists, and property developers.

Segregation was a solution to many problems; it was not just about emotional sentiments, though sentiments were evoked by property developers in crafting their "art" (fearmongering) of their deals.

With so much at stake, the weaponry used by segregationists was like guided heat seeking missiles. Everywhere Blacks went, or were planning to go, the "missiles" sought them out, and the weapons of all institutions were then deployed to take

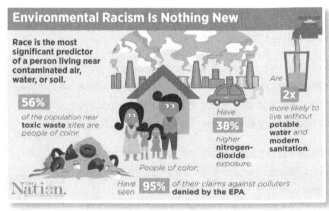

them out—*or not let them in*. Instead, they were moved to locations with bad air, bad water, bad transportation, bad housing, bad schools, and bad outcomes.

Princeton Study (2017): Being Black Doesn't Cause Asthma; the Neighborhood Does

The numbers didn't lie; they showed that black children are twice as likely as others to develop asthma. There was also evidence that low birth weight was a culprit, but could "being black" be a risk factor in asthma, as some believed? Two scholars from Princeton University have concluded that **it's not race, but living conditions**, that accounts for the disparity. The data show the effects of ongoing segregation, which trap African American children in poor neighborhoods, surrounded by pollution.

Janet M. Currie, Ph.D., professor of economics and public affairs at Princeton, and Diane Alexander, Ph.D., of the Federal Reserve Bank of Chicago, made this finding after examining New Jersey health data for low birth weight children of all races living in zip codes where more than half the population was African American. They found that *all* low birthweight children had a higher risk of asthma. New Jersey's industrial history means many black residents live near pollution sources or close to highways that produce harmful soot. Housing in these areas is, on average, 7 years older than housing elsewhere. Currie said these conditions can cause women to have low birth weight babies in the first place.

"The United States continues to be highly racially segregated," Currie said, "with African-American neighborhoods suffering higher poverty, lower average educational attainments, higher unemployment, higher exposure to pollution, and other ills."

Source: Caffrey, M. (2017). Princeton Study: Being Black Doesn't Cause Asthma; the Neighborhood Does. Retrieved from https://www.ajmc.com

Lead Poisoning in Public Housing

Lead poisoning, even at low levels, can lead to lifelong physical and developmental delays for young children. The government banned the use of lead paint in residential homes in 1978, but many older homes still contain lead paint. The risk associated with it increases with the deterioration of the paint, which can chip off into pieces or dust particles that children can ingest.

In 2018, of the roughly 7,000 public housing developments nationwide, lead paint inspections were submitted for fewer than half of them, or about 2,700. But, a spokesman for the HUD inspector general was unable to account for the status of the other 4,000; complexes built after 1978 were exempt. The U.S. General Accountability Office faulted HUD for failing to hold housing authorities accountable consistently and in a timely manner and for awarding lead mitigation grants without taking steps to ensure that the money went to the most at-risk communities.

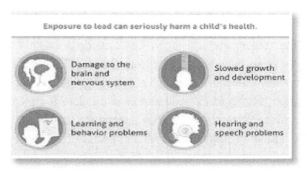

Exposure to lead can seriously harm a child's health.

Damage to the brain and nervous system

Slowed growth and development

Learning and behavior problems

Hearing and speech problems

Targeting Minority, Low-Income Neighborhoods for Hazardous Waste Sites

Race is the biggest indicator as to where a hazardous waste site will be located, and if your race is Black, bingo, that's where it will be located—where Blacks live.

Erikson (2016) wrote an article titled, "Minority, Low-Income Neighborhoods Targeted for Hazardous Waste", in which he cites the longitudinal research of Paul Mohai of Michigan's School of Natural Resources and Environment and Robin Saha of the University of Montana. Mohai and Saha, according to Erikson (2016), wrote two related papers that were published online in the *Journal Environmental Research Letters* that examined the siting of hazardous waste in minority and low-income neighborhoods. They found, after studying 30 years of data, that such neighborhoods and communities in transition are disproportionately targeted by industries that **follow the path of least resistance** when deciding where to locate hazardous waste sites and other polluting facilities. According to Mohai and Saha's research, as referenced by Erikson (2016):

> Several decades of research in the field of environmental justice has established clear patterns of racial and socioeconomic disparities in the distribution of a large variety of environmental hazards. Hazardous waste sites, polluting industrial facilities and other locally unwanted land uses are disproportionately located in nonwhite and poor communities" (para. 13).

The researchers also found that hazardous waste sites are often built in neighborhoods wherein Whites have already been moving out and poor minority residents have been moving in for a decade or two before the project arrives. "Such changes," they suggested, "may result in a further eroding of resources and political clout in these neighborhoods" (para.12), as "demographic change may  represent the weakening of social ties, the loss of community leaders, and weakening of civic organizations".

NIMBYism in more affluent, White communities resulted in industry taking the path of least resistance by targeting communities with fewer resources and political clout—where the poor and people of color live.

Blacks and Hispanic Minorities Bear the Disproportionate Burden of Air Pollution

According to *Science News* (2019), Black and Hispanic Americans bear a disproportionate burden from air pollution caused mainly by White Americans according to a study set to be published in the *Proceedings of the National Academy of Sciences* (PNAS).

The research, led by researchers from the University of Minnesota and the University of Washington, quantifies the racial gap between **who causes air pollution and who breathes it.**

Poor air quality is the largest environmental health risk in the U.S. Fine particulate matter (PM2.5) pollution is especially harmful and is responsible for more than 100,000 deaths each year from heart attacks, strokes, lung cancer, and other diseases.

But not everyone is equally exposed to poor air quality, nor are all people equally responsible for causing it. Researchers found that PM2.5 pollution is disproportionately caused by the consumption of goods and services by the non-Hispanic White majority but disproportionately inhaled by Black and Hispanic minorities. The researchers linked air pollution exposure to the consumption activities that cause it to explore "pollution inequity"— the difference between the environmental health damage caused by a racial/ethnic group and the damage that group experiences.

Specifically, researchers found in 2019 that on average, non-Hispanic Whites experience a *pollution advantage*, meaning they experience approximately 17 percent less air pollution exposure than is caused by their consumption, whereas Black and Hispanic populations bear a *pollution burden* and are on average exposed to about 56 percent more PM2.5 pollution than is caused by their consumption.

Understanding the Pollution Inequity Metric

The pollution inequity metric, according to University of Minnesota researchers, is driven by disparities in the amount of goods and services that groups consume, and in exposure to the resulting pollution. These disparities are influenced by longstanding societal trends, such as income inequality and political representation. Because white Americans consume greater amounts of pollution-intensive goods and services, they are responsible for the creation of more PM2.5 pollution than other racial groups. Further, American blacks and Hispanics tend to live in locations with higher PM2.5 concentrations than white Americans, increasing their average daily exposure to the pollution. In the U.S., racial patterns in where people live often reflects conditions from decades earlier, such as racial segregation.

Source: University of Minnesota. (2019). US black and Hispanic minorities bear disproportionate burden from air pollution. Retrieved from https://www.sciencedaily.com

The pollution problem is inextricably linked to the housing segregation problem; one cannot be understood in isolation of the other. Once Blacks could be isolated from Whites, then Whites could be protected from the environmental injustices that were confined to Black neighborhoods.

POLICIES of Environmental Injustice

Much has happened in the past and much is happening in the present to protect or fail to protect the environment, which affects Black people suffering from environmental injustices.

Presently, the pendulum is swinging in the direction of not protecting the environment or anyone in it. But as we have explained, leveraging the power of the **3Ps** can change its direction.

In a *New York Times* article, "The Trump Administration Is Reversing More Than 100 Environmental Rules. Here's the Full List", Popovich et al. (2020) expose the story of the roll back.

After three years in office, the Trump administration has dismantled most of the major climate and environmental policies the president promised to undo.

Calling the rules unnecessary and burdensome to the fossil fuel industry and other businesses, his administration has weakened Obama-era limits on planet-warming carbon dioxide emissions from power plants and from cars and trucks, and rolled back many more rules governing clean air, water and toxic chemicals. Several major reversals have been finalized in 2020 as the country has struggled to contain the spread of the new coronavirus.

In all, a New York Times analysis, based on research from Harvard Law School, Colombia Law School, and other sources, counts nearly 70 environmental rules and regulations officially reversed, revoked or otherwise rolled back under the Trump Administration, and more than 30 additional rollbacks are still in progress (para 1).

Source: Popovich, N, Albeck-Ripka, L., & Pierre-Louis (2020). The Trump Administration Is Reversing More Than 100 Environmental Rules. Here's the Full List. Retrieved from https://www.nytimes.com/

Patronella and Griffin (2020), in "Communities of Color Bear the Brunt of Trump's Anti-Environmental Agenda," laid out the case of how communities of color continue to be disadvantaged under the current administration as of 2020:

1. **Weakening protections for air and water:** Removed protections for one-third of U.S. drinking water sources: The Trump administration has gutted protections for clean water by weakening the Clean Water Act, finalizing a so-called dirty water rule, and delaying action to protect against toxic chemicals in drinking water. Additionally, under Trump's Environmental Protection Agency (EPA), communities of color in particular are seeing slow and inadequate enforcement of the Safe Drinking Water Act.

2. **Threatening community health and safety:** Undid climate and community protections under the National Environmental Policy Act (NEPA): At the beginning of the year, the Trump administration announced its plans to undermine NEPA—a 50-year-old bedrock law that requires environmental review and public input for federal projects, including for roads and bridges; oil and gas development; and pipeline construction. The proposed changes to the rule include limiting the role of public comment, removing the requirement to consider the cumulative effects of a project, and allowing conflicts of interest. NEPA has been critical in providing communities with a voice in projects that might affect them, and now, the Trump administration hopes to change that by taking away power from the people and placing it in the hands of corporate polluters.

3. **Refusing to take action on climate change:** Rolled back regulations and continued inaction on climate change: The Trump administration has actively worked against climate action at every turn during his presidency, resulting in increased greenhouse

gas emissions and, in turn, increased extreme weather, to the tune of $45 billion of damages in 2019 alone. Trump's efforts to stop climate action at all costs—including withdrawing from the Paris climate agreement, gutting and replacing the Clean Power Plan, and proposing to roll back the clean car standards—mean that these climate impacts are only going to get worse, with the burden placed disproportionately on communities of color; these groups find themselves in worse financial situations after natural disasters such as flooding. Worse yet, the Trump administration has reversed efforts requiring infrastructure projects to be designed to survive the future consequences of climate change (para(s). 2-3).

So, where do Blacks currently stand in respect to environmental injustice? The answer is: approximately where they have always stood, in a place where they lack power through the **Purse**, the **Policies**, and **Persuasion** in sufficient measure to change and improve their situation.

The Power of PERSUASION to Force Change

Basically, what Blacks and their allies can do is protest and endeavor to use democratic systems to persuade stakeholders to act ethically.

Martin Luther King, Jr., reminded us that "the arc of the moral universe is long, but it bends toward justice. Change takes a long time, but it does happen. Each of us who works for social change is part of the mosaic of all who work for justice; together we can accomplish multitudes".

Blacks, COVID-19, Location, and the 3Ps of Power

Zephyrin et al. (2020) published an article titled "COVID-19 More Prevalent, Deadlier in U.S. Counties with Higher Black Populations." In the article, they explained the following:

"Troubling racial inequities have emerged in the COVID-19 pandemic; city and state health departments have raised alarms about the impact on communities of color. In Chicago, African Americans make up 30 percent of the population but 68 percent COVID-19 deaths. Similar trends exist in Milwaukee, Michigan, New Orleans, and other locations" (Zephyrin et al., 2020).

McKinsey (2020), in their article "Black Americans Face Disproportionate Share of Disruption from Coronavirus," also showed that Black Americans are almost twice as likely to live in the counties at the highest risk of health and economic disruption if or when the pandemic hits those counties. McKinsey's (2020) research underscored:

Nationally, Black Americans are not only more likely to be at higher risk for contracting COVID-19 but also have lower access to testing. In addition, they are likely to experience more severe complications from the infection; Black Americans are on average about 30 percent likelier to have health conditions that exacerbate the effects of COVID-19. We also found that 39 percent of all jobs held by black Americans—compared with 34 percent held by white Americans—are now threatened by reductions in hours or pay, temporary furloughs, or permanent layoffs, totaling 7 million jobs (para. 1).

In an article, "Environmental Racism Has Left Black Communities Especially Vulnerable to COVID-19", Casey Berkovitz (2020) has clearly articulated the impact of systemic racism and how the parts fit together in an ecosystem. He stated: "Racism suffuses every system and institution in the United States, and the COVID-19 crisis has highlighted and magnified racial inequality" (para. 1). Berkovitz identifies the factors that make Black communities so vulnerable to COVID-19, and notes the following:

The reasons for these disparities are myriad and interconnected. Black Americans are overrepresented in frontline essential workforces, and therefore face increased risk of exposure; longstanding disparities in wealth and income mean that Black Americans are more likely to need to continue working rather than distance at home; those same disparities, in combination with a lower rate of health insurance coverage, mean Black Americans are less likely to seek care for a sickness that could be COVID-19 due to fear of the cost; and even those who do seek coverage are more likely to face racism from the health care system, resulting in lack of treatment or misdiagnosis. All of these factors exist in addition to preexisting, widespread racial disparities in health outcomes (para. 2).

Climate Change Is Also Unjust

The signs in sympathy for the killing of George Floyd stating, "I can't breathe", had a double meaning for Black people: Many literally can't breathe due to pollution, having asthma, and other conditions. When the problems associated with climate change are factored into the story of Black life in America, it's a perfect storm of injustice.

Can these findings possibly be surprising? No, systemic racism landed Blacks in circumstances and locations where this was bound to happen.

Segregation is not benign. Ultimately, it inevitably has negative societal consequences.

Road to Progress

Blacks have consistently experienced one roadblock after another wherever they were trying to go. But like water, they find the path and roll with that.

From the 1960s onward, when young White student changemakers saw that they could make change happen through their protests, it seemed that change was more possible and easier to accomplish than ever. But it has become exceedingly clear that who is protesting for whom and for what makes all the difference in *whether* and *how* swift a victory might be.

We also see that victories come and go and must be won again. We have witnessed President Trump write the words in various Executive Orders that have wiped out years of accomplishment in housing and in the environment, as well as in other realms of the society.

No, change is not easy, and permanent change is not promised and so the struggles continue.

The good news is that many now have their eyes wide open. Corporations have now been declared to have souls and they are searching them to include a commitment to helping communities as a part of their **ESG** (**E**nvironmental, **S**ocial and **G**overnance) commitments; young White activists have opened their eyes and hearts further in the wake of the killings of so many Black people; and Black people themselves, as their sufferings and exposure to COVID-19 have become even more life threatening, are realizing that they cannot take their feet off the pedals of persuasion.

There is no magic wand and no easy answers, but there are ideas in many areas about how to move forward and take actions in the public and private sectors that can redress some of the existing problems and give us hope.

ESG and the Role of Corporations

One bright spot on the horizon is the prospect of increased ESG investment in initiatives that improve the lives and livelihoods of Black Americans. Large corporations, through their ESG investments, have an important role to play in making investments in the housing and environment sectors that could improve the lives of the low-income population in America.

In "Socially Responsible Investing Accelerates in U.S. Multifamily Space," Bousquin (2020) examined the role of ESG in investing in public housing. He noted that "socially responsible investing is hot" (para.1). Based on data from his firm, McKinsey & Co., Bousquin (2020) said that investment funds connected to some sort of ESG screen accounted for more than $22.89 trillion in 2018, or 26 percent, of assets under management globally. That was up from 21.5 percent of assets in 2012, with ESG investing growing at more than 17 percent annually according to the report.

N.J. Gov. Murphy Signs Environmental Justice Law Designed to Protect Minority Communities

In an Inquirer article, "N.J. Gov. Murphy signs environmental justice law designed to protect minority communities", Kummer (2020), broke the news of the sweeping legislation to protect minorities. He explained the purpose of the legislation, as follows:

The legislation allows the state to deny permits for projects that would have an environmental impact on already "overburdened" communities, defined as those predominated by minority or low-income people. The law, which supporters say is one of the toughest in the nation, would apply to proposals for new or expanded power plants, recycling facilities, incinerators, sludge operations, sewage treatment plants, landfills, or any other major source of potential pollution. The state Department of Environmental Protection would review such projects for "the cumulative impacts" on public health or environmental risk, based on "combined past, present, and reasonably foreseeable" future pollution. Murphy said in a statement that the law sends a clear message that the state will no longer allow Black and brown communities in our state to be dumping grounds, where access to clean air and clean water are overlooked. (Kummer, 2020, para. 2)

Government's Role

There are many issues and opportunities to improve the lives of Black people in respect to improving their access to housing and limiting their exposure to environmental harm. Indeed, many actions are being taken. Two that are highlighted here are in the areas of improving public housing access and investigate mortgage loan denials.

Strategies for Increasing Affordable Housing

Authors Ellen et al. (2020) of the Brookings Institution article, "Strategies for Increasing Affordable Housing Amid the COVID-19 Economic Crisis", note that "even before the COVID-19 pandemic, millions of Americans lacked stable, affordable housing and now, the crisis has highlighted the social and economic costs of this crucial gap in the safety net" (para. 1). The authors also underscore that "people living in poor quality, overcrowded, or unstable housing—or without any home at all—cannot follow public health directives to safely 'shelter in place.' As a result, they are at far greater risk of contracting the virus, along with other chronic illness" (para. 1).

While the article puts forward many recommendations, those that recommend tailoring policy toward local goals, resources, and market conditions are highlighted below. Accordingly, Ellen et al. (2020) provide a framework to guide local decisionmakers in asking and answering critical questions. This framework is particularly interesting because it focuses on engaging the entire ecosystem of stakeholders in housing in order to achieve desired outcomes (para. 29).

✔ What are the highest priorities for the community? Policymakers in high-cost markets may place greater weight on ensuring long-term affordability for properties in appreciating neighborhoods. Communities with an older housing stock will have more properties in poor physical condition that could otherwise become uninhabitable.

✔ What kinds of entities should be eligible to participate? The ecosystem of affordable housing providers varies substantially across communities, including public agencies, nonprofit organizations, and for-profit firms. With appropriate affordability guidelines, any of these entities could be useful partners.

✔ Are local governments prepared to be long-term owners and/or property managers, or is the goal to transfer ownership to non-public-sector owners (either nonprofit or for-profit)? With the exception of local housing authorities, most local governments have little experience with property management and limited staff capacity to take this on.

✔ Are there opportunities to utilize alternative ownership models, such as community land trusts and limited equity cooperatives? These structures can secure long-term affordability and provide greater community voice.

✔ How can public funds be structured to leverage philanthropic or private funds without adding unnecessary complexity? The New York City Acquisition Fund and the Washington Housing Conservancy offer two models for flexible investment vehicles.

✔ How should long-term affordability provisions be designed and implemented? Without deep subsidies, it is difficult to make housing affordable to low-income households. Income-mixing at the project level can increase financial stability, while mixed-income neighborhoods offer residents greater economic opportunity.

Addressing Racial Inequality by Investigating Mortgage Denials

In her article, "Addressing Racial Inequality by Investigating Mortgage Denials", Wallace (2020) starts off by acknowledging that "home ownership has traditionally been one of the main vehicles for accumulating and inheriting wealth in the United States. But not everyone has an equal chance to purchase a home. Since few people have the cash to buy a home outright, their ability to purchase a home is controlled by whether a bank will provide them a mortgage" (para 1).

Wallace explains the situation Black homebuyers are in and what specifically can be done to better understand and address the situation.

A number of factors contribute to the persistent racial inequity in mortgage denial rates. The first is historic. Because of redlining, unequal access to education and jobs, and other systemically racist practices, Black families and other families of color have had a harder time developing generational wealth, either through homeownership or other investments.

This contrasts with people belonging to wealthier families, who are more likely to be able to pull together a larger down payment, which makes getting a mortgage easier. Wealthier families may have an easier time purchasing a home that helps them build more wealth that they can pass to their children, and the cycle continues.

A related issue is that people of color are more likely to have lower credit scores, which also influence mortgage acceptance rates. Research has shown, however, that mortgages applicants who are not white still have higher denial rates than those who are, even when controlling for credit score.

Cities with these kinds of persistent race-based unequal access to housing can use neighborhood data to find areas where partnerships with local organizations can help spread the word about programs that help residents buy homes. They can also identify areas that can benefit from consumer protection regulations to limit credit-damaging predatory loan companies that may operate in those neighborhoods.

The mortgage loan denial data was created by PolicyMap using data from the Federal Financial Institutions Council (FFIEC), collected as part of the Home Mortgage Disclosure Act (HMDA). The data is available to all PolicyMap subscribers.

Source: Wallace, E. (2020). Addressing Racial Inequality by Investigating Mortgage Denials. Retrieved from https://www.policymap.com

The takeaway from this chapter is that there is a lot of work to be done in the short, medium, and long terms to ensure that the protections and benefits of the 14th Amendment of the U.S. Constitution apply to Black people. Doing this work is doing ethics.

CHAPTER THREE

Policing and Ethics

About Chapter Three: **Policing and Ethics**

his was a difficult chapter to write and it will be difficult to read because it shows how policing looks through the lens of the Black American experience—and it is not always a pretty sight.

It picks up from the previous chapter and asks the question: What does bad housing, living in unhealthy polluted environments, and an inability to accumulate wealth cause? It causes festering problems for those in the situation that eventually spill over to others who are not in the situation.

As Black people are often situated in the most dangerous places and circumstances in American life they are among the most feared in society.

Fear is a powerful motivator. Throughout the history of civilization, societies have been built around protecting themselves from the fear of strangers. By "othering" Black people and isolating them into zoned areas, though they have been here all along, they are strangers to many, including to many within the ranks of the police force.

Over the centuries-old systematic "othering" of Black people, they have not only remained as strangers; they have become poor strangers who were increasingly seen by society as poor, dangerous strangers. Dangerous because they were among the have nots who might spill over into the areas designated for the haves.

The last 50 years of empirical research on fear-arousing messaging has shown evidence that high fear messages are generally more effective than low fear messages in determining and changing people's actions, intentions, and attitudes. Arguably, no fear message registers higher than that subliminally and consistently heard in all corners suggesting that Black people should be feared.

When one of the main tools that police have at their disposal is weapons, it becomes too easy to shoot their way into or out of their fear of something. When that which is feared most is Black people, they often become the targets. When Black people engage in behaviors that support the basis of prevailing fears, the entire law enforcement system retaliates harshly, which is as it should be—as long as the treatment is fair, measured, and warranted.

When a police officer chokes the life out of a man by having his knee on the person's neck in the sight of other officers who do not intervene, the entire policing system is called into question, however. Today, many are asking where did we go wrong in policing; what is right and what is wrong; and how can the system be improved?

The subject of policing is one of the biggest and most consequential topics today. This chapter looks only at three issues that are receiving widespread attention during this period of soul searching: the militarization of the police, calls for defunding the police, and qualified immunity to add additional perspective and an ethical lens and magnifying glass through which to see more clearly how these issues impact the policing of Black Americans.

Policing and Ethics

What do bad housing, living in unhealthy, polluted environments, and an inability to accumulate wealth cause? They cause problems that fester until they eventually spill over to others who are not in that situation.

As Black people are often situated in the most dangerous places and circumstances in American society, they are among the most feared in society. Disenfranchisement, as it turns out, has consequences for society as a whole—not just for those who are directly experiencing it. It is like when a vein is cut, the blood spills everywhere. Analogously, though it has been attempted for centuries, it is not possible to fully confine and isolate the "haves" from the "have nots."

> It is reminiscent of an old joke: a man robbed a bank and was brought before a judge who asked, "Why did you rob the bank?" The bank robber replied, "Because that's where the money is."

The situation that society finds itself in today is not a joke, however, and it is not funny. It is a story that has led to the main job of police being to protect the "haves" from the "have nots." The result has been an overzealous policing culture that targets Black people everywhere to prevent them from spilling over into the zones that are inhabited by the "haves."

Too much is being asked of police. They cannot contain the "troubled waters" from spilling over into society just as putting one's finger in a dike cannot hold back the water. Inevitably, the water will flow out and down to the valley floor, and when it gets there, the police are asked to come and clean it up.

But, even more is being asked of the police. They are being asked, as if they were engineers, to design a solution to make water run uphill. Such engineering solutions, while technically possible, never succeed because they are working against the physics of gravitational pull.

The origins of the problems that police are *policing* have many long, wide, and deep roots. The roots are so deep that it would take the most experienced excavation crew to unearth them—and it would take an effort to replant more fertile ground in its place. The police cannot be the excavation crew, the gardeners, nor the engineers who are charged with redirecting the running water—and they cannot provide a solution to the problems that disenfranchisement has caused. Police are not superhuman. In policing the Black community, they often step into a minefield of problems and run up against the aftermath of what systemic racism has created.

By the time the police enter the scene, they are often scared, and those who are policed are also scared. In such a fraught situation, if one thing goes wrong, everything can go wrong in an instant.

The worst-case scenario plays out when lethal weaponry is used by the police to hit the target and bring it down, but if that action is premature or unwarranted, it results in raising the fear and distrust of the police, and society loses.

As the police are intricately woven into the fabric of society, society cannot afford to have its threads unraveled by fear and mistrust. The police force was created to protect society and keep it safe—all of it, not some of it. However, when it increasingly appears that the protection and safety of Black people is not accorded the same weight and

equal treatment as others, the threads of the fabric come unraveled.

It is clear that ethics are on the line, but not everybody is clear on what ethical policing should look like.

Policing is part of an ecosystem everywhere it exists. Whether they are in urban or rural areas, police departments have many stakeholders who contribute to and are collectively responsible for defining and enforcing ethical policing.

Turning Ethical Theory into Practice in Policing

In the article, "Turning Ethical Theory into Practice in Policing," Pumphrey (2016) stated:

> Police work often requires officers to make split-second decisions as part of their daily functions. When in difficult situations, it's essential to have a **solid moral compass** governed by a strong understanding of ethical principles. From racial profiling to crimes involving suspects with mental illness, there are a variety of ethical dilemmas where officers must exercise discretion, appropriate forms of force, and due process (para.1).

How is one's moral compass set?

What cues does one discern that point to true north? Cues are first discerned at home, long before one enters into policing; subsequently, they are discerned from society at large, and ultimately, from the cues signaled within the police force and the ecosystems in which they operate.

Such discernment is through *osmosis*—the process of gradual or unconscious assimilation of ideas and knowledge. Everybody goes into and comes out of this process differently; therefore, different police officers have different moral compasses that have been calibrated differently.

But, there is one thing all police have in common: **weapons**. When they are equipped with weapons, many become convinced that using them is their job.

Tools in the Toolbox

Are ethics in a police officer's toolbox? Is compassion in the toolbox? Is the golden rule, "Do unto others as you would have them do unto you" (King James Bible, 1769, Matthew 7:12), in the toolbox?

In the split second that a police officer has to make a decision, does the officer pull out a moral compass to locate true north, pull out pepper spray or a Taser and use it, or draw their gun and start shooting?

Clearly, if one must stop at that moment of perceived or real danger to pull out a compass to know right from wrong, there is a problem because the compass has not been hardwired in, and hesitation endangers everyone.

The challenge is how society should signal that tools of reason, compassion, and ethical persuasion are just as potent—*and perhaps more effective*—than lethal force.

Could sensitivity training help police officers lead with tools of reason, compassion, and ethics instead of weapons? President Trump advised the following;

On July 28, 2017, President Trump, at a rally, told cops that they should "rough up people more" during arrests. He said, "Please, don't be too nice." He added, "When you guys put somebody in the car and you are protecting their head, you know, the way you put their hand over, like, don't hit their head and they've just killed somebody. Don't hit their head. I said, you can take that hand away, okay?"

That is not a dog whistle: it is a presidential directive. It is a bullhorn blaring, forget about checking your moral compass—just be as rough as you want to without regard for the person's humanity.

The president was not kidding, and we know that because he has repeatedly shown his disdain throughout his presidency for nuance and ethics. In his literal and figurative world of "black and white," there are no gray areas where questions would invoke opportunities to apply reason, compassion, ethics, and sensitivity.

Eventually, on September 22, 2020, he codified his views in opposition to racial sensitivity training in his Executive Order 13950 on "Combatting Race and Sex Stereotyping," which forbade federal government funding for certain "sensitivity training" to address and combat racism.

Maggie Haberman (2020) quoted President Trump's statement on racial sensitivity training in her article, "Trump Moves to Cancel Contracts for Sensitivity Training", in the *New York Times* on September 4, 2020, as follows:

> The president has been a vocal opponent of the Black Lives Matter protests against police brutality that have been held across the nation since late May, calling the movement a "symbol of hate." He has criticized so-called cancel culture, defended the Confederate flag and military bases named for Confederate generals, and accused people of trying to 'erase' American history. "It has come to the president's attention that executive branch agencies have spent millions of taxpayer dollars to date 'training' government workers to believe divisive, anti-American propaganda" (para(s). 5–6).

In stark contrast to the sentiments that were espoused by the president, in her article "Turning Ethical Theory into Practice in Policing," Pumphrey (2016), a professor of criminal justice at the American Military University, stated the following:

> Agencies must do their part to conduct ongoing training so officers can better navigate concepts of right and wrong and use that knowledge to shape their decisions. Ethics training is a cornerstone for policing because it gives officers important insights about how to develop community trust and deal with various liabilities (para. 2).

What is right and what is wrong? Pumphrey (2016) highlights that there are three identifiable branches in the study of ethics to draw from in order to set one's moral compass and to discern what is right and wrong.

- **Metaethics**, which provides the framework for interpreting how "goodness" is defined and what good means when it comes to one's moral philosophy.

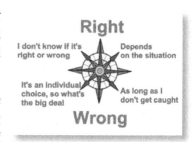

- **Applied ethics**, which examines specific issues concerning judgment and morality. It is best represented as the clear application of theoretical ethics.

- **Normative ethics**, which represents the final branch of ethical theory. It provides the general framework for which individuals are judged by others based on their choices, decisions, and actions (para. 3).

Despite advancements made in the field of professional ethics, at the end of the day, like beauty, ethics are viewed in the eyes of the beholder.

Sadly, if society sanctions undue force against Black people, then it is reasonable to assume, from a normative ethics framework, that such actions are ethical, morally right, and in alignment with societal norms. Thus, while Pumphrey (2016) recommends training as a partial solution for inculcating ethical values into police officers, would the real question be how to *untrain* them from years of believing that certain people, mostly Black people, are the enemy.

But, assuming that ethics training could make a measurable difference, how many hours of training would it take to train police officers to hardwire in a moral compass?

While the precise answer to this question is unknowable because each police officer has a different moral compass setting, the number of hours of ethics training that cadets are provided has been as few as four hours on a one-time basis. Most agencies do not provide ongoing, periodic ethics training, such as mandatory annual scenario-based training.

Is any number of hours of training on ethics sufficient to hardwire in a moral compass, and, if so, how many would that be? How many hours would be sufficient to change the hearts and minds of police officers, to change norms in policing, to save the lives of the many Black people who are needlessly—and, often, unjustifiably—dying at the hands of police officers.

In his article in *Police Chief Magazine* "Teaching Ethics in the Training Academy: A State of the Art Approach," Frederic G. Reamer (2017), an ethics instructor at the Police Department Training Academy in Providence, Rhode Island, sheds light on the history of ethics training in the academy, stating:

> [F]or decades, ethics training in police academies consisted primarily of relatively brief, succinct overviews of the core values that constitute the profession's moral foundation." However, he notes, "ethics trainings in some, but not all, police academies have become more sophisticated and nuanced, reflecting the growth of the broader discipline of professional ethics, applied ethics, or practical ethics" (para. 3).

Reamer (2017) also explained something very important about what police officers must be trained on and how they are trained. From his explanation, one understands that, for the most part, police officers are trained on complex rules and protocols that are "related to core elements of the profession including patrol procedures, investigations, report writing, emergency vehicle operations, defensive tactics, firearm skills, use of force, stress management, human behavior, cultural diversity, and legal guidelines, among others."

But, teaching ethics is a whole other ball of wax—perhaps soft, malleable wax. Typical content in ethics and professional conduct curricula, Reamer (2017) emphasizes, must first include, on the one hand, straightforward guidelines on what to do and what not do (e.g. regarding inappropriate disclosure of confidential information, corruption, excessive use of force, and fraudulent reporting and documentation). However, to be deeply meaningful, ethics education must move far beyond obvious black-and-white issues to explore complex moral challenges, which include gray areas.

There has been a Law Enforcement Code of Ethics for a very long time, but its longstanding existence proves that having something on paper is not the same as having something in one's heart.

The International Association of Chiefs of Police (IACP) adopted the Law Enforcement Code of Ethics at the 64th Annual IACP Conference and Exposition in October 1957. The Code of Ethics still stands as a preface to the mission and commitment law enforcement agencies make to the public they serve. They are :

✔ **Principle #1**: As a law enforcement officer, my fundamental duty is to serve the community; to safeguard lives and property; to protect the innocent against deception, the weak against oppression or intimidation and the peaceful against violence or disorder; and to respect the constitutional rights of all to liberty, equality, and justice.

✔ **Principle # 2**: I will keep my private life unsullied as an example to all and will behave in a manner that does not bring discredit to me or to my agency. I will maintain courageous calm in the face of danger, scorn or ridicule; develop self-restraint; and be constantly mindful of the welfare of others. Honest in thought and deed both in my personal and official life, I will be exemplary in obeying the law and the regulations of my department. Whatever I see or hear of a confidential nature or that is confided to me in my official capacity will be kept ever secret unless revelation is necessary in the performance of my duty.

✔ **Principle # 3**: I will never act officiously or permit personal feelings, prejudices, political beliefs, aspirations, animosities or friendships to influence my decisions. With no compromise for crime and with relentless prosecution of criminals, I will enforce the law courteously and appropriately without fear or favor, malice or ill will, never employing unnecessary force or violence and never accepting gratuities.

✔ **Principle #4**: I recognize the badge of my office as a symbol of public faith, and I accept it as a public trust to be held so long as I am true to the ethics of police service. I will never engage in acts of corruption or bribery, nor will I condone such acts by other police officers. I will cooperate with all legally authorized agencies and their representatives in the pursuit of justice.

✔ **Principle #5**: I know that I alone am responsible for my own standard of professional performance and will take every reasonable opportunity to enhance and improve my level of knowledge and competence.

✔ **Principle #6**: I will constantly strive to achieve these objectives and ideals, dedicating myself before God to my chosen profession... law enforcement.

A closer examination of Principle #1, which states, in part, that the mission of law enforcement "is to protect the innocent against deception, the *weak against oppression or intimidation*, and the peaceful against violence or disorder; and to respect the constitutional **rights of all to liberty, equality, and justice,**" is key. It is the latter point where there have been numerous ethical failures in policing or where the law enforcement ecosystem has broken down.

The weak are often Black people, and they are the very ones who are not always being protected. The opposite is the case; Blacks are often seen as dangerous enemies from whom society needs to be protected. Consequently, the police have a tendency to veer toward the extreme end of the "Use-of-Force Continuum" to out-gun what they assume is facing them.

What is the "Use-of-Force Continuum?"

According to the National Institute of Justice (NIJ) (2009), "most law enforcement agencies have policies that guide their use of force. The policies describe an escalating series of actions an officer may take to resolve a situation. This continuum generally has many levels, and officers are instructed to respond with a level of force appropriate to the situation at hand, acknowledging that the officer may move from one part of the continuum to another in a matter of seconds" (para. 1).

In 2020, the NIJ acknowledged that, broadly speaking, "the use of force by law enforcement officers becomes necessary and is permitted under specific circumstances, such as in self-defense or in defense of another individual or group."

The NIJ also underscored that "there is no single, universally agreed-upon definition of use of force and notes that The International Association of Chiefs of Police has described use of force as the "amount of effort required by police to compel compliance by an unwilling subject." While the NIJ gave an example of a Use-of-Force Continuum in 2009, as shown below, in fact, a universal set of "rules" that governs when officers should use force and how much does not exist. Instead, police officers typically rely on the guidance that they receive from their individual agencies, which means that there is a lot of variation and subjectivity involved in deciding the amount of force that is required. This is the reason why ethics are important and why sensitivity training can play an important role in encouraging police officers to think about how to apply ethics before pulling out their weapons to resolve situations.

An example of how a Use-of-Force Continuum might ideally work was suggested by the NIJ in 2009, as follows:

✔ **Officer Presence** – No force is used. Considered the best way to resolve a situation.
  • The mere presence of a law enforcement officer works to deter crime or diffuse a situation.
  • Officers' attitudes are professional and nonthreatening.

✔ **Verbalization** – Force is not physical.
  • Officers issue calm, nonthreatening commands, such as "Let me see your identification and registration."
  • Officers may increase their volume and shorten commands in an attempt to gain compliance. Short commands might include "Stop" or "Don't move."

✔ **Empty-Hand Control** – Officers use bodily force to gain control of a situation.
  • *Soft technique*: officers use grabs, holds, and joint locks to restrain an individual.
  • *Hard technique*: officers use punches and kicks to restrain an individual.

✔ **Less-Lethal Methods** – Officers use less-lethal technologies to gain control of a situation.
  • *Blunt impact:* officers may use a baton or projectile to immobilize a combative person.
  • *Chemical:* officers may use chemical sprays or projectiles embedded with chemicals to restrain an individual (e.g. pepper spray).
  • *Conducted Energy Devices* (CEDs). Officers may use CEDs to immobilize an individual. CEDs discharge a high-voltage, low-amperage jolt of electricity at a distance (i.e. Taser).

✔ **Lethal Force** – Officers use lethal weapons to gain control of a situation. It should only be used if a suspect poses a serious threat to the officer or another individual.
  • Officers use deadly weapons, such as firearms, to stop an individual's actions.

So, if the continuum is so clear, what remains unclear? Why do things keep going so terribly wrong in policing, as they did in the cases of Breonna Taylor, who was killed on March 13, 2020, and George Floyd, who was killed on May 25, 2020, and in so many other cases?

Reamer (2017) understands this problem and suggests what it takes to inculcate ethics and a sense of right and wrong into the thinking and mindsets of police cadets, but it is not easy because there are too many gray areas.

Thinking Gray While Wearing Blue

Reamer's (2017) recommended strategy, which was set forth in her aforementioned article, identifies five key pillars for training police to help them think about the gray areas that moral dilemmas invoke.

1. **Stimulate the moral imagination.** Reamer quotes bioethics pioneer Daniel Callahan, who states the following:

> A course in ethics can be nothing other than an abstract intellectual exercise unless a student's feelings and imagination are stimulated. Students must be provoked to understand that there is a "moral point of view" . . . that human beings live their lives in a web of moral relationships, that a consequence of moral theories and rules can be either suffering or happiness (or, usually, some combination of both), that the moral dimensions of life are as often hidden as visible, and that moral choices are inevitable and often difficult (para. 7).

2. **Recognize ethical issues.** Police officers, as Reamer explained, have faced disciplinary proceedings, criminal indictments, and prison, in part because of their inability to recognize the moral and ethical elements that are embedded in the scenarios they faced. In some instances, according to Reamer (2017), the officers' judgment may have been clouded because of impairment or because they simply failed to recognize the ethical issues that were involved. In explaining the failure to recognize ethical issues, Reamer (2017) cites the famous "Did you see the gorilla?" experiment by Chabris and Simons:

> In the gorilla sighting experiment, people were given the task of counting the people with white shorts who were playing a basketball game. In the middle of the game, a person dressed as a gorilla walked across the court and no one registered seeing it. Chabris and Simon's research demonstrated that people often do not consciously perceive aspects of their world that fall outside of their narrow attention. Police officers who focus intently on their customary law enforcement duties must be vigilant in their efforts to recognize ethical issues that emerge in their work to avoid what Chabris and Simons call "inattentional blindness."

3. **Develop analytical skills.** Ethical analysis does not come naturally to everyone, and police recruits and officers are no exception. For many, according to Reamer (2017), it is an acquired skill that can be enhanced through rigorous, conceptually oriented, and in-depth instruction that involves real-world cases.

4. **Elicit a sense of moral obligation and personal responsibility.** If ethics training in the police academy is to be effective, it must move beyond vague concepts that have little direct application to policing. Rather, a key goal of training must be to make ethics deeply personal and relevant. The challenge for ethics instructors is to convince recruits that sound moral judgment—and "wrestling" with difficult ethical choices—matters. Recruits must understand that their ethical choices to "do the right thing" really matter.

5. **Develop the ability to respond to ethical controversy and ambiguity.** Inevitably, police officers find themselves facing morally ambiguous dilemmas. When, if ever, for instance, is it permissible for police officers to lie to suspects during an investigation in order to acquire much-needed evidence? What is an officer's ethical responsibility when he or she is concerned that a fellow or superior officer is impaired? How should a conscientious officer respond when he or she encounters blatant corruption in the ranks? Ethics education must seek to enhance officers' ability to navigate such ethically ambiguous circumstances skillfully and with integrity.

The points listed above highlight the difficulty of teaching ethics in general. However, it can be argued that it is exponentially more difficult to teach these concepts as they specifically relate to the policing of Black people when many people have an unconscious bias or unspoken belief that Black lives do not matter as much as other people's lives, and, therefore, they are not entitled to the same treatment as others in society.

Yet, the killing of George Floyd clarified for many that Black lives do matter and that their deaths and the specific manner in which they are killed also matters.

An interesting question to pose is: if the police had shot and killed George Floyd, would that have been a problem for society? Would it have reached the front pages of anyone's news feed? Historical evidence suggests that the answer is no, it would not have mattered because Black people are always shot, and throughout society, people are desensitized to guns and shooting.

> The difference in the Floyd case was *how* he was killed. That one human being could choke the life out of someone with a knee on his neck while he begged for mercy is beyond the grasp and acceptability of most human beings. Putting a reasonable person in the shoes of the police officer under the same circumstances, most could confidently say, "No, I could not and would not have done that—no matter what." It was not an impersonal act like shooting someone; it was deeply personal, as the police officer felt life exiting from a man's body—minute by minute.

In fact, feelings matter, but people must be encouraged and persuaded to feel them—again, this is why sensitivity and ethics training is necessary.

> In my recollection, one of the lessons that was taught in the police academy was to "check your feelings at the door because they can cause favoritism and indecision and slow you down." Over time, however, there has been an increasing recognition that policing requires a balance of thinking and feeling, as both are critical tools in influencing human behavior. In fact, it is thinking plus feelings together that enables one to temper their speed. (Lisa)

Eligibility to Become a Member of the Police Force

Who joins the police force and what qualifications must they have in order to be eligible for such a sensitive, important, and consequential undertaking? While different police departments have different eligibility requirements, an example of one in Arkansas sheds light on an aspect of the problem that does not receive widespread attention. But, are such eligibility qualifications sufficient given the enormity of their tasks?

In accordance with the State of Arkansas Commission on Law Enforcement, the State of Arkansas Civil Service Statutes, and the Little Rock Civil Service Rules and Regulations, applicants for entry-level Police Recruit must meet the following criteria (list is not all inclusive). Candidates must:

1. Be at least twenty and one-half (20 ½) years of age on the date of the written test. Candidates must be at least twenty-one (21) years of age to be hired.
2. Have graduated from a standard high school or possess a high school equivalency certificate General Education Diploma (G.E.D.).
3. Have no felony convictions.
4. Be of good moral character.
5. Have acceptable vision (uncorrected visual acuity must not exceed 20/100 in either eye, correctable to 20/20 or better in each eye).
6. Possess normal hearing and be free of any hearing defect which in the opinion of the physician would adversely affect performance of duty. Hearing may be considered normal when a whispered conversation can be heard at 15 feet.
7. Be a citizen of the United States at the time of hire.
8. Have a valid U.S. Driver's License.

As stated earlier, people come into policing with different moral compass settings. The question that arises from this is how to level set these different compass settings to a place where police are thereby persuaded to lead with ethics and not just weapons.

Know Thyself

Do young police cadets really know themselves, much less the world? While it is convenient to have a definition of when you move from childhood to adulthood at the age of 18, a much more nuanced transition takes place over three decades. From childhood to adulthood people are on a pathway and a trajectory. The question that arises about the judgment of those on the pathway is how far along they are on it, especially when they are confronted with extremely challenging policing situations.

Policing Black people in urban areas is about as challenging as it gets. What is a 20-year-old new recruit, for instance, do when confronted with a dangerous situation—what does the person reach for? It is typically not a moral compass.

An article by Desilver et al. (2020) for the Pew Research Center, "10 Things We Know About Race and Policing in the U.S.," provides survey results from 2016 that underscore the differences in perceptions between the general public and police officers about whether there is a problem in policing Black people. It underscores that ethics are in the eye of the beholder. The sixth finding in the article, in particular, shows the different views that are held by people of different ethnicities, for instance. According to this finding:

In the past, police officers and the general public have tended to view fatal encounters between black people and police very differently. In a 2016 survey of nearly 8,000 policemen and women from departments with at least 100 officers, two-thirds said most such encounters are isolated incidents and not signs of broader problems between police and the black community. In a companion survey of more than 4,500 U.S. adults, 60% of the public called such incidents signs of broader problems between police and black people. But the views given by police themselves were sharply differentiated by race:

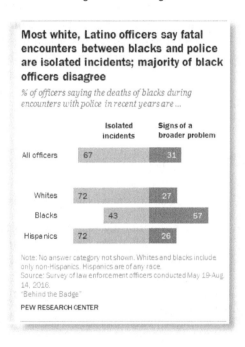

Most white, Latino officers say fatal encounters between blacks and police are isolated incidents; majority of black officers disagree

% of officers saying the deaths of blacks during encounters with police in recent years are ...

	Isolated incidents	Signs of a broader problem
All officers	67	31
Whites	72	27
Blacks	43	57
Hispanics	72	26

Note: No answer category not shown. Whites and blacks include only non-Hispanics. Hispanics are of any race.
Source: Survey of law enforcement officers conducted May 19-Aug. 14, 2016.
"Behind the Badge"

PEW RESEARCH CENTER

A majority of black officers (57%) said that such incidents were evidence of a broader problem, but only 27% of white officers and 26% of Hispanic officers said so (finding # 6, para. 7).

When the Police are Your Friends

There are those who joined the police force with their moral compasses set to true north, because they wanted to do good, and, indeed, there are many caring police officers.

My reflections on being a young police officer. I joined the police force in 1987 in the city of San Marcos, Texas as a reserve police officer at the age of 19. By the age of 21, I had joined the Dallas, Texas Police Department as a full-time police officer.

At the time, many Black people had strong views about policing, and their views were not positive.

For me, policing was a stepping-stone that paved the way for me to do what I really wanted to do: to become a federal law enforcement agent. It worked out. The three years I invested in policing opened the doors for me to spend the next 27 years in federal law enforcement, where I worked at the Bureau of Alcohol, Tobacco and Firearms, at the Immigration and Naturalization Service, at the Housing and Urban Development's Office of the Inspector General (OIG), and, finally, at the US Agency for International Development OIG. At USAID, I held various positions and retired in 2018 as the Deputy Assistant Inspector General for Investigations.

As a Black woman in the late 1980s, it was not easy to get into the federal government; a path had to be carved. I was able to carve one by virtue of my policing experience. People ask me how I could have possibly gone into policing, which was such a maligned profession in the eyes of Black Americans. My answer is: they needed to walk a mile in my shoes.

Policing was not my first career choice; medicine was, but when it became clear how much it cost (both in time and money) to become a doctor—that was not an option for me. Then, I met a woman in policing who I came to respect. She showed me the way forward on the policing path, and I realized that policing created a door opening opportunity that would enable me to shape my future later.

While in policing, I saw and learned many things; some were good and some, not so much. On the positive side, I learned about how local governments work, and I gained insights into social structures and how ecosystems work.

I also began to learn about me—about my likes and dislikes and about how I handle stress. Most importantly, however, I realized that I had much more to learn about the world than I previously knew.

On the negative side, I saw and experienced racism as never before—both inside the police department and in policing situations. Gradually, I began to comprehend what systemic racism means and how it works. I learned about the code names involved in it, the labels of things given to it, the systems that perpetuated it, and about the feelings that people who were both inside and outside of the police force had about it.

No Black person was beyond the reach of systemic racism, and that included me. For instance, by the late 1980s, redlining and housing discrimination that affected Black wealth accumulation was alive and well, and I experienced its negative impact. A White male colleague who graduated from the same Dallas Police training academy class that I had graduated from was approved for an $80,000 mortgage loan. I asked him which mortgage company he used because I was also in the market for a house. However, when I applied for a loan at the same bank, I was only approved for $36,000. I explained to the loan officer that my salary was higher than that of my colleague's because of the incentive pay I received for having earned a four-year university degree and for having received recognition as an outstanding scholar. My colleague had 30 college hours and did not qualify for the pay incentives. We had similar work histories, but his position was lower than mine (he was a dispatcher and I was a reserve officer). Additionally, we were three weeks apart in our age (21), I was single while he was married with a non-working, college student, dependent spouse, and we both had positive credit histories. To deny my loan application was not fair; though I was serving in the protective forces, no one was protecting me.

The loan officer said, "this is the decision of the underwriters." I told her that I would try a different bank, but she cautioned me against that, and she explained that it would be considered "loan shopping" by other underwriters. Furthermore, she warned, it would negatively affect my credit worthiness, and I would be considered a greater credit risk—making getting a loan for any amount very difficult.

Although I entered the police force as a naive young person, I departed with clarity about a number of things. I realized the inherent dangers in policing and that is what made me opt out after three years. I was lucky to have never shot anyone during my time in service, but I was even luckier to not have been shot.

On balance, one thing I now know for sure is that policing is one of the most difficult jobs in the world, but the difficulty of it is multiplied when the ecosystem in which it operates is suboptimal. Ultimately, it is up to local leadership and the stakeholders within the police ecosystem to create the right balance within it and provide the right resources so that the police are not tasked with whole job of protection and safety.

I, like many other Americans, am deeply troubled by how police routinely treat Black people. I have also experienced being treated differently by the police when they did not know that I was one of them or had been among their ranks. I have seen officers continue to get their cues from corners of society—including from President Trump—that signal that Black people are the enemy, and that it is acceptable—even sanctioned—to treat them without humanity.

I also see that while federal and local law enforcement responses to incidents of police using apparent excessive and lethal force have come under fire, they did not receive enough heat in the past to deter such actions. (Lisa McClennon)

At the heart of the matter is the issue of respect. If Black people are not respected by the banking industry that denies them loans, by the housing system that denies them fair housing, by the polluters of the environment who show utter disregard for the lives and health of Black people, and by the healthcare ecosystem itself that has failed Black people, is it reasonable to assume that Black people can expect a more fair and just treatment by the police? The answer and the evidence clearly shows that it is an unreasonable expectation.

This explains why, on average, a Black person is killed in America approximately every 40 hours.

In his article for Brookings Institution, "How Can We Enhance Police Accountability in the United States?", Rashawn Ray (2020) provides data that underscores just how bad the problem is. He states:

Black people are **3.5 times** more likely than white people to be killed by police when Blacks are not attacking or do not have a weapon. George Floyd is an example. Black teenagers are **21 times** more likely than white teenagers to be killed by police. That's Tamir Rice and Antwon Rose. A Black person is killed about every **40 hours** in the United States. That's Jonathan Ferrell and Korryn Gaines. **One out of every one thousand** Black men can expect to be killed by police violence over the life course. This is Tamir Rice and Philando Castile (para. 3).

One of the three important levers of power that Black people reliably have at their disposal to raise their voices against such injustice is **persuasion**, and, so, they march and march—begging the power structures at large to listen and do something.

Crime Rates Have Fallen While Expenditures on Policing Have Risen

Make no mistake, crime is real; it happens, and it has always happened, and it is committed by people throughout society, and it will always be. Every good citizen in society wants to contain and prevent it wherever possible. Fortunately, crime rates have fallen since the early 1990s.

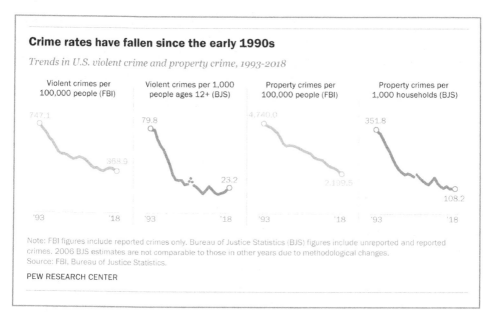

Crime rates have fallen since the early 1990s

Trends in U.S. violent crime and property crime, 1993-2018

Violent crimes per 100,000 people (FBI) — 747.1 ... 368.9

Violent crimes per 1,000 people ages 12+ (BJS) — 79.8 ... 23.2

Property crimes per 100,000 people (FBI) — 4,740.0 ... 2,199.5

Property crimes per 1,000 households (BJS) — 351.8 ... 108.2

'93 ... '18   '93 ... '18   '93 ... '18   '93 ... '18

Note: FBI figures include reported crimes only. Bureau of Justice Statistics (BJS) figures include unreported and reported crimes. 2006 BJS estimates are not comparable to those in other years due to methodological changes.
Source: FBI, Bureau of Justice Statistics.

PEW RESEARCH CENTER

Yet, the level of funding that is allocated for police departments across the United States has not declined, though it might in the future because of upcoming COVID-19-related budget shortfalls, which will impact the availability of funding.

As it stands, in its FY 2019 budget, the Department of Justice allocated **$3.9 billion** in discretionary and mandatory funding for programs to assist law enforcement agencies (LEAs) to address violent crime, opioid abuse, and to help the victims of crime.

> **The Knee on the Neck problem.** Clearly, these expenditures are attempting to solve a problem, and it is acknowledged that real problems exist. The concern is not the money; it is about how to inculcate ethics into the mindset of police so that no police officer would ever believe that it is right or acceptable to go so far as to choke the life out of a person.

This question leads back to the issue of the militarization of the police and whether it is a wise approach.

The Militarization of the Police: What Does Society Gain?

What was society looking for when the police first became militarized? Simply put, it was to fight force with a greater force.

Back in the 1920s, when the police began to use military-style weapons, Black people were not the targets—it was the gangsters. At that time, Black people did not possess the type of weaponry that was involved in high-level crimes. Things changed 50 years later when drugs infiltrated Black neighborhoods. As drugs increasingly infested Black neighborhoods—especially in the public housing complexes where many Blacks were forced into—such areas increasingly became epicenters of crime that eventually spilled over into mainstream society. Guns eventually became as accessible as drugs.

A war on drugs was declared, and as is typically the case, wherever and whenever a war is declared, military-grade weaponry are used to fight it.

In the drug war that began in the 1970s, crack cocaine spread throughout the urban ghettos of America and wiped out the hopes and dreams of generations of their users and victims. Admittedly, it was a scary time for everybody in society—especially for Black people who were both perpetrators and victims of drug-related crimes. But, finally, in the early 1990s, Black people rose up and declared, "enough is enough," and stopped the widespread use of crack cocaine. The Omnibus Crime Control and Safe Streets Act, which gave police agencies money for SWAT units and training, as well as military grade weapons, did not receive much pushback from the Black community because it was helping to reduce crack cocaine-related crime in Black neighborhoods.

In 1991, the then Honorable Charles Rangel, Chairman, Select Committee on Narcotics Abuse and Control House of Representatives, requested the then U.S. General Accounting Office to review the changes in past-year cocaine use between 1985 and 1990 that were reported in the National Institute on Drug Abuse (NIDA) National Household Survey on Drug Abuse. The results showed that the number of cocaine users declined by nearly 60 percent between 1985 and 1990 (from 12.2 to 6.2 million). In addition, the rate that defined current users (those who used the drug within the month before the interview) declined from 47.1 to 26.8 percent.

By the 1990s, however, the die had already been cast for a militarized form of policing, and once such an approach took a foothold, it was difficult to pivot away from it.

Origins of the Militarization of the Police

In the 1920s, during Prohibition, when organized crime began to exploit the lucrative black market in liquor, the golden age of bank robbery, with figures like Bonnie and Clyde, began. Criminals increasingly used submachine guns while the Prohibition-era domestic police departments increasingly used automatic weapons, armored vehicles, and ammo that was developed with the express purpose of being able to penetrate the early bulletproof vests that were worn by gangsters of the era. Overall, crime increased by 24 percent during the first two years of Prohibition.

A few decades later, America saw another significant wave of police militarization during a number of race riots, including the Watts Riots and the 1967 riots in Detroit.

Overkill: Militarized Police Combatting "Super Predators"

Over a 30-year period, beginning in the 1960s, the fear of Black people steadily increased. It came to a head when Black people were labelled as "super predators." It was not just a label, however: it became a mindset that has stuck. But, as Matthew Le Claire (2016) explained in an article featured in the *Huffington Post*, "The Use of the Term 'Super Predator': History and Application," only bad things have resulted from it.

A term and belief with lasting impact. The issue with the term super predator goes back to escalating rates of violent crimes which spawned moral panics about youth in the 70s and 80s; the term was popularized in the early 90s by John J. Dilulio, but was subsequently retired in the late 90s, when the idea of the super predator never came into fruition. Though the term has fallen out of favor with politicians and criminologists, its effects are still evident when examining juveniles within contemporary politics (para. 2).

The 1033 Program and Militarization

With an outstanding and subconsciously embraced notion of Blacks as "super predators," the militarization of the police continued to build, and Black people remained at the center of the bullseye and continue to have a target on their backs.

President Bill Clinton signed into law H.R. 3230 (National Defense Authorization Act for Fiscal Year 1997), which contained Section 1033, which allows the Secretary of Defense to allow the sale or transfer of excess military equipment to local LEAs. As Miller (2019) reported in his article for the Foundation for Economic Freedom, "The Militarization of America's Police: A Brief History," between 1997 and April 2014, $5.1 billion in material was transferred from the Department of Defense to local law enforcement—with ammunition being the most commonly requested.

According to the Defense Logistics Agency (2020), in fiscal 2019, more than $293 million of excess DOD property was transferred to LEAs. The value identified for excess property is based on the original acquisition value, which is what the U.S. government originally paid for the item at the time it was procured. Since the program's inception, the total original acquisition value of property that was transferred to LEAs is **$7.4 billion**.

Civil Asset Forfeiture: A Main Driver in Sustaining the Militarization Strategy

As Miller (2019) explained, "Civil Asset Forfeiture (CAF) is a major driver in the militarization of the police force", CAF is a legal principle that allows police to seize money and property from suspected criminals, which they can do without a warrant because the suspect's property doesn't have the presumption of innocence. In Miller's (2019) view, "CAF is effectively a legally allowed form of theft by police officers." However, a seizure warrant is required for federal cases. The ACLU sheds further light about CAF, explaining:

Forfeiture was originally presented to cripple large-scale criminal enterprises by diverting their resources. But today, aided by deeply flawed federal and state laws, many police departments use forfeiture to benefit their bottom lines, making seizures motivated by profit rather than crime-fighting". For people whose property has been seized through civil asset forfeiture, legally regaining such property is notoriously difficult and expensive, with costs sometimes exceeding the value of the property. With the total value of property seized increasing every year, calls for reform and to rein in the practice are growing louder.

Source: *https://www.aclu.org/issues/criminal-law-reform/reforming-police/asset-forfeiture-abuse*

Rising Concerns about the Over-Militarization of the Police

Finally, we are beginning to scare ourselves. Many in society are beginning to raise questions about the over-militarization of the police and wonder if we are really in a war. Many wonder why we need all of these tanks and military solutions to non-military problems. Why are we applying a tactical solution to a social problem?

High-powered weapons, SWAT teams, and "no-knock" search and arrest warrants are among the police tactics that are becoming increasingly scary to many in society, which raises the question: have we gone too far in the characterization of crime as a war? Have we gone too far in incarcerating and re-incarcerating segments of the population? On the latter point, Pew Charitable Trust researcher Gramlich (2019), in his article "The Gap Between the Number of Blacks and Whites in Prison is Shrinking," provides the following thought-provoking data points:

In 2017, Black people represented 12% of the U.S. adult population but 33% of the sentenced prison population. Whites accounted for 64% of adults but 30% of prisoners. And while Hispanics represented 16% of the adult population, they accounted for 23% of inmates.

Clearly, something is wrong in the way we are policing people of color.

In their article, "Militarization and Police Violence: The Case of the 1033 Program," Miller et al. (2019) said that a tipping point concern about police tactics came in the summer of 2014, when there were protracted protests to the non-response that was associated with the killing of 18-year-old Michael Brown in Ferguson, Missouri. By the second day of the protests, police officers showed up in armored vehicles wearing camouflage, bulletproof vests, and gas masks while brandishing shotguns and M4 rifles. That militarized response led to a wave of criticism from observers, including from former military personnel and politicians from both sides of the aisle.

In response, the federal government launched an investigation that ultimately resulted in Executive Order 13688 (EO). The EO sought to regulate the Department of Defense's 1033 program, which makes surplus military equipment available to state, local, and tribal LEAs at no cost. The EO banned LEAs from acquiring certain equipment and restricted them from acquiring others. It also called for transparency and training regarding the materials that they received.

Some feared that the demilitarized police departments would no longer be able to keep up with drug dealers, rioters, and terrorists.

When then-Attorney General Jeff Sessions announced in 2017 that the Trump Administration's repeal of an Obama-era rule that limited the distribution of certain military equipment (such as tracked vehicles, camouflage uniforms, high-powered rifles, bayonets, and grenade launchers), he dismissed concerns about police militarization as "superficial," according to Bates (2017), as he explained in his article for the Cato Institute "Militarization Makes Police More Violent." Bates (2017) stated that the evidence suggests otherwise, and he noted that militarization makes police more violent—especially against Black people.

Why is Militarization a Problem?

As militarization seeps deep within the culture of policing, the police tend to increasingly rely on violence to solve problems. This mechanism mirrors psychology's classic concept of the "Law of the Instrument," whereby access to a certain tool increases the probability that the tool is used for problems when other tools may be more appropriate.

Ethics and the Use of Force

When ethics are applied to use-of-force cases, it is expected that police officers will balance their responsibilities between being a crime-fighter and a public servant. It must be acknowledged that officers are often placed in situations where their lives are at risk, and their ability to use force is considered an important component for keeping both the officer and community members safe. Officers must ensure, however, that they do not apply unnecessary force and recognize that different situations call for varying levels of what is considered reasonable as per the Use-of-Force Continuum guidelines. Ethics that are built into police training through continuing education reinforces the need to take reasonable and appropriate measures—even under stress.

There are two U.S. Supreme Court case decisions that are often cited when discussing the use of force in policing. The first, *Tennessee v. Garner* (1985), set a precedent that a police officer can only use deadly force with probable cause to believe that a suspect poses a serious threat or physical harm to officers or citizens. In the second case, *Graham v. Connor* (1989), the Supreme Court justices focused on the concept of "reasonableness," stating that the use of force is often something that is determined by a split-second decision. They ruled that several factors must be considered when determining reasonableness, including the severity of the crime, the threat posed to officers, whether the suspect was resisting arrest, and if the suspect was attempting to flee the scene.

These two cases set the precedent involving the use of force in policing and helped shape the Law Enforcement Code of Ethics. Law enforcement officers need to demonstrate lawful authority and a lawful, objective reasonableness before utilizing force.

"Defunding" the Police?

How did we get here? It has been a long, winding, and bumpy road where the carnage of Black people is laying on the sides of the road.

The unfortunate label of "defunding" speaks to a broader issue. It is a recognition that, on one hand, "to he who much is given, much is expected." On the other, it is a recognition that too much has always been expected of the police—they are not "the engineers, the gardeners, or those that can make the water run uphill." More importantly, they are not the cause of the disenfranchisement of Black people; they could be more aptly referred to as "the cleanup crew."

But, the mess they are attempting to clean up and contain is way beyond their capacity to do so. The term "defund the police" expresses an ill-informed but well-intentioned desire of some to suggest that a share of the budget that is allocated to the police be redirected...and this is where is gets complicated.

There is no magic wand. The reasons that Black people are disenfranchised in America have multiple origins from over long periods of time. As a result, there are multiple problems that Black people face that have now been multiplied and exacerbated during the COVID-19 pandemic. Such problems are experienced at every level by Black people—from housing, to the environment, to healthcare, to the treatment of women, and throughout all aspects of living life in a modern capitalistic society where Black people lack capital.

The easiest solution to all of this, as it seemed to be for advocates in the heat of the moment, was to "take **some** of the money from the police and reallocate it."

As Brookings Institution Fellow, Rashawn Ray (2020), explained in his article "What Does Defund the Police Mean, and Does It Have Merit?":

An unfortunate misnomer. "Defund the police" means reallocating or redirecting funding away from the police department to other government agencies funded by the local municipality. That's it. It's that simple. Defund does not mean abolish policing. And even some who say abolish, do not necessarily mean to do away with law enforcement altogether. Rather, they want to see the rotten trees of policing chopped down and fresh roots replanted anew (para. 1).

In essence, the moniker "defund the police" is a societal cry for help to stop the unwarranted, unethical, and immoral abuse of Black people. While the solutions to the broader issues of poverty that lead to crime and punishment are multifaceted and complicated, one thing that can be concluded by many about policing today is that something is not right, and something must be done about it now.

Yet, it must be underscored that within the police force, there are differing views on the extent of the problems that Black people have in the first place. This, in turn, leads to the question of why and whether Black people should be afforded any special consideration in how they are treated by the police.

The article by Silver et al. (2020) for the Pew Research Center, "10 Things We Know About Race and Policing in the U.S.," shed light on the differing views held on whether more changes are necessary—presumably, in any regard—for Blacks to gain equality.

In the four years since that study was undertaken, things have changed—even though some minds have not.

For one thing, COVID-19 happened, and it made everything worse and revealed the extent of the problem that Black people have.

While the term "defund the police" is a misnomer, the costs associated with wrongful deaths are mounting and may cause police departments to de facto defund themselves at the rate they are going.

The recent payouts to families of those who were wrongfully killed were some of the largest in history and show that it is neither morally nor fiscally sustainable to continue down this road. A few recent civil awards provide a hint of the magnitude of the problem.

Police, public divided by race over whether attaining equality requires more changes

% saying that ...

	Our country has made the changes needed to give blacks equal rights with whites	Our country needs to continue making changes to give blacks equal rights with whites
White officers	92%	6%
Black officers	29	69
All whites	57	41
All blacks	12	84

Note: No answer category not shown.
Source: Survey of law enforcement officers conducted May 19-Aug. 14, 2016; survey of U.S. adults conducted Aug. 16-Sept. 12, 2016.
"Behind the Badge"
PEW RESEARCH CENTER

$20 million: This is believed to be one of the nation's largest one-time settlements involving someone being killed by police. As reported by Alexander (2020), "Prince George's County settled with the family of 43 year old William Green, who authorities say was shot six times with his hands cuffed behind his back in the front seat of a police cruiser by Cpl. Michael A. Owen Jr. Owen was arrested the day after the January 27, 2020 shooting and

has been fired. He is awaiting trial on charges of second-degree murder". It turns out, Black Lives Do Matter, after all.

$12 million: This settlement with Breonna Taylor's family is the highest-ever settlement paid by Louisville, Kentucky, which came six months after Taylor was killed inside her apartment as police officers executed a "no-knock" search warrant for drugs that was unrelated to Taylor. As she lay in bed, her boyfriend heard what he

thought were intruders and shot at them. The police then shot Taylor six times as she lay in her bed.

$6 million: The City of Cleveland agreed to pay $6 million to the family of Tamir Rice. On November 22, 2014, *Tamir Rice*, a 12-year-old African American boy, was killed in Cleveland, Ohio by Timothy Loehmann, a 26-year-old White police officer. *Rice* was carrying a replica toy gun; Loehmann shot him almost immediately after arriving at the scene.

$5.9 million: New York City agreed to pay Eric Garner's family $5.9 million. On July 17, 2014, Eric Garner died in New York City after Daniel Pantaleo, a New York City Police Department (NYPD) officer, put him in a prohibited chokehold while arresting him. Video footage of the incident generated widespread national attention and raised questions about the appropriate use of force by law enforcement.

On June 24, 2020, The *Los Angeles Times* Editorial Board printed the article "A Very Abbreviated History of Police Officers Killing Black People." It listed and examined the many cases of the killings of Black people, including those above, among others, where there were apparent miscarriages of justice and evidence of police misconduct. There are too many on the list to include here, but suffice to say, there are valid reasons for advocating for "police reform," and no single reason is more persuasive than the preservation of life. It is noted that advocates of police reform are not just Black people; they are Americans of all colors whose moral compasses are pointing to true north in a new direction of policing—one that respects the lives of everyone in society and their constitutional rights to liberty, equality, and justice.

Black People as Consumers of Police Services

For argument's sake, let us assume that some would actually advocate for "defunding the police" for real. Who would lose and who would gain in such a proposition?

Before answering the hypothetical question, it is important to be reminded that one of the important legs of the stool of policing is protection. Do Black people need the police's protection? Yes, they do—both from the crime they perpetrate against each other and the crimes that others, including the police, commit against them.

Specific data that show how people of different ethnicities use 911 Emergency Assistance can be found at the local level. In general, however, it is known that people of all ethnicities use the service. It is when the police arrive that the outcomes for those who called differs depending on the caller's ethnicity and on the nature of the problem and reason for the call.

Too Many Guns and Too Much Concentration of Them in Certain Areas

No topic on the subject of militarization can be complete without mentioning the proliferation of guns in America—and here, it is not just about the police being militarized; the people are also militarized.

In an article for the *Guardian* "Want to fix gun violence in America? Go local," authors Aufrichtig et al. (2015) provide a map that shows the state of America's gun violence as of five years ago. As the authors observe, America's gun violence epidemic can seem overwhelming. There were more than 13,000 gun-related homicides in the U.S. in 2015, across nearly 3,500 cities and towns. But, the toll of this gun violence was not distributed equally. Half of America's gun homicides in 2015 were clustered in just 127 cities. The conclusion is that "*like income inequality, murder inequality in America is stark*" (para. 15). The article cites Lauren Krivo's views, which are expressed as follows:

> **Gun violence is a regressive tax** that falls heaviest on neighborhoods already struggling with poverty, unemployment, and failing schools. The unequal burden of violence is also marked by intense racial disparities. "It's not about race, per se, it's about how other conditions are racialized and are racially inequitable (para. 16).

Aufrichtig et al. (2017) further quote Krivo, who opines, "Most people don't understand how few predominantly white communities have conditions that are anywhere near the levels of disadvantage that are common in non-white communities, and particularly black communities" (para. 17).

Guns are everywhere in American society and reaching for them to solve problems happens too often—not just by the police, but also by those who hold and use guns for nefarious purposes. The police use guns to protect themselves from the gun-toting public, in part. But, many in the public also tote guns to protect themselves from the police.

Qualified Immunity

Is qualified immunity tantamount to a "get out of jail free pass"—or, more accurately, is it a "never go to jail pass?" That is the question and concern.

Before the killing of George Floyd, it was probably not an exaggeration to say that most ordinary citizens in the U.S. had not heard of the term "qualified immunity." Today, the term is too familiar.

As explained by Cornell University's Legal Information Institute (LII), "Qualified Immunity" is a type of legal immunity, where 'immunity' is freedom from legal obligation to perform actions or to suffer penalties, as in immunity from prosecution" (para. 1).

Qualified immunity balances two important interests—the need to hold public officials accountable when they exercise power irresponsibly and the need to shield officials from harassment, distraction, and liability when they perform their duties reasonably. Cornell's LLI provides further information about what is involved in qualified immunity:

> Specifically, qualified immunity protects a government official from lawsuits alleging that the official violated a plaintiff's rights, only allowing suits where officials violated a "clearly established" statutory or constitutional right. When determining whether a right was "clearly established," courts consider whether a hypothetical reasonable official would have known that the defendant's conduct violated the plaintiff's rights. Courts conducting this analysis apply the law that was in force at the time of the alleged violation, not the law in effect when the court considers the case. Qualified immunity is not immunity from having to pay money damages, but rather immunity from having to go through the costs of a trial at all. Accordingly, courts must resolve qualified immunity issues as early in a case as possible, preferably before discovery (para. 2).

Tim Miller (2007), a constitutional law professor at the Federal Law Enforcement Training Center, explained in a 2007 podcast how qualified immunity works. Basically, according to Miller (2007), if a person is injured or killed and someone files a lawsuit seeking damages, the court determines if the officer violated the person's rights. If the answer is no, then the suit is dismissed. If the answer is yes, then the court then decides if the "right" that was claimed to have been  violated was clearly established by law and whether the action of the police was what a reasonable officer on the scene might would have done under the similar circumstances?

How High is the Bar for Qualified Immunity?

The short answer is that it has varied over time. In an article for *Newsday*, "What Does Qualified Immunity for Police Officers Mean?", Brune (2020) explained:

"In a 1967 ruling, the Supreme Court said police and other public officials would be immune from lawsuits, but that immunity was qualified — it would only protect the officials if they acted in "subjective good faith" in their acts or conduct identified by the plaintiffs" (para. 11). In 1982, however, Brune (2020) stated that "the high court raised the bar for plaintiffs with an 'objective' test: Plaintiffs could overcome officials' qualified immunity only by showing their conduct "violate[d] clearly established statutory or constitutional rights of which a reasonable person would have known" (para. 12).

"The court said in another ruling that lawsuits should be permitted only to officials who are incompetent or knowingly break the law. And a 2009 decision has led lower court judges to quite literally parse whether a police officer knowingly violated a 'clearly established' law" (Brune, 2020, para 13).

Today, "Qualified Immunity faces a growing chorus of critics, who blame the courts' interpretation of what it takes to show police violated a 'clearly established' law to succeed" (Brune, 2020, para. 15). Reuters analyzed data in 2020, Brune explained, which revealed the following:

Courts tend to protect the police. A Reuters analysis recently found that appellate courts appear to have increasingly protected police in excessive force cases—with the courts shifting from approving police immunity in 44% of those cases in 2005-07 to 57% of them in 2017-2019.

Brune (2020) cited examples of failed efforts to challenge qualified immunity, as follows:

Challenging Cases in Which Qualified Immunity Was Granted. An unusual "cross-ideological" dozen-member collaboration that includes the NAACP Legal Defense Fund, the libertarian Cato Institute, and the gun rights Second Amendment Foundation have filed briefs in support of appeals to the Supreme Court. Those briefs back challenges in cases in which immunity was granted to inept cop accidents, apparent police illegality and simply brutality, including:

▶ An appellate court panel protected a Georgia deputy who aimed at an unthreatening dog but shot a 10-year-old child instead because no prior case matched those "unique" facts, though one judge protested that no "competent" officer would shoot at a dog surrounded by kids.

▶ An appeals court ruled that officers might have been "morally wrong" but didn't have "clear notice" that theft violates the Fourth Amendment in blocking a California homeowner's suit against police for allegedly stealing $225,000 in cash and rare coins while executing a search warrant.

▶ An appellate court dismissed a homeless man's suit against police in Tennessee who sicked a dog on him after he surrendered while sitting with his hands in the air because raising his hands wasn't enough to put them on notice that releasing the dog on him was unlawful.

Source: Brune, T. (2020). What does qualified immunity for police officers mean? Retrieved from https://www.newsday.com

Sometimes you lose and sometimes you win. A big win for justice recently happened when the court rejected qualified immunity for cops who shot a "motionless" Black man 22 times.

In an article for *Forbes*, "Court Rejects Qualified Immunity For Cops Who Shot A "Motionless" Black Man 22 Times", Sibilla (2020) reported, "More than seven years ago, Wayne Jones was stopped by police in West Virginia for not walking on the sidewalk. Less than half an hour later, Jones was dead, after police tasered, choked, beat, and shot him 22 times while he lay on the ground" (para. 1).

The family received more than the $3.5 million settlement; they received justice when the court denied qualified immunity. According to Sibilla (2020), the court ruled as follows:

> The Fourth Circuit U.S. Court of Appeals unanimously rejected qualified immunity for the officers, which would have enshrined the "fear-based use of deadly force, which we cannot accept." "Non-cooperation with law enforcement has never given officers carte blanche to use deadly force against a suspect," Judge Henry Floyd wrote for the court. "Although we recognize that our police officers are often asked to make split-second decisions, we expect them to do so with respect for the dignity and worth of black lives," he added (para. 2)

On the other side of the coin is how the police feel about qualified immunity. According to the International Association of Chiefs of Police, "Qualified immunity is a foundational protection for the policing profession and any modification to this legal standard will have a devastating impact on the police's ability to fulfill its public safety mission" (Brune, 2020, para. 30).

In the meantime, New York City paid $94.6 million for Section 1983 civil rights claims in 2019, $100.2 million in the year before, $95.2 million for police misconduct lawsuits under state law in 2019, and $117.8 in 2018. In addition, local governments have negotiated settlements to avoid the costs and time of a federal civil rights trial, such as New York City's $5.9 million payout to the estate of Eric Garner.

The good news is that some scholars argue that the pressure of higher payments may lead cities and counties to provide better training to officers and give more oversight of their police departments.

What is the Relationship Between the Use of Excessive Force and Qualified Immunity?

Rodriguez's (2020) article for the ACLU "Lower Courts Agree — It's Time to End Qualified Immunity" precisely answered the question. He explained that qualified immunity is one reason why police are emboldened to use excessive force without fear of repercussions. According to Rodriguez (2020), "they know the law protects them, even if they may be violating the Constitution. Senseless shootings will continue occurring because police officers are essentially allowed to gun down Black people with impunity". He also said, "this is the abhorrent cost our society pays for qualified immunity" (para. 11).

> On a personal note, when I joined the police force, if I believed that I would be liable for doing the job that the government asked me to do in the way they asked me to do it, I would not have taken on the risk of entering law enforcement. I lived and worked under the impression that any policing tool I used had to be used within the rules. Staying within the confines of the rules was a creed that I adhered to in life—both while on duty and off duty. I know firsthand that it is possible to act ethically in all circumstances—no matter how dangerous situations appear and whether they require a split-second decision. It is always possible to do the right thing if you seek to do it. (Lisa)

The Road to Progress in Policing

Change is never easy, but it is especially hard to make the many changes that are necessary in the law enforcement ecosystem to address problems in policing Black people when some police officers believe that in so doing, they are not only responding to mere incidents, but rather are responding to putting down the "enemy" at large.

One need not look any further than to compare the treatment of those that stormed Capitol Hill on January 6, 2021, versus the treatment of Black Lives Matter protesters. The former was more than a protest, it was an insurrection, yet those who stormed the capitol were treated with kid gloves. The same cannot be said of the handling of the those who peacefully protested against the killing of George Floyd. Black Lives Matters protestors were met with a gauntlet of police presence and enforcement whereas White insurrectionists were not perceived as a great threat.

There are two conclusions that can be drawn. The first is that the police are capable of moderating their responses when they choose to, and the second is that the response to—*not only actions of Black people*—but also to events that support Black people, will be handled in the most draconian manner because Black people are often seen as the "enemy" and are therefore not prioritized for protection or support.

The road to progress must acknowledge what road we are currently on to realize that we need to get off of it and get on another one.

Fortunately, there are many throughout the society who are making "U turns" to get on a better road. Campaign Zero, for instance, is putting up new road signs showing another path. In June 2020, in response to the killing of George Floyd and others, Campaign Zero launched an "8 Can't Wait" campaign, which is a database that tracks how eight policies to curtail police violence are employed in major cities. The eight policies are:

1. Ban chokeholds and strangleholds.

2. Require de-escalation.

3. Require a warning before shooting.

4. Require that all alternatives be exhausted before shooting.

5. Require officers to intervene when excessive force is being used.

6. Ban shooting at moving vehicles.

7. Establish a Force Continuum.

8. Require comprehensive reporting.

This is just the beginning; change is in the air and in the hearts, minds, and plans of many in all corners of the society, including within the entire ecosystem of policing.

One powerful voice being raised is that of the National Organization of Black Law Enforcement Executives (NOBLE), which is shining a light on a new road to take.

NOBLE Indeed

On December 15, 2020, NOBLE and John Jay College of Criminal Justice (John Jay) released a report, "Future of Public Safety (https://www.jjay.cuny.edu/future-public-safety). It details nine points of consensus among law enforcement, activists, union leaders, and elected officials to realize a more racially-just system of public safety and policing in America.

In the report, John Jay and NOBLE share recommendations to help chart a new course for our country where communities of color feel equally protected, respected, and cared for. The report, centered on fairness, is designed to serve as a framework for action and support for local governments, community members, law enforcement leaders, businesses, philanthropic institutions, and activists as they work collaboratively to create a new age of public safety.

Beginning in September, 2020, NOBLE and John Jay brought together a diverse range of speakers for a series of six public conversations to identify points of consensus around what the future of public safety ought to look like.

- Everyone wants the same thing: to be safe

- Healthy communities are safer communities. Public resources must be invested in the areas that are most likely to create healthy communities.

- We must decriminalize mental health, homelessness, and substance abuse and invest in building an effective network of social services in communities.

- There must be a cultural shift in policing away from thinking of officers as "warriors" and instead as guardians who are there to protect the communities they serve.

The good news is that progress is being made in reimagining policing in these areas.

Progress is also being made at the state and local levels as well. While there are substantial reforms underway in states like Illinois, Ohio, Oregon, Pennsylvania, and Washington, to mention a few, one example, in New Jersey, is highlighted below because it focuses on an important aspect of the policing problem, the use of force by police, which has a disproportionately negative impact on Black people.

New Jersey AG to Announce Overhaul of Statewide Police Use of Force Policies

New Jersey's use of force policies govern all 38,000 state, county, and local law enforcement officers in New Jersey. In December 2020, the AG issued new policies in accordance with the following core principles:

1. The Sanctity of Human Life and Serving the Community. In serving the community, law enforcement officers (hereinafter "officers") shall make every effort to preserve and protect human life and the safety of all persons. Officers shall respect and uphold the dignity of all persons at all times in a non-discriminatory manner.

2. Force as a Last Resort and Duty to De-Escalate. Force shall only be used as a last resort when necessary to accomplish lawful objectives that cannot reasonably be achieved through verbal commands, critical decision making, tactical deployment or de-escalation techniques. Force shall never be used as a retaliatory or punitive measure.

3. Duty to Use Only Objectively Reasonable, Necessary, and Proportional Force. Officers shall use the least amount of force that is objectively reasonable, necessary and proportional to safely achieve the legitimate law enforcement objective under the circumstances.

4. Duty to Use Deadly Force Only as an Absolute Last Resort and Duty to Avoid Actions Which Create a Substantial Risk of Death or Serious Bodily Injury. Deadly force shall only be used as an absolute last resort and in strict compliance with this Policy. Other actions by law enforcement that create a substantial risk of death or serious bodily injury must be avoided or employed only under the strictest of conditions.

5. Duty to Intervene and Report. Every officer, regardless of rank, title, seniority, or status, has an affirmative duty to take steps to prevent any use of force that is illegal, excessive, or otherwise inconsistent with such policies, regulations, and laws, if possible, before a fellow officer uses excessive, illegal, or otherwise inappropriate force. Every officer has a duty to immediately report any improper use of force.

6. Duty to Render Medical Assistance. After any use of force, and when the environment is safe, officers shall promptly render medical assistance to any injured person consistent with the officer's training and shall promptly request emergency medical assistance for that person, if needed or requested. Officers also have a duty to monitor individuals for potential medical intervention after any officer uses force.

7. Duty to Report and Review Uses of Force. Every use of force must be reported and receive a meaningful command level review as set forth in a written department policy that includes review by the law enforcement executive. The law enforcement executive shall also conduct an annual review and analysis of the overall use of force by the department.

In addition to the foregoing, new legislation has been enacted in 41 states from 2014-2019, according to Campaign Zero, and at least 107 laws have also been enacted in the same period to address police violence.

The House of Representatives Has Also Passed Sweeping Policing Reform

There is nothing like having to "walk a mile in someone else's shoes" to get people on the right road. What happened on Capitol Hill on January 6, 2021, where insurrectionists planted the confederate flag, put many truisms into stark relief about the unfair manner in which many Black people are policed. While the legislation put forth by the House on June 25, 2020 was already an imperative, the need for it to move forward just became more imperative.

> In addition, on June 25, 2020, the House of Representatives passed a sweeping policing bill H.R. 7120), which targeted racial bias and use of force. The bipartisan vote was 236–181 to approve the measure, which was the most sweeping federal intervention into law enforcement in years. It would eliminate legal protections that shield police officers from lawsuits, make it easier to prosecute them for wrongdoing, impose a new set of restrictions on the use of deadly force, and effectively ban the use of chokeholds. It is noted, however, that Republicans said that the bill is a federal overreach into policing that will never pass the Senate.

What a difference a day makes—especially when the day was January 6, 2021 on Capitol Hill. With all that has happened, it's a safe bet to assume that the foregoing, and perhaps even stronger legislation, will pass.

Indeed, it has come to pass that today, as perhaps never before, the importance of acting ethically and with integrity in all matters is what will save our society. We are, after all, one country with one destiny.

CHAPTER FOUR

Switching the Light On:
The Ethical Example of the Harlem Children's Zone® (HCZ®)

About Chapter Four: **Switching the Light On: The Ethical Example of the Harlem Children's Zone® (HCZ®)**

he preceding chapters have described systemic racism and how the **3Ps** (**P**urse, **P**olicies, and **P**ersuasion) are leveraged to endeavor to break it down. But, its walls are hard to penetrate and the modus operandi of it, which entails isolating, targeting, and destroying Black people wherever they are, has been hard to overcome.

This chapter focuses on a success story, the Harlem Children's Zone®, and how it is succeeding in undoing some of the damage caused, in part, by systemic racism in one area of Harlem.

It shows what "doing ethics" entails in practical terms and the steps a leader must take to make a difference in just one of the zones in Harlem where Black people have been isolated, targeted, and partially destroyed.

Instead of marching in the street, the creator of the Harlem Children's Zone®, Geoffrey Canada, marched into the homes, neighborhoods, and into the minds and hearts of those living in targeted blocks in Harlem to persuade Black people to have hope. He did not march in there empty-handed in 1990; he entered with a plan and concrete strategy for rescuing the future of the children and their communities.

The theory of change of the HCZ® model holds that the success of Black children and the strength of their community go hand-in-hand and that their respective needs are inseparable and must be addressed together to break the cycle of generational poverty and to give children and their families a shot at the American dream.

The approach aims at providing comprehensive, critical support to children and families and reweaving the very fabric of community life.

The HCZ® Project began as a one-block pilot in the 1990s; today it encompasses 100 blocks in Harlem. With bold ambition, careful planning, and a strong infrastructure, it set out to address *not just some but all* of the issues children and families were facing within a finite geographic area: crumbling apartments, rampant drug use, failing schools, violent crime, and chronic health problems.

The challenge is to continue to replicate the model and to go further and deeper into zones where it is needed, not just in Harlem, but throughout the society.

In the words of HCZ® founder Geoffrey Canada (August 2020, *Time Magazine*):

I keep challenging America: If we can do it and if you care about these children, why aren't we ensuring that it is happening at scale across this country? That's the next part of the work.

Switching the Light On: The Ethical Example of the Harlem Children's Zone® (HCZ®)

Undoubtedly, Black people have suffered from systemic racism throughout their existence in America, which has led to all manner of problems in Black society and between it and other communities within society.

Once zoned into specific areas, Black people were "othered" and easily targeted by many forces, including the evil force of drugs. The backstory of why the Harlem Children's Zone® needed to be created has to do with the devastation of Harlem caused in part by drugs and associated incarceration.

Quite simply, the drug epidemic turned off the former bright and dazzling lights of Harlem. Prior to the infestation of drugs, Harlem was one of the most famous urban Black communities in America. It prospered and gained international recognition as a center of African American music, art, and literature. Perhaps such acclaim is the reason drug dealers targeted Harlem, as people there had disposable income to pay for drugs before the drugs robbed them of it.

The Harlem Children's Zone® arrived on the scene long after Harlem's glory days, in the same way a clean-up crew arrives after a hurricane—to "build back better." HCZ®'s master building plan started with building a foundation of support inside the hearts and minds of people in the community. The design was planned to give them hope and encouragement, and to help them reimagine that their neighborhoods could be safe again and that their children could graduate from high school and go on to university and succeed. It was a straight climb up a mountain of problems as high as Mt. Everest, but the mountain had to be scaled because everything was at stake.

A figurative typhoon hit Harlem, causing the kind of damage that only a force of that magnitude could cause and it lasted throughout the 1980s to the early 1990s. Mustain (2017) described just how hard-hit New York was during the height of the crack scourge in an article for the *New York Daily News* titled, "When the Crack Scourge Swept New York City." He explained that "by several measures, the city was brought to its knees [in 1988]. It was the worst year ever for murder. Nearly 40% of the 1,896 homicides were [crack] related, and it was the worst year ever for total violent crimes". With a crime total of 152,600 incidents, New York had as many victims as Syracuse had people, Mustain states (para. 11).

"Though no part of the city was safe from an addict in thrall, the worst peril was in the poorest neighborhoods," according to Mustain (2017), and the worst part was its impact on families (para. 11).

> Crack ripped apart families the same way it did neighborhoods. Reports of Domestic violence increased 24% in 1988 and were up 150% since 1985, the dawn of crack. Child abuse and neglect petitions shot up 19% and were up 156% since 1985. Some kids never got a chance to be rescued; a record 133 died of abuse and neglect. More than 5,000 were born with severe ailments caused by their crack-pipe mothers (para. 12).

Tragically, "the young abused the old and attacks against the elderly by youthful relatives shot up 44%." In effect, "crack had 'wiped out certain ethics' that even criminals once had" (Mustain, 2017, para. 12).

The law enforcement system fought back to the extent it could. As Mustain (2017) reported, "the system was arresting, indicting, trying, convicting and jailing more people than ever." The boss of the police anti-crack unit, which had opened for business in May 1986, "kept a chart of crack-dealer

arrests on his office wall, and in June 1988 it showed that his unit had arrested 13,200 sellers, an average of one every 85 minutes for 25 months," according to Mustain (para. 15).

Mass incarceration in Black neighborhoods exacted another toll. In a report titled "Neighborhood, Crime, and Incarceration in New York City," Fagan et al. (2004) explained in their article for Colombia Law School that a persistent application of drug enforcement produced consistently elevated rates of prison admissions that were well above what might be expected given the overall decline in crime and homicide since 1993. They also explained that "incarceration begets more incarceration, and incarceration also begets more crime, which in turn invites more aggressive enforcement, which then re-supplies incarceration. It is, quite literally, a vicious cycle" (p. 74).

> **The Three Strikes law was the opposite of too little too late; it was too much too late**. In the U.S., habitual offender laws (commonly referred to as three-strikes laws) were first implemented on March 7, 1994, as part of the Justice Department's Anti-Violence Strategy. These laws require an offender of both a serious violent felony and two other previous convictions to serve a mandatory life sentence in prison. The three-strikes law significantly increased the prison sentences of persons convicted of a felony who had previously been convicted of two or more violent crimes or serious felonies and limited the ability of these offenders to receive a punishment other than a life sentence.

By 1990, the tide was already turning against crack, but by then it was rare to find a family in many urban Black neighborhoods that had not suffered from the results of the crack epidemic in the decade before in some way. Harlem was no exception.

The ravage of drugs added to a perfect storm of forces that engulfed Harlem, which included suburbanization, economic decline, epidemic disease, and advantageous municipal public policy.

The master building plan conceived by the Harlem Children's Zone® was not shaped around the assumption that only the purse and policies—two of the three important levers of power—could be used as building material. It also used the lever of persuasion to convince Harlem neighborhood residents that the vision of the HCZ® model, to save the children and the neighborhoods, could be realized.

Understanding who had to be persuaded first was key. It was not the powerful leaders in City Hall, but the people with damaged homes and lives in Harlem neighborhoods.

Fagan et al. (2004) explained exactly what the damage was in their article for Colombia Law School, "Neighborhood, Crime, and Incarceration in New York City." It was not just drugs that ravaged neighborhoods, it was the incarceration of so many Black people from certain areas. They explained the impact of this incarceration as follows:

> The effects of concentrated imprisonment can be observed in the everyday lives of those directly affected—the children and relatives of inmates, for example—but also vicariously in the lives of their neighbors who intersect with the families of inmates and parolees. When high incarceration rates are internalized into the ecology of small, homogeneous neighborhoods, it adversely affects their economic fortunes, political participation, family life, and normative orientation (p.73).

The creator of Harlem Children's Zone®, Geoffrey Canada, had to overcome many obstacles to convince the disenfranchised residents of Harlem that they had the power within to change their circumstances. By jumping in and acting, Canada showed the world what *doing ethics* looked like: it looked like a stakeholder in the Black community, stepping up and throwing down the gauntlet to "build back better."

In helping Harlem to fight its way back to a better place, Harlem Children's Zone® was envisioned not only as a way to switch the light on; *it was instrumental in turning the dark off*. It created a new pathway for eventually moving 100 blocks in Harlem out of the darkness and into the light.

But as the only light that comes on by itself is the sun, a switch had to be flipped to turn on the light. Geoffrey Canada flipped this switch. He stated:

> The Harlem Children's Zone® has always been driven by the belief that the success of our children and the strength of the community go hand in hand. Their needs are inseparable and must be addressed together to break the cycle of generational poverty and give our kids a real shot at the American dream. (www.hcz.org)

The breakthrough approach of the Harlem Children's Zone® was an acknowledgement and understanding that what was in "the zone" in Harlem was toxic and prevented children from succeeding, and that what was needed was a holistic approach for detoxification.

In an August 2020 *Time Magazine* interview with Tyree Boyd-Pates titled, "Tyree Boyd-Pates in Conversation with Geoffrey Canada: America's Future Is Predicated on Knowing the Full History," Geoffrey Canada was quoted as follows:

> It took me decades before I realized we needed something so encompassing that no one would want to do it: to re-create what we call middle-class environments for poor people. People would say, 'We can't afford to do that!' But I'm like, wait. We did that already. We built a middle class for Whites. We got them homes and free college. Why shouldn't we think we can afford to do that for a people who have been systematically denied opportunities? (para. 17)

Canada knew that it would be costly to accomplish the HCZ® dream, but the dreams of others have been realized throughout the history of America. Now, it was time to turn the nightmares of Black people into an opportunity to realize the American dream.

As noted in "Whatever It Takes," the Harlem Children's Zone® white paper (2014):

> The gravitational pull of negative forces is so strong on already fragile families that only a small fraction of the children in these neighborhoods thrive. These exceptional young people are labeled resilient and are justly celebrated for beating the odds. But by definition, most children are not exceptional. Most poor children lack the means to overcome these crushing forces and reach their potential. Instead, they grow up ill-prepared to find good jobs with decent wages as adults, and many fall into substance abuse or end up incarcerated (p. 10).

Indeed, in Harlem and in most other locations in America, once the Black population was contained in isolated zones, resources could be spent in other more desirable areas instead of in those zones.

The HCZ® approach was designed to switch on the light to guide Black people out of the darkness in which they lived.

> Aimed at providing comprehensive, critical support to children and families and reweaving the very fabric of community life, the HCZ® project began as a one-block pilot in the 1990s. With bold ambition, careful planning, and a strong infrastructure, it set out to address *not just some, but all* of the issues children and families were facing within a finite geographic area: crumbling apartments, rampant drug use, failing schools, violent crime, and chronic health problems. (*www.hczpromise.org*)

The mission is being accomplished against all odds.

How High Were the Odds? A Picture of Black America in 1970 Paints the Image

HCZ® was formed from another organization, the Rheedlen Centers for Children and Families (Rheedlen Centers), which began in 1970. For twenty years prior to carving out HCZ®, Canada worked with the Rheedlen Centers. During that time, he was "schooled" on every aspect of the problems facing children, their families, and their neighborhoods in Harlem.

Canada learned that the barriers facing children and families in the community were both internal and external, and immeasurable and measurable, so he formulated a maximum strength antidote to cure the problem.

The picture of Harlem, and of Black urban areas throughout the United States in the 1970s when the HCZ® precursor organization was established, was bleak due to: substandard housing, bad jobs, poor education and healthcare, excessive crime and unfavorable prospects for Black people.

The damage of having been "othered" and zoned out of the mainstream was measurable by many statistics, but the damage it had on the human psyche and the loss of hope it caused was immeasurable. However, the condition of the places and spaces of Black people were not unknown; they were designed for failure through systemic racism.

Paradoxically, two years before HCZ®'s predecessor, the Rheedlen Centers, was formed in 1970, a breakthrough in Black America's ongoing fight for equality occurred.

It took the 1968 assassination of Martin Luther King Jr. to force change when riots broke out in cities around the country. Rising against this tragedy, the Civil Rights Act of 1968 outlawing housing discrimination was signed into law. The National Advisory Commission on Civil Disorders, better known as the "Kerner Commission," was formed to deliver a report to President Johnson in 1968 that examined the causes of civil unrest in African American communities. The report named "white racism" as the factor that led to "pervasive discrimination in employment, education and housing." The report's authors called for a commitment to the realization of common opportunities for all within a single [racially undivided] society.)

But was the call for a commitment to "the realization of common opportunities for all within a single racially undivided society" answered?

By 1970, it was so bad in Harlem that there was a mass exodus from it. Shipp (1991) in the article "Harlem Battles Over Development Project," wrote the following in *The New York Times:*

> Since 1970, an exodus of residents has left behind the poor, the uneducated, the unemployed. Nearly two-thirds of the households have incomes below $10,000 a year. In a community with one of the highest crime rates in the city, garbage-strewn vacant lots and tumbledown tenements, many of them abandoned and sealed, contribute to the sense of danger and desolation that pervades much of the area (para. 12).

The Harlem Zone Prior to 1970

Location, location, location. Racial=spatial. Isolate, target, and destroy. These words are familiar, as are their intent, practices, and applicability to Black people regardless of location, but especially in Harlem.

The reason that the Harlem Children's Zone® emerged was because Harlem was submerged.

The Harlem story is long and with a familiar arc.

To bend the arc towards justice, many groups mobilized in Harlem in the 1960s to protest for better schools, jobs and housing. Some were peaceful protests and others were not, but none were successful until the Chairman of the House Committee of Education and Labor, Adam Clayton Powell Jr., used his position to direct federal funds to various development projects in Harlem. The result was large public housing, with the largest concentration built in East Harlem. Sadly, such large public housing projects later became concentration points for crime and had to be torn down.

The education structure also came tumbling down. In the 1960s, about 75% of Harlem students tested under grade level in reading and 80% in math. In 1964, residents of Harlem staged two school boycotts to call attention to the problem. In central Harlem, 92% of students stayed home.

This is the world that the Harlem Children's Zone® was born out of and dared to reimagine.

This world is described in graphic detail in "Whatever It Takes," the Harlem Children's Zone® white paper (2014):

> In disadvantaged communities many children face a daily barrage of negative influences. The reality for most children in devastated communities is this: they live in substandard housing; they move frequently because their parents do not have secure jobs that pay a living wage; their schools are failing; their playgrounds are filled with broken glass, drug needles, and used condoms; roaches, rats, and mice infest their homes and schools; their healthcare consists of trips to the ER when they have asthma attacks; their walk to school is a dangerous obstacle course where they dodge drug dealers and gangs; at night they pray that stray bullets do not shatter their bedroom windows; their parents work hard, but in minimum-wage jobs without benefits; without a neighborhood supermarket, they buy either overpriced produce or unhealthy but inexpensive meals at McDonald's (p. 13).

"Chaotic and depressing environments like these overwhelm most families," states the report (HCZ®, white paper, 2014, p. 13). Therefore, the HCZ® model was developed to address multiple aspects of the problems. According to HCZ®, "unless sufficient means and resources are invested to substantially improve the lives of the poor, the cycle of poverty will continue with each generation and small-scale, uncoordinated efforts will not work" (p. 14). It was also explained in the report that "community-wide crises demand a community-wide holistic approach that addresses all issues affecting the crisis simultaneously…[and] The Harlem Children's Zone® takes this approach" (para. 15).

Leadership Matters

One definition of genius is making the extraordinary ordinary. It was extraordinary for most Black school-age children in Harlem to come from wholesome and healthy families that aimed for academic achievement in target Harlem zone neighborhoods. It therefore became the mission of the HCZ® to make academic achievement and better neighborhoods *ordinary* in 100 blocks in Harlem. Just as a brick building is built block by block, the HCZ® model endeavored to build a better foundation in the hearts, minds, souls, and reality of the children and their families in the neighborhoods of Harlem.

About Geoffrey Canada, Master Builder. Canada was born in the South Bronx, the third of four sons born to Mary Elizabeth Canada, a substance abuse counselor, and McAlister Canada. The marriage of his parents ended in 1956 and he was raised by his mother. His father played little part in the life of his children and did not contribute to their financial support. Canada was raised among "abandoned houses, crime, violence and an all-encompassing sense of chaos and disorder."

When Canada was in his mid-teens, his mother sent him to live with her parents in Wyandanch, New York. He attended Wyandanch Memorial High School. During his senior year, he won a scholarship from the Fraternal Order of Masons. He holds a Bachelor of Arts degree in psychology and sociology from Bowdoin College, graduating in 1974, and a master's degree in education from the Harvard Graduate School of Education. Canada's brother Derrick Canada was a Harlem Globetrotters player. (www.hcz.org)

Geoffrey Canada was not born with a silver spoon in his mouth. He witnessed the mean streets and what was behind them, resulting in his desire to *do something* to flip the switch.

What is the Relationship Between HCZ® and Ethics? Doing ethics emphasizes that ethics is an activity—something you do—rather than a body of knowledge that one possesses. Ethics cannot be all talk and thought, it must be put into action. HCZ® is an example of doing ethics—of doing the right and moral thing. Helping one's fellow man is one of the highest callings of humanity and the best example of "ethics is as ethics does."

Time Magazine featured Geoffrey Canada in its "The New American Revolution" series in August 2020 in the piece titled, "Tyree Boyd-Pates in Conversation with Geoffrey Canada: America's Future Is Predicated on Knowing the Full History."

Before the conversation got started, Geoffrey Canada expressed how he sees the overall and historical situation of Blacks in America, stating the following:

[It] frustrates me so much when I'm talking to people about the condition of African Americans: they think of slavery as such ancient history—like, "Didn't you get over that?" But it was just a blink of the eye in which I can reach back in history and touch that period. Through my grandmother, I have talked to a person who talked to an enslaved person.

> Since then, so many forces have been working against us: President Hayes pulling the troops out of the South after Reconstruction, the slaughter and the absolute reign of terror that continued right through when I was born in 1952. And policies like the GI Bill, which built the white middle class by giving out free college and low-interest mortgages—but African Americans couldn't get any loans for houses. In New York and northern New Jersey, there were 67,000 mortgages insured by the GI Bill—but less than 100 for nonwhite people. All of this Black history shaped my life and helped me do what I ended up doing (para. 2).

Today, a member from the younger generation joins Canada in ensuring that HCZ® continues to thrive—Kwame Owusu-Kesse. He took over as Chief Executive Officer of the Harlem Children's Zone on July 1, 2020, while Canada serves as president.

But Owusu-Kesse is not new to the mission of or being involved with HCZ®, as prior to assuming his current role he served as its chief operating officer for six years.

In addition, he is not new to or unfamiliar with the poverty, single parenthood and family struggles facing the children in the zone as he was a child of such circumstances. But he was fortunate in that he escaped. He obtained his bachelor's degree in economics from Harvard University and then begin his career at Morgan Stanley as an analyst. During his third year with the bank, he was chosen for an externship at HCZ®. After completing this externship, Mr. Owusu-Kesse returned to Harvard to receive a Master's in Business Administration from the Harvard Business School and a Master's in Public Policy from the Kennedy School of Government. But then he did something extraordinary—he returned to HCZ®.

His choice to return to HCZ® is an example of *doing ethics*—jumping in to help where help is needed. For him and the leaders and supporters of HCZ®, it is not about philosophizing, but rolling up one's sleeves to do real work that is hard but important for future generations.

The Harlem School Zone® Vision for Success

From the beginning, the vision for the HCZ® was all encompassing.

> To provide comprehensive, critical support to children and families and *reweaving the very fabric of community life,* the HCZ® Project began as a one-block pilot in the 1990s. It set out to address not just some, but all the issues children and families were facing within a finite geographic area: crumbling apartments, rampant drug use, failing schools, violent crime and chronic health problems. (www.hcz.org)

Today, CEO Kwame Owusu-Kesse joins Canada, who now serves as president, in ensuring that the HCZ® dream is not a mirage.

As stated in "Whatever It Takes," the Harlem Children's Zone® white paper (2014), the HCZ® model "created a new paradigm for fighting poverty, intended to overcome the limits of traditional approaches. [Its] model focuses primarily and intensively on the social, health, and educational development of children" (p. 4).

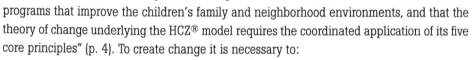

To help support that development, HCZ® explains in its white paper that it "provides wraparound programs that improve the children's family and neighborhood environments, and that the theory of change underlying the HCZ® model requires the coordinated application of its five core principles" (p. 4). To create change it is necessary to:

- Serve an entire neighborhood comprehensively and at scale. Engaging an entire neighborhood helps to achieve three goals: it reaches children in numbers significant enough to affect the culture of a community; it transforms the physical and social environments that impact the children's development; and it creates programs at a scale large enough to meet the local need.

- Create a pipeline of support. Develop excellent, accessible programs and schools and link them to one another so that they provide uninterrupted support for children's healthy growth, starting with prenatal programs for parents and finishing when young people graduate from college. Surround the pipeline with additional programs that support families and the larger community.

- Build community among residents, institutions and stakeholders, who help to create the environment necessary for children's healthy development.

- Evaluate program outcomes and create a feedback loop that cycles data back to management for use in improving and refining program offerings.

- Cultivate a culture of success rooted in passion, accountability, leadership and teamwork.

It took many years and a deep understanding of what was needed to envision and perfect the HCZ® model. It took vision, programming, infrastructure, financing, understanding, cajoling, trial and error, hard work and dedication, passion and commitment, public–private partnerships, and ultimately proof of concept followed by results.

> It wasn't easy. It was tantamount to waging a war on the totality of circumstances that created the situation that the HCZ® model was fighting to overcome. The failure to wage the war would not have just been an ethical failure; it would have been tantamount to acquiescing in the status quo, one that was undoubtedly leading to a continuation of **isolating, targeting,** and **destroying** the Black people of Harlem.

The world has taken notice of the HCZ® model because it is doing the hard work of enfranchising the disenfranchised and of making the extraordinary ordinary.

Communities of the disenfranchised exist around the world and their circumstances are not dissimilar to those of Harlem. It boils down to "the haves and the have nots" in society and what to do about them. Therefore, it is not surprising that since 2003, as reported by HCZ®, "more than 500 U.S. groups and 186 international delegations have visited the Harlem Children's Zone® to learn about HCZ®'s model of comprehensive educational development of children and families in economically disadvantaged communities" (www.hcz.org).

It is also not surprising that many have studied and questioned the HCZ® approach and its success stories, including its costs. Had the same amount of scrutiny, concern and energy been placed in trying to understand and help the people of Harlem before HCZ® was created, it would have not been necessary to create it.

It is important to remember what winning looks like in the particular war being waged by HCZ®; it has many faces and many parts that can only be assessed over time.

But perhaps no one will ever be able to measure what a mother, father, child, extended family member or neighbors might think when they are able to recalibrate their possibilities equations because of the HCZ® program. In their minds and their equations, once they witness a child being plucked out of destitution and put on the road to success it changes everything. When they see such a child placed in a car on this road to success, that child, figuratively speaking, becomes the driver, who then begins to steer everyone around the neighborhood to places where they can breathe more freely, see the beauty of the roadside and imagine a better place when they alight from the car.

When one child succeeds in HCZ®, that success multiplies throughout the child's community and cannot be simply measured by a child's entrance or success in college. Another aspect of this success is its ability to encourage others in the community to think and be influenced to see and pursue the positive possibilities in life.

The main goal of the HCZ® mission is "to provide comprehensive, critical support to children and families and reweaving the very fabric of community life." (www.hcz.org)

There are many threads to pull in such a tapestry. One of the most important threads creates a tipping point on a neighborhood-level scale. This concept of a tipping point is explained in the HCZ® white paper as follows:

> **What is a tipping point?** It is the moment of critical mass, the threshold, the boiling point. By serving thousands of children in a 97-block neighborhood (by 2014), the HCZ® Project can reach that critical mass and help take the entire community across the threshold that separates dysfunctional from supportive environments. To reach a critical mass, HCZ® programs were designed to serve about 65% of the total number of children in the neighborhood (p. 14).

However, some things can be easily measured, while some things cannot. Sometimes there is a reliable form of measurement, and sometimes there is not.

One commonly used measurement applies to a portion of the HCZ® model. It measures and compares HCZ®'s education outcomes and costs to other models, especially to charter schools.

As of 2017, HCZ®'s Promise Academy® charter schools had a 97% college acceptance rate, which is phenomenal by any standard. Here is how the program works:

> About HCZ®'s Promise Academy® Charter Schools. When students enter HCZ®'s Promise Academy® K–12 Charter Schools, a promise is made to help each one get to and through college. Students receive a high–quality, standards–based education, and their families also have access to HCZ®'s comprehensive network of support, including counseling, benefits assistance, and other social services. Admission is determined by a lottery, which gives preference to Zone residents to ensure that we are supporting children and families with the deepest needs. Because early intervention and consistent support are critical, HCZ® first opens admission to three–year–olds, who are then enrolled in the HCZ®'s Three-Year-Old Journey program, followed by HCZ®'s Harlem Gems® Pre-K program, to make sure they start school ready to excel. (www.hcz.org)

Some choose to think of HCZ® as merely a charter school, but it is much more and encompasses a full suite of wraparound services and programs mentioned below.

EDUCATION
Early Childhood • The Baby College® • The Three-Year-Old Journey • Harlem Gems®
Elementary School • Promise Academy® • K–12 Charter Schools • Peacemakers
Middle School • Promise Academy® • K–12 Charter Schools • A Cut Above
High School
Promise Academy® • K–12 Charter Schools • TRUCE® Media • Employment and Technology Center
College Preparatory • College Preparatory Program • Center for Higher Education & Career Support
Family & Community
• HCZ® Community Centers
• Beacon Community Center
• Housing Development and Community Centers

A full description of these programs is available on the HCZ® website: (www.hcz.org).

The work of HCZ® is not static nor stale. To keep it that way, HCZ® states that it tracks 600 goals each year and that it is constantly gathering data and reviewing its results, as are others.

A few highlights reported on the HCZ® website show some of the results as of FY 2016. They include those listed below, but studies are constantly ongoing and underway.

Achievements in "The Children's Zone®—One Family, 25,000-Strong":

✓Worked with 12,509 children and 12,498 parents, grandparents, aunts, uncles, friends and neighbors.

Achievements in "Early Childhood Education: Beginning at Birth for a Lifetime of Success":

✓325 caregivers—including 82 fathers—graduated from The Baby College®, which is a nine-week series of workshops for new and expectant parents on early brain development, health and nutrition, safety and discipline, stress management, and the importance of talking and reading to their babies. After graduation, ongoing support was provided to new dads and community leaders through a weekly Father's Council.

Achievements of "K-12: Building Confidence, Character and College Readiness":

✓Worked with 10,147 K-12 students, including 2,120 students at two Promise Academy® Charter Schools and 8,027 students in traditional New York City public schools through HCZ® in-school and afterschool programs. Of those, 2,904 were students in our Peacemakers program, which provides all-day classroom support at the seven traditional public elementary schools in the Zone.

Achievements of "From College Success to Career Competitiveness" included:

✓The graduation of 114 students from college, including 80 from four-year schools and 34 from two-year schools. Worked with 913 students in 207 colleges and universities across the country, providing individualized academic advising, social services, financial guidance, emergency support, health and wellness activities, and a variety of career readiness workshops and professional opportunities. Helped 201 HCZ® college students obtain paid internships at 57 organizations and conducted a series of workshops for parents of HCZ® high school and college students to help them navigate the financial aid process.

Achievements of "Healthy Harlem" included:

✓Engaged 9,229 children of all ages in regular physical activity and health and nutrition education. In addition, 3,185 adults participated in fitness and cooking classes, support groups and HCZ®'s monthly farmers' markets.

As explained in its FY 2016 report, HCZ® did not become a national model for social change overnight. Up to that point, it took seventeen years of constant evaluation and improvement, round-the-clock commitment from staff and the unwavering partnership of loving, supportive parents.

Shining a Light on a New Pathway

President Barack Obama recognized the accomplishments of the Harlem Children's Zone®, stating that it is "an all-encompassing, all-hands-on-deck, anti-poverty effort that is literally saving a generation of children." Beyond praising it, he took efforts to replicate it.

In 2008, inspired by the immense progress of The Harlem Children's Zone® toward breaking the generational cycle of poverty, President Obama proposed the creation of "Promise Neighborhoods," which used HCZ®'s "cradle to college" approach.

The initiative sought to help selected local communities improve outcomes and opportunities for children and families in defined neighborhoods by following the HCZ®'s paradigm to improve every aspect of life in impoverished communities. Its purpose, which directly mirrors that of the HCZ® model, states:

> All children growing up in Promise Neighborhoods have access to effective schools and strong systems of family and community support that will prepare them to attain an excellent education and successfully transition from college to career. (www.hcz.org)

In 2010, the Obama administration allocated $75 million in the federal budget for the program. More than 330 communities across the nation applied for Promise Neighborhood planning grants. Twenty-one communities were awarded one-year grants from $400,000 to $500,000. Planning grantees were given a year to produce a strategic paradigm to address the issues specific to their community in pursuit of an implementation grant.

Results of this program have been analyzed by the U.S. General Accountability Office (2014) in "Education Grants Promise Neighborhoods Promotes Collaboration but Needs National Evaluation Plan," and others have also analyzed it.

In the case of Promise Neighborhoods as well as that of HCZ®, there is always room for improvement. But one thing is clear: creating HCZ® was a game changer in a game that was rigged against Black people from the start.

Ongoing Analysis and Research on the HCZ® Model

Many studies about HCZ® have been and are being undertaken. One important study is a longitudinal study by Mathematica that began in spring 2010. It examines students' outcomes and school experiences as they progress from early childhood programs through Promise Academy® charter schools.

Specifically, the study focuses on the extent to which programs are implemented as intended and the extent and nature of family involvement and the characteristics of students' families and home environments.

As shown on Mathematica's website (www.mathematica.org), the following research questions guide the longitudinal study:

Characteristics of students and families:

1. What are the demographic characteristics of the students?
2. What are the home environments of the students like?
3. What are the naturally occurring patterns of participation in HCZ® programs?
4. How do students' cognitive and behavioral outcomes compare to national norms?
5. How do students perceive themselves, their abilities and aspects of their school environments?

Group differences in outcomes:

1. What are the subgroup differences in students' outcomes?

Student outcomes over time and predictors of the outcomes:

1. How do the students' outcomes change over time?
2. What factors predict student and family outcomes?

As of September 2020, the results of the study were not yet available.

Mathematica is systematically studying many program elements of the HCZ® model. One set of results from its series of longitudinal studies is available in "Results of The Impact of Healthy Harlem on the Prevalence of Child Overweight and Obesity and Contributing

Factors: Interim Evaluation Report" (Mabli et al., 2017). The full results are on Mathematica's website. Some of its findings include those mentioned below:

> **About the Healthy Harlem Program.** HCZ® recognizes that childhood obesity is a critical public health problem, and that obesity can derail children's ability to reach their full potential. HCZ® has promoted healthy, active lifestyles since 2001 by offering increased opportunities for physical activity in school and afterschool settings, sports instruction and seasonal sports teams, nutrition education, and access to fresh produce.
>
> Although these efforts met with some success, the urgency of the issue was heightened in school year 2010–2011 when HCZ® found that nearly half (45%) of students 12 and older who participated in HCZ® programs were overweight or obese. In 2011, HCZ® received funding from The JPB Foundation to design and implement a comprehensive program for promoting healthy lifestyles. HCZ® contracted the Bridgespan Group, also funded by The JPB Foundation, to create (1) a blueprint for the program and (2) a basic plan for implementing the program. Using this guidance, HCZ® continued developing plans for the program.
>
> The result is Healthy Harlem, a multifaceted program implemented in HCZ®'s after-school sites, where students receive additional instruction, physical activity, a snack and an opportunity to socialize for several hours after school each day.
>
> Source: Mabli, J., Bleeker, M., & Fox, M.K. (2017). The Impact of Healthy Harlem on the Prevalence of Child Overweight and Obesity and Contributing Factors: Final Report. Mathematica Policy Research.

In short, Mabli et al. (2017) found the following:

Healthy Harlem had positive, significant impacts on student outcomes. Specifically, the program:

✔ Increased students' nutrition knowledge and self-efficacy related to physical activity, and these increases have been sustained over three years.

✔ Had some positive impacts on other measures of self-efficacy and social support.

✔ Generally increased students' levels of fitness, although there is some variation by gender.

✔ Reduced BMI z-scores and the prevalence of overweight and obesity among students who were overweight or obese at baseline and received both Get Fit and Prevention components.

Responding to the COVID-19 Crisis

Concern about the whole circumstances of the child and their environment, by definition has entailed a focus on health. Therefore, it is not surprising that HCZ® was selected as a 2020 Audacious Project grantee and that it received $26 million towards HCZ®'s ongoing national COVID-19 relief and recovery efforts.

The award will be applied toward HCZ®'s goal of raising $50 million to support the implementation of ongoing COVID-19 relief efforts in Harlem and six U.S. cities. HCZ®'s newly launched William Julius Wilson Institute (WJW) at HCZ® will serve as the platform for this national effort, which is described on HCZ®'s website as follows:

> **About Harlem Children's Zone® COVID-19 Program.** "HCZ® is delivering emergency resources and services designed to address the needs of Black communities disproportionately affected by COVID-19," said Anna Verghese, Executive Director of The Audacious Project at TED. She stated, "at a time when efficacy and fast action are critical, their comprehensive approach and deep community ties are paramount to building an equitable recovery and resilient future. We are grateful to be able to support their work both in Harlem and as their model expands across the country."
>
> "The Audacious investment serves as an incredible vote of confidence in the national leadership role of Harlem Children's Zone® and is a testament to the impactful work of our amazing partners," said Kwame Owusu-Kesse, CEO of Harlem Children's Zone®. "Furthermore, it underscores our model's critical element—targeting neighborhoods with comprehensive services—which unlocks the great potential in our communities and ensures a pathway to social and economic mobility.
>
> As the COVID-19 pandemic hit, it became clear that it was disproportionately affecting Black Americans. HCZ® swiftly conceived and implemented a comprehensive multi-pronged approach to emergency response and recovery, focusing on five crucial areas to help offset the pandemic's impact and unfathomable effects on its community."
>
> Source: Harlem Children's Zone. (2020). Harlem Children's Zone® COVID-19 Program. Retrieved from www.hcz.org

HCZ'®s accomplishments since 1990 show that it is never too late to enter the game, no matter how badly the game is rigged. Being in the game, endeavoring to make a difference is *doing ethics*.

The Road to Progress

HCZ® is not only on the road to progress; it is paving the road as it travels on it.

As Geoffrey Canada said (August 2020) in a *Time Magazine* interview:

> I keep challenging America: if we can do it and if you care about these children, why aren't we ensuring that it is happening at scale across this country? That's the next part of the work.

Now, America must decide which America it wants to be—the one that ensures the promise of the 14th Amendment to the U.S. Constitution is kept for all Americans, or not.

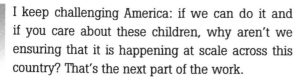

CHAPTER FIVE

Ethical Environmental, SOCIAL, and Governance (ESG) Investing

Environmental · Social · Governance

About Chapter Five: Environment, SOCIAL, and Governance (ESG) Investing

The ascension of ESG investing has come along at the right time, just when it is needed most. It is needed by society as a whole, but it is especially needed by the part of society that has so many needs on so many levels.

This chapter focuses on the largest companies in America that are in a position to make ESG investments. In 2019, when corporate executives signed on to a new corporate purpose that emphasizes that customer value, investing in employees, fair and ethical supplier relationships, and care for the community and environment are *also* the purpose and responsibility of a business, in addition to long-term shareholder value, a new day dawned.

In the light of the new day, the hope in Black America is that the new corporate purpose coupled with new momentum in the ESG movement will lay the ground for more investments in the communities of Black America, as well as in Black people—as employees, as Board members, as business partners, and as targets for ESG investing in many areas.

The term ESG, may not be familiar to many but many of the terms associated with its predecessors are. ESG is the latest evolution from sustainability, corporate responsibility, the triple bottom line, and the old standby, "green". ESG is an embrace and maturation of these concepts that has evolved into operational practices that include disclosing and benchmarking data.

ESG's scope, practices, and relevance to capital opportunities have led to a substantial shift in the way companies measure and disclose their performance and in the priority investors give to investments that emphasize "doing good while doing well".

Whereas all three of the baskets of issues, environmental, social, and governance, are inextricably linked, this chapter focuses on the social factors (S-factors) in ESG, as actions taken in accordance with their intentions have the potential to address community and business concerns of immediate relevance to the current predicament of Black America in the time of COVID-19.

Within the framework of making ESG investments, social criteria look at the company's business relationships. Does it work with suppliers that hold the same values as it claims to hold? Does the company donate a percentage of its profits to the local community or encourage employees to perform volunteer work there? Do the company's working conditions show high regard for its employees' health and safety? Are stakeholders' interests taken into account? Are their board of directors diverse?

Who could have known that by March 2020, seven months after 181 leaders of Fortune 500 companies signed the new corporate purpose statement that the need for them to act on it would be so great when COVID-19 hit? This chapter shows how some corporate leaders are acting on the new corporate purpose by leveraging their ESG investments and by acting ethically.

Ethical Environmental, SOCIAL, and Governance (ESG) Investing

O n August 19, 2019, the Business Roundtable released a new statement on corporate purpose. Its preamble stated:

> Americans deserve an economy that allows each person to succeed through hard work and creativity and to lead a life of meaning and dignity. We believe the free-market system is the best means of generating good jobs, a strong and sustainable economy, innovation, a healthy environment, and economic opportunity for all.

This struck a new deal. It challenged the often-quoted Friedman doctrine, which says that a corporation's ONLY responsibility is to its shareholders. In contrast, the new purpose emphasizes that customer value, investing in employees, fair and ethical supplier relationships, and care for the community and environment are *also* the purpose and responsibility of a business, in addition to focusing on long-term shareholder value.

The new purpose lit a fire under the **E**nvironmental, **S**ocial, and **G**overnance (**ESG**) movement that began in 2004. The pandemic and civil unrest in 2020 fanned the flames of the fire and elevated the role of corporations as critical stakeholders and partners in saving society. Consider this:

The world's 500 largest companies generated $33 trillion in revenues and $2.1 trillion in profits in 2019. They employed 69.9 million people worldwide and were represented by 32 countries.	The federal debt at the end of the 2018/2019 fiscal year, ending September 30, 2019, was $22.7 trillion. The portion that is held by the public was $16.8 trillion. Interest on the debt was $404 billion.

What does this picture show? It shows that without big corporations stepping up and stepping in to help meet societal needs, we cannot thrive as a society. A snapshot from the live U.S. Debt Clock (*usdebtclock.org*), as of November 2020, paints a dreary picture, one that undoubtedly suggests a growing need for corporations to do social good.

US National Debt	Debt per Citizen	Debt per Taxpayer
$27,274,830,637,023	$82,506	$218,798

Who could have known that seven months after 181 leaders of Fortune 500 companies signed the new corporate purpose statement that the need for them to act on it would be so great when COVID-19 hit? The challenge now is acting on corporate purpose commitment in the time of coronavirus.

What should a company's purpose be when the purpose of so many is now survival? For years, enlightened executives have sought the sweet spot between their responsibility to maximize profits on behalf of shareholders and their desire to find a purpose across environment, social, and governance (ESG) themes on behalf of a broad range of stakeholders, including customers, employees, and communities. COVID-19 has now upped the ante.

How Bad is the Impact of COVID-19?

It is catastrophically bad, in all markets, in all sectors, and on all citizens in the U.S.—and it rages on. As it wreaks havoc on the economy and society, it is revealing a truth that has been cloaked in the shadows, which is the deep divide between the haves and the have nots in society.

It is a tale of two Americas. On the one hand, there were 621 billionaires as of 2019 with a combined wealth of **$2.9 trillion**.

In contrast to the enormous wealth of a few, an article for the Pew Trust, "Poverty Grew in One-Third of Counties Despite Strong National Economy," Henderson (2019) reported that the poverty rate grew in 30% of counties between 2016 and 2018, based on Pew's Stateline analysis of U.S. Census Bureau county estimates (para. 2). This is what it looks like in minority communities, according to Henderson.

The poverty rate is the percentage of people in households earning less than the poverty threshold, which is currently $25,750 per year for a family of four. But that was before COVID-19. Though official estimates of income and poverty for 2020 will not be available until September 2021, it is clearly getting worse.

In an article entitled "Unemployment Rose Higher in Three Months of COVID-19 Than It Did in Two Years of the Great Recession," Pew researcher Kochhar (2020) explained the following:

> The COVID-19 outbreak and the economic downturn it engendered swelled the ranks of unemployed Americans by more than 14 million, from 6.2 million in February to 20.5 million in May 2020. As a result, the U.S. unemployment rate shot up from 3.8% in February – among the lowest on record in the post-World War II era – to 13.0% in May. The rise in the number of unemployed workers due to COVID-19 is substantially greater than the increase due to the Great Recession, when the number unemployed increased by 8.8 million from the end of 2007 to the beginning of 2010 (para. 1).

How Does COVID-19 Impact ESG Investing?

As COVID-19 continues to wreak havoc, especially within communities of color and even more dramatically in Black American communities, corporate leaders are recognizing and acting on the need to weight their ESG efforts more heavily on the social S-factors. The crisis, in effect, is serving as a wake-up call that is accelerating the need for a different approach to investing.

Over the long run, COVID-19 could prove to be a major turning point for ESG investing, or strategies that consider a company's environmental, social and governance performance alongside traditional financial metrics," said Jean-Xavier Hecker and Hugo Dubourg (2020), Co-Heads of ESG & Sustainability within J.P. Morgan EMEA (Europe, Middle East, Africa) Equity Research, in their article titled, "Why COVID-19 Could Prove to Be a Major Turning Point for ESG Investing" (para. 5).

J.P. Morgan polled investors from 50 global institutions, representing a total of $12.9 trillion in assets under management (AUM), on how they expected COVID-19 to impact the future of ESG investing. The results show that 71% of respondents indicated that the virus would increase awareness and actions globally to tackle high impact. Hecker and Dubourg (2020) further commented:

> We believe that pandemics and environmental risks are viewed as similar in terms of impact, representing an important wake-up call for decision makers. The impacts of the COVID-19 crisis on the real economy and the financial system highlight the limits of most forecasting models, which do not deal well with non-linear, complex systemic risks, said Hecker and Dubourg (para. 8). As action and awareness of long-term sustainability risks are likely to increase in the longer run in the aftermath of the COVID-19 crisis, this should be a positive catalyst for ESG.

Now it gets interesting. First, here is a clarification on what ESG is.

Defining ESG

Essentially, as Chen (2020) of Morningstar (a funds research and rating firm) explained, "Environmental, Social and Governance (ESG) criteria are a set of standards for a company's operations that socially conscious investors use to screen potential investments" (para. 1). **E**nvironmental criteria consider how a company performs as a steward of nature. **S**ocial criteria examine how it manages relationships with employees, suppliers, customers, and the communities where it operates, and **G**overnance deals with a company's leadership, executive pay, audits, internal controls, and shareholder rights.

Today, ESG is a movement and, as in any movement, there are steps along the way. Some of the critical steps on the pathway toward ESG included raised ethical concerns about where to *invest*, or where to *disinvest* from to ensure that corporations were "doing good while doing well." Critical milestones leading to the pathwat of ESG are discussed below.

Ethical Considerations as the Underpinnings of ESG. Historical decisions of where financial assets would be placed were based on various criteria, financial return being predominant. However, there have always been other criteria for deciding where to place money—from political considerations to heavenly reward, as a soul-searching pursuit. In the search, in the 1950s and 60s vast pension funds managed by the trade unions recognized the opportunity to affect the wider social environment using their capital assets. The International Brotherhood of Electrical Workers invested their considerable capital in developing affordable housing projects, while the United Mine Workers invested in health facilities.

But early searches for the "corporate soul" did not stop there. Corporations also began to consider what not to do in order to act more ethically and in alignment with their "corporate souls."

Disinvestment: A Demonstration of the Ethical Corporate Soul. Morally, in the 1970s, the worldwide abhorrence of the Apartheid regime in South Africa led to one of the most renowned examples of selective disinvestment along ethical lines. As a response to a growing call for sanctions against the regime, the Reverend Leon Sullivan, a board member of General Motors, drew up a code of conduct in 1971 for conducting business with South Africa, which became known as the Sullivan Principles. This led to a mass *disinvestment* by the U.S. from many South African companies, and the resulting pressure applied to the South African regime by its business community added great weight to the growing impetus for the system of apartheid to be abandoned.

Milton Friedman asked, "what does 'soul' have to do with it", in the 1960s and 1970s as he observed the prevailing mood of philanthropy. He argued that social responsibility adversely affects a firm's financial performance. He contended that the valuation of a company or asset should be predicated almost exclusively on the pure bottom line (with the costs incurred by social responsibility being deemed non-essential).

In 1988, James S. Coleman definitively answered Milton's question of why corporations should do "good while doing well," and he won the argument that ultimately helped lay the foundation for the ESG movement. His article in the *American Journal of Sociology* titled, "Social Capital in the Creation of Human Capital," challenged the dominance of the Friedman Principle of "self-interest" in economics and introduced the concept of social capital into the measurement of value.

The notion of leveraging the power of collective investors to encourage companies and capital markets to incorporate environmental and social challenges into their day-to-day decision-making was reborn through the ESG movement in 2004.

There is a clear nexus between ESG and ethical investing, as Kenton (2020) explained in his article titled, "Ethical Investing." Accordingly, he explained that "ethical investing refers to the practice of using one's ethical principles as the primary filter for the selection of securities investing" (para. 1). He acknowledged, however, that ethical investing depends on the investor's views and that "ethical investing is sometimes used interchangeably with socially conscious investing; however, socially conscious funds typically have one overarching set of guidelines that are used to select the portfolio, whereas ethical investing brings about a more personalized result" (para. 2). On balance, the key takeaways Kenton (2020) underscores are that:

- ✔ Ethical investing is the practice of selecting investments based on ethical or moral principles.

- ✔ Selecting investments based on ethics offers no guarantee of performance.

- ✔ Ethical investors typically avoid investments from "sin" stocks and companies involved with stigmatized activities, such as gambling, alcohol, smoking, or firearms.

- ✔ Analyzing investments according to ethics should also include reviewing whether the company's actions align with their commitment to ethics and their historical, current, and projected performance (para. 2).

Metrics and ESG

The next jump in the evolution of ESG was being able to measure and quantify that doing good helped corporations to do well.

> **Rating Goodness**. Asset managers and other financial institutions increasingly rely on ESG ratings agencies to assess, measure, and compare companies' ESG performance. Recently, data providers have applied artificial intelligence to rate companies and their commitment to ESG. Each rating agency uses its own set of metrics to measure the level of ESG compliance, and there is, at present, no industry-wide set of common standards.

Today, while few question whether doing good is the *right* thing to do, some still question whether it is good for the bottom line, and while there are many ways to measure its impact on the bottom line, there is no consensus about such measurements.

Here is what we know for sure, as Lefkovitz (2020), a *Morningstar* analyst, wrote in his article titled, "ESG at a Tipping Point" for the CFA Institute on July 20, 2020, "mutual funds and exchange-traded funds (ETFs) designated as sustainable attracted $46 billion of inflows in the first quarter of 2020 amid the market turmoil of 2020's first quarter. Some had predicted that ESG would be exposed as a bull market luxury that was easy to champion only during boom times. They thought that when markets plunge, priorities like securing retirement savings would dominate investors' hierarchy of needs" (para. 3) to the exclusion of ESG investing. To the contrary, crises tend to accelerate trends, as Lefkovitz (2020) explained:

> **Crises Tend to Accelerate Trends**. The upheavals of 2020—from the global pandemic to the movement for racial justice and the ongoing threat of climate change—have undoubtedly helped propel environmental, social, and governance (ESG) investing into the mainstream. ESG-related topics have never been so central to the investment conversation. Assets are growing and the connection between ESG and risk is strengthening (para. 1).

But even before the COVID-19 crisis engulfed the nation, the ESG movement was already steadily marching forward and was on the rise. Prior to the crisis, the Harvard Law School Forum on Corporate Governance's "2020 Global and Regional Corporate Governance" took a pulse of how corporations were articulating the ESG agenda at the beginning of 2020. It was observed that for the first time, the focus on the "E" and the "S" of environment, social, and governance (ESG) was the leading global trend.

Russell Reynolds Associates' Global Head of the Board Consulting and Effectiveness Practice Rusty O'Kelley and Board member Anthony Goodman (2020) posted the trends and classified them into five main groups. The issues within these groups were identified based on the work of Russell Reynolds Associates, which entailed interviewing 40 global institutional and activist investors, pension fund managers, proxy advisors, and other corporate governance professionals to identify the corporate governance trends that would impact boards and directors in 2020. The five main groups of global trends identified in 2020 were:

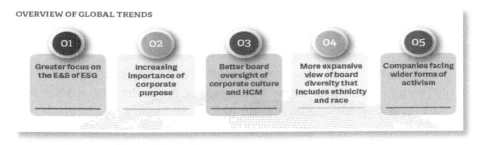

Source: Harvard Law School. (2020). 2020 Global and Regional Corporate Governance Trends. Retrieved from https://corpgov.law.harvard.edu

Some of the key issues involved in these trends, as reported by O'Kelley and Goodman (2020) are summarized below.

✔ Trends in Group 1: Greater focus on the "E" and "S" of the ESG group. Beyond the global emphasis on good governance, Russell Reynold's survey results showed that environmental and social issues are taking the greatest precedence for investors, though the question remains about how to execute on them. In the meantime, boards are expected to strengthen their oversight and knowledge of "material" E and S matters and to disclose their connection to the business in the form of risks and opportunities.

✔ Trends in Group 2: Increasing importance of corporate purpose. Corporate purpose and stakeholder considerations are business norms. In August 2019, according to the Russell Reynolds survey, 181 out of 188 member CEOs of the U.S. Business Roundtable signed on to an amended "Statement on the Purpose of a Corporation" putting aside the traditional view that maximizing shareholder returns is priority one. This was followed by a December announcement from the World Economic Forum updating their 2020 Davos Manifesto (last published in 1973) to center on principles that guide companies into the Fourth Industrial Revolution.

✔ Trends in Group 3: Better board oversight of corporate culture and Human Capital Management (HCM). Investors, according to Russell Reynolds, are asking what the board is doing to ensure the culture is robust and can withstand transformation and change. "Investors would like more transparency on board involvement in culture and HCM to determine whether boards are providing adequate oversight." Russell Reynolds also suggests "that data and analysis on corporate culture will play a key part in this oversight by boards and that directors should appreciate the impact of culture on hiring, retention, and productivity."

✔ Trends in Group 4: More expansive view of board diversity, which includes ethnicity and race. Considerable strides have been made globally calling for greater board gender diversity. Russell Reynolds advises that "institutional investor voting power grew dramatically and so did demands for gender diversity, and that boards will begin to experience additional pressure to consider ethnic and racial diversity."

✔ Trends in Group 5: Companies facing wider forms of activism. Globally, investor activism, according to the Russell Reynolds survey, "continues to evolve and grow, creating a kaleidoscope of styles and approaches that change year to year. What remains constant is that directors must maintain a degree of vigilance and be ready to respond to activists or assuage the concerns of investors" para(s). 1–5.

Russell Reynolds expects to see increased activism success rates and greater influence from both the traditional "activist" investors and from larger non-governmental organizations (NGOs).

As can be gleaned from the foregoing, the ESG movement was heading in an increasingly activist, "social capitalism" direction even before COVID-19.

Examples of common ESG issues, according to the CFA Institute, a global association of investment professionals that offer financial analysts certification, include, in summary, the following examples, as reported in CFA's guide, "Environmental, Social, and Governance Issues in Investing: A Guide for Investment Professionals" (2015, p. 4).

ENVIRONMENTAL ISSUES	SOCIAL ISSUES	GOVERNANCE ISSUES
Climate change, carbon emission	Customer satisfaction	Board composition
Air and water pollution	Data protection and privacy	Audit committee structure
Biodiversity	Gender and diversity	Bribery and corruption
Deforestation	Employee engagement	Executive compensation
Energy efficiency	Community relations	Lobbying
Waste management	Human rights	Whistleblower schemes
	Labor standards	

Among these issues, in the time of COVID-19, the need for corporations to address **community relations S-factor** issues is garnering the greatest attention.

> **About the "S" Factors in ESG.** Social criteria look at the company's business relationships. Does it work with suppliers that hold the same values as it claims to hold? Does the company donate a percentage of its profits to the local community or encourage employees to perform volunteer work there? Does the company's working conditions show high regard for its employees' health and safety? Are other stakeholders' interests considered?

Today, there is growing recognition that doing good helps corporation to do well, and that is the true bottom line, and while ethical considerations figure in, a growing number of investors see ESG issues affecting the financial results. As investors and corporate leaders see it today, climate change poses risks and opportunities; workforce relations affect a company's competitive positioning; and checks and balances on corporate management lead to better decision-making. As Lefkovitz (2020) noted, it is not surprising that the CFA Institute encourages all investment professionals to consider ESG factors, and it views their integration as being "consistent with a manager's fiduciary duty to consider all relevant information and material risks in investment analysis and decision-making" (para. 7).

Things Have Clearly Changed in Corporate America

The bigger the game, the more corrupted the soul of the hunter. Once a truism, there is clearly a new game in town. The soul of the hunter has been tamed by accepting the new corporate purpose.

Consistent with the new purpose, corporations are increasingly being held responsible for "doing good" for society while doing well for themselves—which are compatible goals.

Kenneth Frazier, the chief executive of Merck said, "I actually don't see that big a conflict between meeting the needs of shareholders and meeting the needs of society." He cautioned, however, that the role of the chief executive has never been more complex or more consequential. "Business leaders," he emphasized, "are reshaping the internet, reimagining health care, upending transportation, and more. Being a chief executive is no longer just about running a company. It means taking political stands on everything from immigration to gun rights. Such political stands have the potential to lead to ethical dilemmas and point to the need for strong corporate governance to make and enforce the right choices and behavior.

The lanes of corporations, government, and society used to be on parallel tracks. Today, the tracks intersect at every turn, not just within our country but between our country and others.

The days when the corporate hunter could go out and shoot the game, bag it, go home, and put it on the wall are long gone. Today, we are living in an ecosystem of connections that are as interdependent as veins in a body.

Big corporations are at the center of our lives and in all aspects of our lives, from controlling our social media connections to having their algorithms influence and manipulate our thinking and buying and selling behavior. There is no separation between corporate

America and anyone's personhood, and there is less separation between corporate America and the government. The latter point is particularly noteworthy as what is happening or not happening in the government is key to setting the ESG agenda because, in a sense, the ESG agenda picks up where the government leaves off—and a lot is being left off. Consider this:

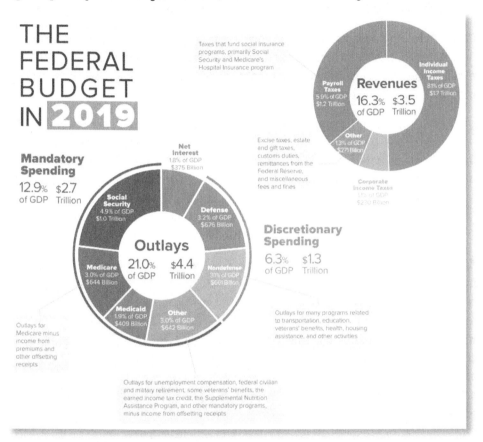

What does this budget imply in the time of COVID-19? It suggests that we cannot necessarily rely on the federal government alone to solve the growing social and economic problems in society; rather, addressing them is an all hands-on deck endeavor.

As Fiona Reynolds (2020) underscored in a *Fortune* article, "Big Investors, We Can't Fight Poverty or Protect the Planet Without You," when public sector leaders neglect the importance of addressing Sustainable Development Goals (similar to ESG goals), they can be voted out at the ballot box, but the private sector cannot hide. Not surprisingly, at this time, Reynolds notes:

Many investors and corporate leaders, along with elected officials and governments, clearly recognize their inherent responsibility to respond to these tumultuous times with solutions that foster change and help us to address some of the most pressing and urgent issues we face, ranging from climate change, human rights abuses, inequality, and social inclusion (para. 3).

Corporations can no longer be seen as doing their thing over *there*; they are increasingly doing things over *here* that impact our thoughts, our vision, and our happiness. In the old model of commerce, corporations responded to our demands, but today it is increasingly the other way around, and the "tail is wagging the dog."

Take Amazon, for instance, in its steady march toward being everything to everyone; it has become a reflection of society. At first, we demanded, and it supplied; now, in the truest manifestation of "the tail wagging the dog," it supplies, and then we demand. In yet another case of "the tail wagging the dog," with Facebook, we are no longer face-to-face. Instead, in a Wizard of Oz behind the curtain way, algorithms now determine, which posts are sent to whom, thereby controlling who has the opportunity to "like" us.

As corporations have moved deeply into our personal lives and into our psyche and feelings of recognition and self-worth, it is only natural that the light is reflected back onto the corporations causing us to ask: Who are you, really? Who is your wizard, and does your wizard have a heart and a soul?

It has become personal. A line has been crossed. Corporations are not "socially distant" from us, and they do not always mind their manners; they just open the doors to our homes and lives and march right in uninvited—they are in our "faces", in our business, and in our souls. Now, society wants to know more about their souls and wizards behind their curtains.

Gelles (2018), in an article for the *New York Times* entitled "Merck C.E.O. Ken Frazier on Death Row Cases and the Corporate Soul," quoted Ken Frazier, who said that, "there are lots of examples of companies that have lost their way because they've sort of lost their soul, which is a funny word to use, but companies do have souls" (para. 22). But Ken Frazier does not only talk about the "soul of corporations;" he ensures that as a leader of one of the nation's largest corporations, he sets the example of doing the right thing.

An example of Ken Frazier acting in accordance with his convictions was demonstrated in 2017 when he resigned from the President's Manufacturing Council. As David Gelles (2018) reported in his article for the *New York Times*, "The C.E.O. Who Stood Up to President Trump: Ken Frazier Speaks Out," the events that led to Mr. Frazier's confrontation with the president centered on an event that happened in Charlottesville, Virginia in August 2017 when White nationalists convened to protest the removal of a statue of Robert E. Lee. Bloody fighting broke out as they clashed with counterdemonstrators, one of whom was killed when a self-described neo-Nazi drove his car into a crowd of people.

"Mr. Trump, speaking at a veterans' event at one of his golf clubs, condemned the violence but did not criticize the White nationalists chanting neo-Nazi slogans... He blamed 'hatred, bigotry and violence on many sides'" (Gelles, 2018, para. 10).

Ken Frazier then resigned from the Manufacturers Council making the following statement:

When we speak of the corporate soul and heart, we are essentially talking about moral values. Therefore, it is important to understand these concepts in a corporate context and their relationship to ESG investing.

> **Statement from Kenneth C. Frazier, chairman and chief executive officer, Merck:**
>
> "I am resigning from the President's American Manufacturing Council.
>
> Our country's strength stems from its diversity and the contributions made by men and women of different faiths, races, sexual orientations and political beliefs.
>
> America's leaders must honor our fundamental values by clearly rejecting expressions of hatred, bigotry and group supremacy, which run counter to the American ideal that all people are created equal.
>
> As CEO of Merck and as a matter of personal conscience, I feel a responsibility to take a stand against intolerance and extremism."

Moral Values and Economic Value. Investors consider ESG issues for various reasons. Some may see them solely as economic risks and opportunities—a source of economic value. Others see ESG issues not just as risks and opportunities but also as a matter of moral values. Those motivated by moral values may not wish to become complicit in actions they find objectionable, or they may actively attempt to make a positive impact on

society or the environment. A fundamental point in the "value versus values" debate is that all investors pursue the same economic value (even if with different investment objectives and time horizons), but they inevitably have different moral values. The different exclusionary screens used in investing explain the different values being implemented in investing.

COVID-19 Demands that 2020 Be the "Year of the S-Factor"

In ESG investing, issues such as climate change (part of the "**E**-factor") and the composition of corporate boards (part of the "**G**-factor") become a key component of investor decision-making. However, while some companies have long focused on social issues, such as the treatment of employees, worker safety, and community involvement (part of the "S-factor"), these issues have generally featured less prominently in investment decisions than environmental and governmental factors. Until now.

The events of this year have changed the landscape, elevating the social component of ESG investing to the forefront. That is why 2020 will be the "year of the 'S-factor.'"

The two major events of 2020 so far—a worldwide pandemic and urgent efforts to confront the problem of systemic racism—have spurred corporations to take the new statement of purpose announced by the Business Roundtable and quickly put it into practice. What has followed is a redoubled focus on employees and communities.

Corporate profits and shareholder returns have suddenly taken a backseat to employee health and safety. Companies of varying sizes made bold commitments to retain their workforce despite economic uncertainty, and some vowed to even increase benefits and support to their employees.

Communities also took center stage after the death of George Floyd. Protests decrying racism against Black people and the need for police reform erupted across the country and, eventually, the world. Corporations took notice. Fortune 500 companies, as well as many others, made significant donations to organizations dedicated to fighting racism, while at the same time making commitments to improve diversity and inclusion practices within their own corporate walls.

At this moment, as in the days of the robber barons, the growing needs in society contrast with the growing wealth of the wealthiest in society. Woods (2020), in his August 23, 2020 article for *Businessinsider.com* "How Billionaires Got $637 Billion Richer During the Coronavirus Pandemic," shows how much richer they have become and why. He explained:

- Forty million Americans filed for unemployment during the pandemic, but billionaires saw their net worth increase by half a trillion dollars.

- This is not the first-time billionaires have seen gains while others dealt with loss, and it tends to tie back to two things. First, the government disproportionately gives more aid to larger companies.

▦ Then, when the stock market bounces back, the unequal bailouts mean that the wealthy still have money on hand to invest and thus profit, while the middle and lower classes do not.

▦ Wealth-friendly tax laws and loopholes then keep those billionaires at the top. Knowing all of this, some are advocating for policies to help level the playing field and create change

In contrast, the picture of the other America, in which most people dwell, is quite grim. It is a picture of the have nots. The picture was painted by Morath et al. (2020) in their October 5, 2020 article for the *Wall Street Journal,* "The COVID Economy Carves Deep Divide Between Have and Have Nots." The article underscores the following:

A two-track recovery is emerging from the country's pandemic-driven economic contraction. Some workers, companies, and regions show signs of coming out fine or even stronger. The rest are mired in a deep decline with an uncertain path ahead (para. 1).

Corporate Leadership On the S-Factors of ESG Investing

Every day that COVID-19 rages on and wreaks havoc throughout society, the S-factors of ESG investing becomes more important. A lot is already being done through ESG investments. In his article for *Morningstar,* "The Number of Funds Considering ESG Explodes in 2019," Hale (2019) reported:

Overall, as reported in Morningstar's 2019 *Sustainable Funds U.S. Landscape Report,* there were 564 ESG Consideration funds with $933 billion in assets under management at the end of 2019. Twenty-three of the funds have more than $1 billion in assets. Most (302) are equity funds spanning U.S., international developed, and emerging markets. But another 223 are fixed-income funds and the balance a smattering of allocation, commodities, and convertibles funds (para. 3).

Hale (2019) says that the explosive growth of funds "reflects the widespread recognition among asset managers of the materiality of ESG factors in evaluating investments", suggesting that ESG factors are relevant to all investments" (para 4). This view is illustrated by the CFA Institute's paper (2018) "Positions on Environmental, Social, and Governance Integration," which stated:

The CFA (Chartered Financial Analysts) Institute encourages all investment professionals to consider ESG factors, where relevant, as an important part of the analytical and investment decision-making process, regardless of investment style, asset class, or investment approach. Moreover, the CFA Institute's view is that factoring ESG into the investment process is consistent with a manager's fiduciary duty to consider all relevant information and material risks in investment analysis and decision-making (para. 3).

Accordingly, as Hale (2019) reported, large ESG investments were made in 2019 and are growing.

The 10 Largest ESG Consideration Funds

Fund	Morningstar Category	AUM USD Mil
MFS Value	Large Value	51,936
JPMorgan Core Bond	Intermediate Core Bond	31,850
MFS International Intrinsic Value	Foreign Large Growth	29,869
Templeton Global Bond	Nontraditional Bond	26,894
MFS Growth	Large Growth	25,570
Franklin Growth	Large Growth	17,093
ClearBridge Large Cap Growth	Large Growth	15,729
JPMorgan US Equity	Large Blend	15,698
Hartford MidCap	Mid-Cap Growth	14,625
JPMorgan Core Plus Bond	Intermediate Core-Plus Bond	14,437

Source: Morningstar Direct. Data as of 12/31/2019.

The advice of the CFA Institute is being heeded as more ESG funds are coming online. It also appears that the funds are *doing well through doing good* as Sustainalytics, a leading ESG researcher recently acquired by Morningstar, found that 72% of the ESG indexes held up better than their broad market parents for the five-year period through year-end 2019.

Nevertheless, naysayers persist. Influential investor Warren Buffet of Berkshire Hathaway is one corporate leader who is not convinced that investing in ESG is the way to go. With a portfolio value calculated to be $202,411,166,000. Buffet has a loud voice, and he has used it to speak out against the ESG movement. As Armstrong (2019), in his article, "Warren Buffett on Why Companies Cannot be Moral Arbiters," for the *Financial Times* in December 2019 reported, Buffet said that:

> [I]t was wrong for companies to impose their views of "doing good" on society. What made them think they knew better? It's very hard to do. If you give me the 20 largest companies, I don't know which of the 20 behaves the best, really. I've been a director of 20 publicly owned [companies] and I think it's very hard to evaluate what they're doing (para. 4).

However, a misunderstanding many be at the heart of the debate. ESG fund managers and corporate leaders are not imposing their views of "doing good on society;" rather, it is society that is demanding that corporations do good by responding to their needs. The push-pull equation therefore goes in the other direction than that suggested by Buffet: Society is *pushing* corporations to act on its new corporate purpose by paying greater attention to the S-factors, and ESG fund managers and corporate leaders are *pulling* those requests and considerations into their investment portfolios and corporate decisions.

Leadership Matters

ESG is a broad tent and an evolving field. As ESG assets grow and performances continue to impress, it will increasingly come under greater scrutiny, and due diligence will be necessary to understand whether an index or strategy uses exclusionary screens or positive ESG selection, or whether it focuses on a particular issue—or a combination of all of these elements. Company-level ESG researchers may come to divergent conclusions because their methodologies vary. As such considerations hover in the background, the need for corporations to address S-factor needs is looming in the foreground.

If the ESG movement needed any wind beneath its wings, Larry Fink, CEO of BlackRock Capital—which had $7.4 trillion of assets under management in 2019, blew the wind in a direction that lifted the ESG movement when he said the following in his Annual CEO Letter in 2019:

> Purpose is not a mere tagline or marketing campaign; it is a company's fundamental reason for being and what it does every day to create value for its stakeholders. Purpose is not the sole pursuit of profits but the animating force for achieving them.

JP Morgan, which had $2.98 trillion of assets under management in 2019, announced in March 2020 that it would invest $200 billion in sustainable financing.

> J.P. Morgan announced that it would integrate ESG into all of its asset management portfolios. The investment manager also announced that it would launch new ESG-focused strategies. The decision by the investment bank came on the heels of a similar decision by BlackRock to integrate ESG into all of its investment decisions. CEO of JP Morgan, Jamie Dimon, said: "We take ESG seriously. We're not doing this to respond to the short term or the long term. We think it's the right thing to do. We want to be a measured voice, a mature voice in solving society's problems."

When Fink and Dimon talk, "the street" listens, but the good thing is that Fink, Dimon, and many others on Wall Street, despite the naysayers, are listening to the people *in the street* and are responding to their needs.

Here is a perfect example of how J.P. Morgan is putting its money where its mouth is and showing the world how to execute on the new corporate purpose in accordance with the principles of ESG— and with heart and soul.

JPMorgan Chase is making a $30 billion commitment it says will help address U.S. wealth inequality, especially in traditionally underserved Black and Latino communities.

 ▶ The bank's pledge is a combination of loans, investments, and philanthropy over five years that it says goes beyond what it would do in the normal course of business.

 ▶ The great bulk of JPMorgan's dollar commitment is tied to housing: The bank says that it will provide $14 billion in loans and investments for 100,000 affordable rental units and make $12 billion in mortgages that it would not otherwise.

"Systemic racism is a tragic part of America's history," said Jamie Dimon, CEO of JPMorgan.

Diversity on Corporate Boards Could Make a Big Difference

One result of systemic racism has been the systematic exclusion of Blacks from having a seat at the boardroom table. Despite pledges to nominate more members of underrepresented ethnic and racial groups, companies have made little progress over the last five years.

Eavis (2020), in an article for the *New York Times*, "Diversity Push Barely Budges Corporate Boards to 12.5%, Survey Finds", reported that the boards of the 3,000 largest publicly traded companies remain overwhelmingly White, and that underrepresented ethnic and racial groups made up 40% of the U.S. population but only 12.5% of board directors, according to an analysis by the Institutional Shareholder Services' ESG division. Eavis also reported that "Black directors make up just 4% of the total, while Black women make up just 1.5% of the more than 20,000 directors included in the analysis…" (para. 3).

Since the death of George Floyd, many chief executives have backed efforts to tackle racial injustice. Eavis (2020) highlights an initiative that many executives are taking to increase the number of Black people on their boards.

A group of 44 executives and organizations last week announced the "Board Challenge," a campaign that calls on companies to add a Black director within the next 12 months. One of the supporters of that effort is Tony West, the chief legal officer for Uber and a former senior Justice Department official in the Obama administration. According to Mr. West, "The real test will not be in the commitments that we're making right now in this moment of heat, but what the commitment will be over the long term when the protesters have gone home." (para. 4).

In describing how the system of board placements works, Eavis (2020) explains that "A lot of power rests with the big investment houses that vote in board elections through the shares they own and manage." He singles out Larry Fink, the chairman and chief executive of BlackRock, the world's largest investment manager, for instance, who has spoken about "the critical importance of diversity and inclusion."

Stakeholders in promoting corporate board diversity are not just corporate executives, they include local governments as well. Eavis (2020) gives the example of how the State of California is taking a stake in promoting board diversity.

Lawmakers could also act. The California Legislature recently passed a bill that would require companies with headquarters in the state to have at least one board member from an underrepresented ethnic group, or who identifies as gay, bisexual, or transgender, by the end of 2021. A spokesman for Gov. Gavin Newsom declined to say if he intends to sign the bill. The measure is modeled on a 2018 California law that requires companies to appoint at least one woman to their boards (para. 5).

In an article titled, "Turning 'ESG' into 'ESGD': How Investors Can Support Diversity with their Dollars," Fleischmann (2020) suggests that "prioritizing environmental, social, and governance considerations in investing is not enough." He asserts, "if we truly want to change the systems that drive systemic inequities in our country, we need to proactively add considerations of race and diversity to all areas of our lives, including in the way we invest (para. 3).

Flesischmann states that will require adding a "**D**" (diversity) to ESG, as it would signal prioritizing diversity and justice to foster a more inclusive society. He explains how adding a "**D**" would work:

Our approach to the "**D**" in "ESGD" doesn't have to be one-size-fits-all. Nor does it imply that "D" stands alone and separate from the "E," "S," or "G." Having top-line billing for diversity is important so that diversity doesn't just get measured by numbers in the workforce, but rather is integrated specifically as a lens to look at the "**E**" (think of the water crisis in Flint, Mich.), or the "**S**" (zeroing in on the social impacts of businesses on Black communities), and the "**G**" (promoting people of color for corporate boards). Some investors might consider prioritizing investments in Black-owned businesses. Others might invest in companies that serve primarily Black communities. Still, others might focus on companies that commit to anti-racism policies—from racial equity training, to pay equity, to lobbying for criminal justice reform, to ensuring Black Americans have a voice in democracy by making Election Day a paid company holiday (para. 7).

ESG and "**D**" are issues whose time has come. As the year 2020 closes and the pandemic rages on, it is likely that next year will also be the "year of the S-Factor." The expectation is that many companies and wealthy individuals will join the ESG movement, or what it inspires, and seize opportunities to do the right thing.

The Road to Progress in Addressing S-Factors in ESG Investing

Corporations are addressing the S-Factors in ESG investing in different ways. As they do, hovering in the background are many loud voices that are increasingly jolting corporations into a rude awakening. One of the loudest noises in 2020 from a societal perspective was the one that silenced George Floyd in May 2020. It was a profound moment in history when the eyes of corporate leaders in America were opened wide to see the importance of their new corporate purpose as never before, and many knew what to do: They stepped up and stepped in and listened to the voices in the streets of America.

Whether their investments were always channeled through their ESG vehicles is not clear, but what is clear is that their response and actions were consistent with the reason that ESG exists: It is to do good while doing well.

Every day something good happens in the realm of ESG, and it gives us hope and shows us what *doing ethics* looks like. Some of the immediate "soul awakening" S-factors community support initiatives taken by corporations after people took to the streets in protest over the killing of George Floyd and of the increasing examples of police brutality against Black people, for instance, have included the following.

- PayPal pledged $530 million to support Black and minority-owned businesses. The bulk of the money—$500 million—will be devoted to the creation of an economic opportunity fund that will invest in Black and underrepresented minority businesses and communities.

- Apple announced the $100 million Apple's Racial Equity and Justice Initiative on June 11, 2020, which will challenge the systemic barriers to opportunity and dignity that exists for communities of color and, in particular, for the Black community.

- Google and Amazon announced grants totaling $22 million to activist and racial justice organizations.

- Walmart announced a $100 million donation over five years through a new center on racial equity.

- SoftBank Group Corp is launching a $100 million fund to invest in "companies led by founders and entrepreneurs of color."

▶ Sony Music Group announced the launch of a $100 million fund to support social justice and anti-racist initiatives around the world.

▶ Warner Music Group, in partnership with the Blavatnik Family, announced the launch of a $100 million fund to support charitable causes related to the music industry, social justice, and campaigns against violence and racism.

▶ Universal Music Group announced that it will invest in a $25 million "Change Fund" to support the Black community as well as a Task Force for Meaningful Change (TFMC) to help fight for equality, justice, and inclusion.

▶ UnitedHealth Group said that it will pay for the college education of George Floyd's children and donate more than $10 million to help Twin Cities neighborhoods hurt by recent riots, including a $5 million donation to the YMCA Equity Innovation Center of Excellence.

▶ Comcast CEO Brian Roberts says that the company will commit $75 million in cash and $25 million in media over the next three years to "fight injustice and inequality against race, ethnicity, gender identity, sexual orientation, or ability."

▶ Target pledged $10 million to organizations such as the National Urban League and the African American Leadership Forum.

▶ Fashion Nova pledged $1 million in donations throughout 2020 to various organizations, including Black Lives Matter, NAACP Legal Defense and Educational Fund, and Know Your Rights Camp.

▶ The Pokémon Company International announced that it will donate a minimum of $5 million to nonprofit organizations that focus on improving the lives of children with a focus on diversity, equity, and inclusion.

▶ Whataburger is designating $1 million of their charitable fund to their internal Feeding Student Success program, which facilitates scholarships and programs aiding Black and minority students.

These are just a few examples of what happens when corporations act with "soul" and in alignment with their newly declared purpose of doing good while doing well. There are many other examples throughout corporate America, and although some go through the ESG investment channel, others are part of the ESG-inspired movement of doing the right thing, as shown in the examples cited below.

> **Thinking Out of the Box to Get into the Box**. In a unique and innovative collaboration, Lowe's is teaming up with Daymond John of ABC's "Shark Tank" to: call all diverse small business owners to pitch their products to Lowe's executives for a chance to land them on Lowes.com... or to secure shelf space in Lowe's stores. Marketing support to reach millions of homes across America will also be provided. In addition, Lowe's is teaming up with Daymond John to help give small businesses the ultimate lift with the chance for mentoring, networking, and other opportunities.

Others from the sports world are also stepping up and stepping in to do the right thing in this time of need.

LeBron James Gets $100 Million Investment to Build Media Empire. "The King" and his longtime business partner Maverick Carter have formed a new company, SpringHill, with an unapologetic agenda: A maker and distributor of all kinds of content that will give a voice to creators and consumers who have been pandered to, ignored, or underserved.

> SpringHill is named for the Akron apartment complex where James and his mom moved to when he was in sixth grade. It consolidates the Robot Co., a marketing agency, with two other businesses.

Such actions are part of a movement, one in which many CEOs are speaking out and doing more. At a recent Yale School of Management CEO Summit, CEOs spoke out.

Ken Frazier, CEO of Merck stepped down from President Trump's Advisory Council in the aftermath of Charlottesville and spoke up in an important CNBC interview. Frazier's goal in speaking up was to explain to viewers what the source of the anger is for many African Americans. He said that when the African American community views the video of George Floyd, they see an African American being treated as less than human.

Frazier said, "this is a defining moment for our country when it comes to the issues of race," and added that he worries that our democracy is "at a very fragile state." He sees the business community playing a key role in getting through this time and in providing opportunities to the African American community. "The business community can take leadership when it comes to concrete actions around things like police reform and access to capital…[these are some] of the issues the business community can unilaterally make an impact on.—Kenneth C. Frazier, Chairman, President & CEO, Merck & Co.

Other CEOs commended Frazier for speaking up and agreed with his message. Paul Polman, former CEO of Unilever, stressed the importance of CEOs as advocates. During his time at the helm of Unilever, he was also vocal in making the case that businesses need to be more environmentally and socially conscious.

Doug Parker, CEO of American Airlines, concurred. Parker said that White people are not good at having difficult conversations about racism and therefore often avoid having such conversations. But, because of their role, CEOs are always in the public spotlight and have an obligation to initiate important conversations on race, even if it is uncomfortable. "We do have an obligation. Sometimes we can convince ourselves that it's not really my responsibility as a CEO to opine on this or make a statement on this, because when it comes to diversity and inclusion, we might think, 'Well, it's not going to matter, because who am I to be making these statements?' It does matter."—Doug Parker, Chairman & CEO, American Airlines

Former IBM CEO and current executive chairman Ginni Rometty reiterated Ken Frazier's words that focused on healing, reconciliation, and action. She was emphatic in stating that all organizations need to do more. Rometty encouraged CEOs to listen to successful Black leaders, who often feel an immense burden on behalf of their community not to fail or let others down. "I think for all of us, whatever we have done, it is not enough on the listening, the healing, the reconciliation.… It is not enough…we have much more to do on the listening piece and on learning." —Virginia M. Rometty, Executive Chairman, IBM

Joanne Lipman, former editor-in-chief of *USA TODAY* and author of "That's What She Said", drew parallels to the #MeToo movement. Initially, #MeToo was viewed as a female issue. But it was finally recognized that it was an issue for everyone, just as confronting racism is increasingly seen as an issue for everyone. Speaking and listening is a start, but actions must follow with a focus on jobs and opportunities.

Other ways that companies can provide opportunities is through greater access to capital. Goldman Sachs has been extremely focused on getting capital into underserved communities through a series of long-term programs, including the company's 10,000 Small Businesses program and 10,000 Women program. Also, when SBA's PPP came out, Goldman Sachs worked with community development organizations and financial institutions to deploy just under $600 million in capital. This is going to businesses that have an average of four employees and take loans averaging $62,000; about 60% of these loans are in communities of color. "We see an enormous imbalance in the way capital is allocated to people of color...I think these are things where we can make a difference through actions over a long period of time by consistent investment." —David M. Solomon, Chairman & CEO, The Goldman Sachs Group

What Will Happen After the Pandemic and the Headlines Fade?

Indra Nooyi said that the real test is how people and companies will behave when the collective crises we now face are over. Will we change?

Prior to the pandemic, Nooyi stated that we referred to many individuals as "hourly workers." Then, during the pandemic, many of these people became the backbone of our country and were termed "essential workers." We admire them and clap for them. But what happens when the pandemic has concluded? Will we give these individuals higher wages? Will we provide health insurance and more workers' rights? Will we treat them differently?

Additionally, once the protests about police brutality and racism subside, what changes will truly be made? "What happens when we come out of this pandemic; are we going to be a different humanity? Or, are we going to be like a rubber band and snap right back to the way we were?...I'm hoping and praying that as we come out of the pandemic, we imagine a very different society—that has a conscience and that makes money. I'm not against making money, but not money at all costs on the backs of workers." —Indra K. Nooyi, Chairman

A lot of good is being done within both the practice and spirit of ESG. One important development in its practice, for instance, is the requirement for more diverse board members, which Nasdaq has acted upon.

Nasdaq-listed companies will be required to publicly disclose board-level diversity statistics through Nasdaq's proposed disclosure framework within one year of the SEC's approval of the listing rule and to have two diverse directors within four years of the SEC's approval of the listing rule.

Amazon is also staking a big claim in "doing the right thing" by having recently launched a $2 billion Housing Equity Fund to benefit moderate- to low-income families and individuals in three communities Amazon calls home: Washington State's Puget Sound region; Arlington, Virginia; and Nashville, Tennessee.

At the individual gift-giving level, perhaps no one has staked a greater claim in living up to a moral persuasion of sharing one's wealth with those who are in need than MacKenzie Scott, former wife of Amazon's Jeff Bezos and the third richest women in the world. She has donated more than $4 Billion since December 2020 to many causes, including to those that address systemic inequities that have been deepened by the COVID-19 crisis. The causes her foundation has given to include debt relief, employment training, credit and financial services for under-resourced communities, education for historically marginalized and underserved people, civil rights advocacy groups, and legal defense funds that take on institutional discrimination.

Doing the things cited above are examples of *doing ethics*—not of merely talking about them, or philosophizing about them, but of actually doing things that are ultimately for the better good of society (*e pluribus unum*—all for one!)

C H A P T E R   S I X

Imperiled Black-Owned Businesses, COVID-19, and Ethics

About Chapter Six: **Imperiled Black-Owned Businesses, COVID-19, and Ethics**

T his is a difficult story to tell because the facts of the matter pull at our heart strings and make us realize the inescapable truth that systemic racism has landed Black-owned firms in the most unenviable position of near extinction during the time of COVID-19.

When one asks the question of "how did we get here? One begins to see a common theme: The data are systematically not collected to reveal the extent of the problem. Now, the facts of the matter are laid bare as we walk in any urban area where Black-owned businesses are located and see one boarded up business after another.

The truth is that many Black-owned firms, and many of their owners, are being wiped out by COVID-19. Many were fragile and imperiled before the pandemic, but the pandemic did something that no other barrier they faced ever did all at once: It took away their customers, their dreams, and many of their lives.

This chapter sheds light on why COVID-19 is the end of the line for many of the nation's 2 million Black-owned firms. Previously, when at the end of their ropes, they would tie and knot and hang on but in the face of COVID-19 the rope won't hold.

In the story of Black-owned businesses this chapter makes it clear that being in a capitalism nation without capital is a curse. It's also a vicious cycle: Black firm owners can't get bank loans because they never got bank loans. As a result, of the 2 million Black-owned firms, only 124,000 firms of them employ workers. For the others, the owners and their families are the workers. Yet Black-owned businesses are a net gain for society and when their dreams die, they are replaced by nightmares, for themselves and for the society as a whole.

The wisdom of thought leaders is shared throughout in telling the story and in putting forth urgent recommendations for addressing the problems facing Black-owned firms, including their apparent inability of those with employees to have been able to access the government Paycheck Protection Program (PPP). Magic Johnson was so upset about it he gave the U.S. Small Business Administration $100 million to lend to Black Businesses. Imagine that.

Though there is a lot of sadness in this story, there is also a lot of hope. In fact, ethics is about hope and the heart, and many in the public and private sector have opened their hearts, minds, and wallets to step in to help Black-owned businesses.

While small and minority businesses as a whole have also suffered during this pandemic, we chose to focus on Black businesses because many are owned by those that don't have a "bench", meaning as many are non-immigrants they lack networks, financing and other external supports that immigrants have. As a result, they are among the most reliant on government interventions.

Imperiled Black-Owned Businesses, COVID-19, and Ethics

When small businesses catch a cold, Black-owned businesses catch pneumonia. That's because it's always been hard for them to catch a break.

To be a business in a capitalist nation without capital is a problem.

The phrase "too big to fail" is familiar. What is not as familiar is the reality that Black-owned businesses are often "too small to win" but too important to fail in their communities, so when they get to the end of their rope, they tie a knot to hang on.

Black business owners have had to overcome a lack of business networks, a lack of capital, a lack of knowledge, and a lack of working space, but one thing they have never lacked is nerve. They had the nerve to forge their way into business ownership from the lowest level of self-employment to the highest levels of industry, against all odds.

> According to the 2018 Annual Business Survey (ABS), which is conducted by the U.S. Census Bureau and the National Science Foundation, there were over 2 million African American-owned firms in 2017 in the United States. By contrast, in 1969, the first year that the Census reported data on Black-owned firms, there were 163,000 that had total receipts valued at $4.5 billion. It is noteworthy that in 1969, of the 163,000 firms, 82 percent were "employer firms, meaning they had employees, whereas in 2017 only 124,000 of the 2 million Black-owned firms had employees. It appears that today, as contrasted with the past, many Black-owned firms are primarily self-employment vehicles.

It has always been a long, hard road for Black-owned businesses, but in the time of COVID-19, the road is washing out—and so are they.

As Florant et al. (2020) underscores in the article, "COVID-19: Investing in Black Lives and Livelihoods" (2020), "the pandemic is imposing an additional burden on Black

Americans, who already deal with a vicious cycle of structural barriers and disadvantages." The article emphasizes that "Black Americans have worse health outcomes and are less likely to build wealth due to factors such as under-resourced community institutions, poor environments for investment, lower rates of career advancement, overrepresentation in lower-wage jobs, and a lack of inclusion in the financial system". Collectively, "this makes them more susceptible to the health and economic effects of the pandemic, even though they are among the most poorly positioned to surmount the challenges—a double bind".

Florant et al. (2020) provide further insights into the overall problem that Blacks face at every stake of the wealth building process, noting:

> [As] the impact of the pandemic moves from health to economic consequences, black Americans will likely sustain more damage across every stage of the wealth-building journey. Crucially, 39 percent of jobs held by Black workers (seven million jobs in all) are vulnerable as a result of the COVID-19 crisis compared with 34 percent for White workers. Forty percent of the revenues of black-owned businesses are located in the five most vulnerable sectors—including leisure, hospitality, and retail—compared with 25 percent of the revenues of all U.S. businesses.

In the report, "Double Jeopardy: COVID-19's Concentrated Health and Wealth Effects in Black Communities," the Federal Reserve of New York (2020) zeros in on the specific impact that the pandemic is having on Black-owned firms, observing that (p.1):

> The effects of the pandemic on small businesses amid forced closings, modified re-openings, and weakened demand, are well documented. Nationally representative data on small businesses indicate that the number of active business owners fell by 22 percent from February to April 2020, the largest drop on record. The number of Black business owners plummeted from 1.1 million in February 2020 to 640,000 in April. The loss of 440,000 black business owners representing 41 percent of the previous level. Latinx business owners fell by 32 percent and Asian business owners dropped by 26 percent. In contrast, the number of white business owners fell by 17 percent.

The owners of the landmark D.C. restaurant Ben's Chili Bowl don't need to rely on research to understand how COVID-19 is impacting Black businesses that operate in Black neighborhoods; They are living it. After 60 years in business, weathering all storms, COVID-19 is hitting the restaurant with the force of a super typhoon. If it is barely hanging on, imagine how the virus is hitting Black-owned firms of lesser standing and fewer years of experience? Berkon (2020) takes the pulse of the restaurant's owner, as her heart races.

Landmark D.C. Restaurant Ben's Chili Bowl: Hit Hard by COVID-19

The restaurant has accomplished a lot in the last 60-plus years. It's fed everyone from leaders of the civil rights movement to entertainment superstars to busloads of hungry tourists. Its owners have launched a charitable foundation, collected awards, and expanded the operation from one location to eight. Now Ben's may do something it's never done: Close.

"We're suffering a great deal. It's very, very, very difficult for us right now," says Virginia Ali, who co-founded the restaurant with her late husband Ben Ali. Apart from Thanksgiving and Christmas, the original U Street location has been open every day since 1958.

Ben's Chili Bowl has weathered past recessions. It has survived civic unrest and held out as the blocks around it gentrify. But as the coronavirus keeps public life shut down, the restaurant is facing its toughest challenge yet.

All Chili Bowl locations except the original are currently closed. Company revenue has plummeted. Three-quarters of staff were home as of April 2020.

Source: Berkon, A. (2020): After Six Decades, Ben's Chili Bowl Faces Its Greatest Challenge Yet: Coronavirus. Retrieved from https://www.wamu.org

Ben's Chili Bowl is not the only Black-owned business suffering, most are suffering.

At the beginning of the pandemic in March 2020, *Forbes* took the pulse of how some Black-owned firm owners were being impacted at that early stage. In its article, "13 Entrepreneurs of Color Share How COVID-19 Has Impacted Their Business" (2020), firm owners shared a snapshot of what was happening to them and how they felt about it. A few of their comments are mentioned below.

■ **Micki Webb, founder of Get Psyched:** COVID-19 brought my entire industry to a screeching halt. My clients are staffing agencies placing contractors in school districts to fill in gaps as special education teachers, school psychologists, paraeducators, etc.

While permanent school staff are being paid during the closures, most contracted staff are suddenly without pay and my staffing agency clients and myself [are] now without revenue.

▨ **Nusrat Alam, co-founder of I am Perspective:** We had two large conferences scheduled for 3/28/20 and 4/25/20 that had to be cancelled. Our work was mainly interactive, and we can no longer work with groups of people in any forum. "I Am Perspective" Radio is also impacted because it is preventing us from having guests travel to [the] recording studio.

▨ **Nayoka Simone, founder of Nyrai Interior Designs:** COVID-19 impacted my business due to the significant decrease in client connections. This virus has forced me to scale back on my face-to-face in-home consultations, shopping for my clients and meeting with vendors. My clients are very visual and hands-on, so this restricts this option. Customers that were once willing to open their doors, are now no longer comfortable with letting people into their homes [because] this virus can be potentially fatal.

▨ **Tony Weaver, Jr., founder of Weird Enough Productions:** With COVID-19 leading to widespread school closures, we're unable to bring our program to students during the school day. These months are the peak of the academic sales cycle, but education leaders have much bigger problems to tackle right now.

It's probable that many small businesses, no matter who their owners are, were experiencing similar problems at that time—and still today. But there is a difference for Black firm owners: Many have no financial cushion and most likely started their firms on a "shoestring" with minimal financing, which makes them more vulnerable to shocks.

The reasons that Black-owned businesses are disproportionately negatively impacted by COVID-19 have their origins in the systemic racism Blacks experience throughout society and in business. As a result, many Black business owners are classified as "necessity entrepreneurs," meaning that they "had" to go into business to survive when they could not obtain viable employment. Many of their businesses are stuck at the margins of society, with the owners just trying to be lucky enough to catch whatever falls their way. For the 124,000 firms that actually employ workers, they are the lucky ones, even though many of thom havo aloo bccn disadvantaged by systemic racism In multiple ways.

In an article, "More than Half of Black-Owned Businesses May Not Survive COVID-19", Lennihan (2020) draws on Brookings Institution scholar Andre Perry to explain why it is so difficult for Black-Owned businesses to survive. According to Perry:

> Andre Perry, in his book, "*Know Your Price: Valuing Black Lives and Property in America's Black Cities*", (2020) says the lack of wealth in the Black community has had a huge impact on its ability to survive the pandemic. Because a lot of Black business owners don't have the kind of equity due to structural racism, they have less of a cushion to withstand this particular moment in time. He also underscores that if Black businesses and individuals had the same type of cushion as their White counterparts, they would not be in this situation.

It follows, under the circumstances, that Black-owned employer businesses are smaller and have fewer employees, lower average revenues, and lower average payroll expenditures than American businesses overall. Their average annual revenues of $1 million are 84% smaller than the average revenues for all firms; their average of 10 employees compares to 22 employees for all firms, while their annual payroll per employee is almost $30,000 as compared to $51,000 for firms overall.

There are historical roots of the problem that help explain how and why Black-owned businesses have underperformed as well as immediate factors that explain why they have been hit 2.5 times harder by COVID-19 than other businesses. In its report, the New York Federal Reserve points to three main baskets of issues to help explain the current predicament of Black-owned businesses (pp. 1-2):

- Volumes of COVID-19 cases coincide with Black-owned business locations: two-thirds of counties with high levels of Black business activity pre-COVID-19 are in the top 50 COVID-affected areas. Data from counties nationwide show Black-owned firms are more likely to be located in COVID-19 hot spots, whereas white-owned firms are less likely to be in the most heavily affected areas.

- The Paycheck Protection Program (PPP), the federal government's signature relief program for small businesses, has left significant coverage gaps: these loans reached only 20% of eligible firms in states with the highest densities of Black-owned firms, and in counties with the densest Black-owned business activity, coverage rates were typically lower than 20%.

- Weaker cash positions, weaker bank relationships, and preexisting funding gaps left Black firms with little cushion entering the crisis: even the healthiest Black firms were financially disadvantaged at the onset of COVID-19.

There is a lot to unpack in these three bullet points. Indeed, they are like bullets to the heart of Black businesses.

But let's focus first on the PPP program. To be clear, it is not clear exactly how many Black-owned businesses have been able to access the program because the Small Business Administration (SBA) that oversees the PPP has not ordered the private banks charged with disbursing the money to keep records about the ethnicity of recipients.

> As was reported in *Bloomberg News* in June 2020, the SBA's inspector general released a report noting that of $659 billion that Congress has approved for PPP loans — which are meant to allow small businesses to keep workers on their payrolls instead of firing or furloughing them— about $425.8 billion had been disbursed. The inspector general pointed out that the legislation authorizing PPP funding mandated that the SBA prioritize lending to rural, minority and women-owned businesses, but that didn't appear to have happened. Why not? Because the SBA decided not to order private banks charged with disbursing the money to do so, according to the inspector general. And, his report noted, "because SBA did not require demographic data to identify PPP borrowers in underserved markets, it is unlikely that SBA will be able to determine the loan volume to the intended prioritized markets."

Outraged by the inability of minority firms to access the PPP, hip-hop media mogul Sean Diddy Combs launched the "Our Fair Share" platform to help minority businesses access much-needed PPP funds. The goal of the platform is to walk firms through the process of the application and lend them a hand to ensure that they understand that the opportunity exists.

Combs and others who know that Black businesses can hardly catch a break are stepping up to try to help them and to slow down the rapid rise of firm closures.

Black-owned firms are not the first to catch a break but they are the first to catch a lot of what "hits the fan," and a lot of that has come their way in the form of institutional racism, which is largely to blame for these circumstances. Discrimination in banking relationships and lending decisions has, in cumulative and generational ways, imposed specific barriers to Blacks that have limited their entry, diversification, and growth in business.

The problem is plain for the world to see: Black businesses are hurting today for historical and current reasons. In his article explaining that half of Black-owned firms may not survive COVID-19, Lennihan (2020) cites the Economic Policy Institute and Kristen Clarke to highlight some of the reasons why Black-owned firms are at such a disadvantage.

> As the Economic Policy Institutes notes, "The disparate racial impact of the virus is deeply rooted in historic and ongoing social and economic injustices. Persistent racial disparities in health status, access to health care, wealth, employment, wages, housing, income, and poverty all contribute to greater susceptibility to the virus—both economically and physically".

> Kristen Clarke, president and executive director of the Lawyers' Committee for Civil Rights Under Law, says "Black Americans are still recuperating from the economic collapse of 2007-2009, which had a staggering impact on Black wealth. Unlike other communities, African Americans are not as equipped today to recover from a second period of economic collapse" (para. 12).

Why have Black-owned businesses apparently been unable to access more help from the PPP given the disproportionate negative impact they are facing under COVID-19?

The answer to this question underscores how a lifetime of injustices has led to yet another specific injustice in the inability of Black-owned firms to access the PPP.

> The pandemic has served to exacerbate these structural inequalities affecting Black business ownership. Since the lockdown's onset, according to the Economy League (2020), Black-owned businesses have been impeded from accessing cash relief programs—like the (PPP)—because of the ways in which these programs rely on existing banking. They also privilege firms with employees over sole proprietorships. Yet, even Black-owned firms with employees faced barriers to access. As of April 2020, 40 percent of Black business owners reported that they were not working compared to only 17 percent of white business owners. The pandemic has only amplified existing inequities for Black business owners. (www.economyleague.org)

As a Black woman who grew up in Philadelphia in the 1960s as the daughter of two entrepreneurs, I don't have to read external research reports to know what Black businesses have experienced—I have witnessed it firsthand.

My Family's Business: Drexel Products, circa 1950s and 1960s

My parents, Judson and Sylvia Freeman, met a Black man who was a chemist and had graduated from one of the historically Black colleges and universities (HBCUs) in Atlanta, Georgia. It was probably Morris Brown College, as my father had attended that college for a time until he ran out of money and wasn't able to complete his studies. The chemist could not get a job and decided to put his knowledge of chemistry to use by creating formulas for Black cosmetics and hair care products.

He tried to get a loan to go into business but, sadly, was unable to obtain one. In one of his last acts before he committed suicide, he sold his formulas to my parents. My parents, with no formal knowledge of chemistry, decided to go into business to make and sell the products for which they had formulas from the chemist. Their products included hair grease, perfume, face powder, and other personal care products. Did they have employees? Yes: We, their children, were their "employees." Every Saturday morning of my childhood, I went straight to work in our basement, helping to mix and stir things and to affix labels on the jars. We had to hurry because the seller's agent for my parents was a woman who would be there at 3 p.m. sharp each Saturday to take the merchandise to sell through her networks at churches and beauty salons and door-to-door throughout the neighborhoods of Black communities in West Philadelphia.

I recall that every Friday, I had to go to in person to pay the installment loan that my parents took out from the Household Finance Corporation (HFC) to finance their business. I didn't know it at the time, but the HFC was the only institution in Black neighborhoods that lent to people like my parents. I never knew that my parents weren't able to get a standard loan from a bank. I assumed that the HFC was a bank, but it was more like a payday lender with exorbitant rates.

In the end, although it was a really good business, when the likes of large White-owned companies realized that they could make good money from selling Black personal care products to Blacks, small entrepreneurs like my parents couldn't obtain the capital to compete and scale up, so they sold out.

Interestingly, years later, Korean immigrants also realized that there was a lot of money to be made in selling hair to Blacks. After all, in the 1960s, one of their leading exports was human hair. Two decades later, they moved into inner cities in locations like West Philadelphia, where they purchased little shops that had been abandoned by the previous Jewish owners and became the new merchants. Unlike Blacks, Koreans did not have to rely on banks for capital; they had ethnic lending networks and relatives that supplied their capital. Remember, many Blacks weren't immigrants—they arrived on America as slaves, and there is a big difference in terms of having or lacking a network of support on which to rely. Many Blacks had no choice other than to rely on unreliable banks to supply capital; they had no "bench," no network, and very little hope. (Sharon Freeman)

While the foregoing depicts an experience from the 1960s, the experience of many Black-owned firms in Philadelphia today is not much different from the past.

As reported in the Pew Charitable Trust's "State of the City" report on Philadelphia in 2019, poverty remains a persistent challenge in Philadelphia. "The city's poverty rate has been stuck in the 26% range for the past five years, a time period wherein the rate has dropped in many other cities. Philadelphia has nearly 400,000 residents living below the poverty line, a fact that affects numerous aspects of city life."

Poverty in Black neighborhoods is one reason why COVID-19 has hit Philadelphia's Black businesses so hard: They were fragile in the first place. In an Economy League (2020) article on "The Impact of COVID-19 on Greater Philadelphia's Black-Owned Businesses," it was underscored that "while some Black-owned firms have been able to take advantage of federal, state, and local cash relief programs, many have been forced to close their doors forever." The article provides a broader context of the state of Black businesses in Philadelphia, noting:

- In 2017, 20.3 percent of Greater Philadelphia's population identified as Non-Hispanic Black, but only 2.5 percent of all employer firms were Non-Hispanic-Black-owned.

■ The City of Philadelphia had the highest rate of Black-owned employer firms in the region in 2017 at 5.4 percent; even though Non-Hispanic Black residents made up 41.3 percent of the population in 2017.

■ Regional Black-owned businesses show higher than average concentrations in the health care and social services sectors, the transportation and warehousing industry, the administrative support and waste management industries, educational services, and the arts and entertainment industry.

■ Researchers estimate that roughly 40 percent of Black-owned businesses nationally have closed due to the pandemic-induced recession; others predict up to a 60 percent attrition rate.

Here is why this matters so much: In the Philadelphia region, as one example, a 40% attrition rate among Black-owned businesses would equate to a loss of 1,135 firms, $993 million in regional revenue, 12,735 jobs, and $345 million in wages. A 60% attrition rate would equate to the loss of 1,702 firms, $1.5 billion in regional revenue, 19,102 jobs, and $517 million in wages. This would be catastrophic.

All the while, the "American dream" for many Black businesses is turning into a nightmare.

Against all odds, some have weathered all the storms that have come their way ... but survivors weren't in little row boats—they were in aircraft carriers.

Today, there are six Black billionaires out of the 615 billionaires in America. Some Black-owned firms have even climbed to the top of the ladder in their respective fields, one of the most successful to date being World Wide Technology (WWT), Inc., a Maryland-based IT products and services firm founded in 1990 that had, in 2018, an annual revenue of over $11 billion and over 5,000 employees. But WWT is an exception in addition to being exceptional.

The other side of the story paints a grim picture, however, and harkens back to the Lennihan (2020) article that predicts that half of Black-owned firms cannot weather the COVID-19 storm. As cited in the article:

> For the masses of Black-owned businesses, however, COVID-19 has hit them hard and is the third strike that has counted them out. Research at the University of California, Santa Cruz, based on data of the National Bureau of Economic Research, found that 41 percent of Black-owned businesses—some 440,000 enterprises—have been shuttered by COVID-19, compared to just 17 percent of white-owned businesses. "I knew it would be bad, but I didn't think it would be this devastating," says Robert W. Fairlie, author of the UC Santa Cruz report and a professor of economics at the university (para. 4).

Fairlie, as referenced in the Lennihan article, explains that half of all Black families have less than $9,000 in total wealth, while the median wealth for white families is $130,000. "If you need $10,000 to get through a rough period, you can do it if you have $130,000," he said...and, "if you have only $9,000, that makes it impossible." Perry is cited in the Lennihan article, noting: "Blacks receive business loans at about half the rate of their white counterparts, and when received it's at higher interest rates" (para. 17).

Earnings of Blacks in the Labor Force

Businesses, large and small, are established by people, and if those people don't have money or can't access any, that's a problem.

Salaried employment as a basis for accumulating wealth has not been a viable path for many Blacks to accumulate it.

Data from the United States U.S. Bureau of Labor (BLS) (2018) tells the story. The data from its "Labor Force Characteristics by Race and Ethnicity 2018" report shows that as a result of the pattern of racism

that Blacks have experienced, they have considerably lower wages than Whites and Asians. The median usual weekly earnings of full-time wage and salary workers in 2017 were $655 for Hispanics, $682 for Blacks, $890 for Whites, and $1,043 for Asians. Among men, the earnings for Whites ($971), Blacks ($710), and Hispanics ($690) were 80%, 59%, and 57%, respectively, of the earnings of Asians ($1,207). The median earnings of White women ($795), Black women ($657), and Hispanic women ($603) were 88%, 73%, and 67%, respectively, of the earnings of Asian women ($903).

The earnings disparity across the major race and ethnicity groups for men held for nearly all major occupational groups, according to BLS data (2018). For example, the median usual weekly earnings of Asian men ($1,662) and White men ($1,458) working full time in management, professional, and related occupations (the highest paying major occupational groups) were considerably higher than the earnings of Hispanic men ($1,166) and Black men ($1,099) in the same occupational groups.

The median weekly earnings for women by race and ethnicity groups were relatively close across a number of occupations, the data show. For example, among women in service occupations, the earnings were $515 for Asians, $505 for Whites, $484 for Blacks, and $475 for Hispanics. By contrast, in management, professional, and related occupations, the earnings of Asian women were higher than those for women in other race and ethnicity groups.

Salaried Employment of Blacks During COVID-19

According to the BLS's "Supplemental Data Measuring the Effects of the COVID-19 Pandemic on the Labor Market" (2020), as of July 2020, in general:

> People employed in service occupations were among the most likely to have been unable to work due to the pandemic. Of those employed in July 2020, 1 in 5 service workers were unable to work at some point in the last 4 weeks because of employer closures or cutbacks due to the pandemic. Within service occupations, 33 percent of workers in personal care and service occupations and 24 percent of workers in food preparation and serving related occupations were unable to work because of pandemic-related closures or lost business.

The BLS 2020 supplemental data also provides the following insights:

> Self-employed workers were much more likely than private wage and salary workers and government workers to have been unable to work because of pandemic-related closures or lost business. About 27 percent of the self-employed in July were unable to work because of the pandemic, compared with 11 percent of private wage and salary workers and 6 percent of government workers.

The pain of this reality has no doubt hit Black people the hardest. Whereas some business owners "moonlight" from salaried employment to have a business on the side, now, as they are sidelined from their employment, their businesses are suffering both from a lack of cash infusions from the business owners and a lack of customers to support the businesses due to COVID-19.

The bottom line remains: At every turn and in every regard, Black people just can't catch a break.

COVID-19 Created the Perfect Storm

For the most part, with Black-owned firms already being fragile, COVID-19 is proving to be the "straw that breaks the camel's back." Blacks have persevered through everything, navigated around every roadblock, made a way out of no way—but then came COVID-19, the perfect storm. Clouds have hung over the heads of Black businesses from the very beginning, but COVID-19 has done something that other singular barriers did not at once accomplish: **It has taken away their jobs, their businesses, their customers, and many of their lives.**

The New York Federal Reserve's (2020) report sheds further light on the dark predicament of Black-owned businesses, explaining the following salient facts (p.2):

- **Black Business Activity is Geographically Concentrated.** Black business activity is geographically concentrated in the U.S. and is correlated with Black population density. Research shows that Black populations are typically clustered in metropolitan hubs and the number of cities that are majority-Black has grown over the past decade. Forty percent of receipts from Black-owned businesses are concentrated in just 30 counties, roughly one percent of all counties in the country. Examining the same 30 counties, we find that roughly two-thirds (19 of 30) are areas with the highest numbers of COVID-19 cases. Given the high geographic concentration of firm activity and the Black population in general, business disruptions in these places can have outsized effects on African American well-being at large.

- ■ **Covid-19 Cases Coincide with Black Business Locations.** A broader analysis of counties across the United States shows a correlation between Black business density and COVID-19 incidence. It shows that there is a positive relationship between COVID incidence and the share of a county's businesses that are Black-owned, an indication that areas with higher concentrations of Black businesses are more likely to be facing larger direct (longer forced closures, COVID-19 symptoms) and indirect (social distancing, fewer customers) effects of the pandemic.

But why are Black businesses located where they are? There are two reasons. First, that is where their customers are. Second, the primary market knowledge they have historically had is what they can observe around them. They haven't always had license to freely walk around in other neighborhoods to observe what people are buying and selling, which largely remains the case today. In fact, four dreaded words in the life of Black people who dare to go somewhere they don't belong are **"Can I help you?"** This was—and still is—understood to mean "What are you doing here? You don't belong here."

The Nerve to Walk into Bonwit Tellers

I remember walking into the swanky Bonwit Tellers store in Center City Philadelphia when I was a high school student. My mother warned me to dress up and look my best. I did that, walked in, and held my breath in anticipation of being asked to be asked the "dreaded question." But being the child of entrepreneurial parents, and thereby mistakenly believing that I was both free and rich, when the question came, I simply replied, "Show me where the size 5 dresses are, please." Had I been born and raised in the South, I probably would have been more deferent and would not have had the nerve to go into that store. In fact, when my mother was 90 years old, it occurred to me to finally ask her how it had been growing up in the South, in Atlanta, in 1920s and 1930s. I asked her, "Mom, how bad was the racism you experienced? Did people hit you? Were you scared to walk down the street"? She said, "No, none of that happened because we were too poor to be where we didn't belong, and as long as you stayed in your place, and 'knew your place,' there was no problem."

Black businesspeople "knew" their place, and their place was often the only place they knew.

Their place was in crowded locations in Black communities with ample opportunities to enter into low-barrier-to-entry businesses that sold goods to meet the basic and lifestyle needs of the local population. Selling such goods and services was as far as their money stretched and as far as their knowledge and networks extended. They knew their market and their customers. Importantly, they had "societal permission" to meet the needs of the customers in their neighborhoods—that is, until larger White-owned businesses decided to compete with them.

When Black businesses were left alone, they created businesses out of everything: house parties, dinners, clothing sales, etc. They replicated everything in the White world but in a much smaller way that relied on self-financing.

Before there was Uber or cell phones, there were "Jitneys," guys with cars who waited outside the supermarkets to offer to take you home for a fixed price. There were many such "on-and off-the-books" businesses in Black neighborhoods, so much so that some mistakenly believed that segregation was more viable for these little Black-owned businesses. In a way, they weren't wrong because, indeed, segregation was very good for keeping small businesses very small; however, if a business sought to grow, it had to extend its goods and services beyond the neighborhood and operate somewhere it "didn't belong."

And now, we are here. "Volumes of COVID-19 cases coincide with Black-owned business locations: two-thirds of counties with high levels of Black business activity pre-COVID-19 are in the top 50 COVID-affected areas," the New York Federal Reserve said.

Despite this, the coverage gaps in the PPP have left many Black-owned businesses out of the government relief bonanza. According to the New York Federal Reserve's (2020) report, "Double Jeopardy: COVID-19's Concentrated Health and Wealth Effects in Black Communities":

> These loans reached only 20% of eligible firms in states with the highest densities of Black-owned firms, and in counties with the densest Black-owned business activity, coverage rates were typically lower than 20%, the Fed report showed. At the same time, Black-owned firms, already smarting from a Great Recession that hurt them badly, entered the crisis with weaker cash positions, weaker bank relationships, and preexisting funding gaps. Even the healthiest Black firms were financially disadvantaged at the onset of COVID-19 (p. 4).

Essentially, Black business owners are denied financing because they really need financing because they never got financing. Think about that. Yes, it is circular but so is the reality of the circumstances of Blacks in America. August 28, 2020, marked the fifty-seventh anniversary of Martin Luther King's famous "I Have a Dream" speech. Today, Blacks are continuing to dream and hope that they can obtain financing for their businesses, but, in many cases, their dreams continue to be just that: dreams.

In "Why the Racial Wealth Gap Persists, More Than 150 Years After Emancipation", Schermerhorn (2019) identifies many factors that help explain the problem. In fact, there are many reasons why it exists, a few include the following:

> The wealth gap of Blacks today can be traced back to Jim Crow-era practices that include redlining and job discrimination that segregated African Americans from higher paying jobs and homeowner ownership opportunities that ultimately prevented wealth building. The 1935 Social Security Act did not afford coverage to domestic and agricultural workers, many of whom were African American, and its requirements for residency and payroll information also excluded the large number of African Americans working menial, "off the books" jobs and migrating north at the time.

The income from such "off the books" jobs—then and now—has counted many Blacks out when they want to be counted in to access government programs. By being "off the books" they lack proof of the income they make.

But even when Black salaried income is "on the books" it typically accounts for a lot less than that of their White counterparts.

Today, the median wealth for white families is about 12 times that for Black families, averaging around $140,000, and 1 in 4 Black households have zero or negative net worth compared to the less than 1 in 10 White families without wealth. Even more concerning is that by 2053, the median wealth for Black families is projected to fall to zero. If Black people from these households seek financing from banks, they will not get it because they need it but never got it before. It's circular, indeed.

What is the Ethical Case for Supporting Black-Owned Firms?

They matter to their communities and to society!

Supporting them is the right thing to do, where "right" is operationally defined as being that which is just, moral, ethical, fair, humane, and consistent with the expressed aims of our founding documents. In the words of Franklin D. Roosevelt:

> "The test of our progress is not whether we add more to the abundance of those who have much. It is whether we provide enough for those who have too little."

But it's hard to get "there" from "here." As the sentiments conveyed on the Robert Schlankenbach Foundation (2020) website state:

The unfortunate fact is that there is no one cause and therefore not one solution. Racism in the U.S. is complex and multifaceted, and it would be a mistake to describe any single reform as an overall solution. Economic measures are not a panacea; improving material circumstances will not cure the racial biases – implicit or explicit.

But, while they are insufficient, economic solutions are necessary for making progress on racism in the U.S. The material conditions of the Black community reflect and perpetuate centuries of racism, and thus those conditions need to be addressed as part of any effort to root out continued systemic racism. This is why Dr. Martin Luther King, in his 1967 address "Where Do We Go from Here", was so insistent on the elimination of poverty as a tool.

In addition to moral and ethical justifications, there are also practical and smart reasons to encourage and support Black-owned businesses.

The framers of the Constitution, many of whom were entrepreneurs, understood the importance of supporting entrepreneurship as a foundation upon which to build the greatness of the nation, and they weren't wrong. They knew, and we have seen, that business success starts with an individual, one who has the desire to achieve and who dares to turn their dream into reality. Such individuals come in all hues, from all races and all cultures. One never knows which individuals might be able to soar. The trick is to ensure that everyone has wings to fly.

A few examples of Blacks who have laid the foundation for great entrepreneurial successes, both their own and those of others, show what's possible when human potential is unharnessed and unleashed:

Dr. Shirley Jackson, for instance, an American physicist who received her Ph.D. from the Massachusetts Institute of Technology (MIT) in 1973, was the first African American woman to earn a doctorate in nuclear physics at MIT. Her experiments in theoretical physics paved the way for numerous developments in the telecommunication space, including the touch-tone telephone, the portable fax, caller ID, call waiting, and fiber-optic cables. Her work laid the foundation for many businesses that changed the world.

Lonnie Johnson's example shows that it's possible to be an entrepreneur and a rocket scientist simultaneously. He invented the most famous water gun—the Super Soaker—and he wasn't even a toymaker; he was an aerospace engineer for NASA with a résumé boasting a stint with the U.S. Air Force, work on the Galileo Jupiter probe and Mars Observer project, and more than 40 patents. He was also working on the Johnson Thermoelectric Energy Converter, which converts heat directly into electricity—and while accomplishing all of this, he created a toy that gave us fun and proved that there are no limits to the human imagination and potential.

The common thread between the successes of both Dr. Shirley Jackson and Lonnie Johnson is education. One cannot talk about Black business formation and success without addressing the subject of education because the educational attainment of business owners is often a success factor in business as well as a reason to be self-employed (or not). The discrimination that Blacks have suffered in the education and housing ecosystems of America has placed them in locations and positions to fail. Richard Rothstein's 2014 article, "The Racial Achievement Gap, Segregated Schools, and Segregated Neighborhoods – A Constitutional Insult," explains these connections.

Impact of Education and Housing

Schools that the most disadvantaged black children attend are segregated because they are located in segregated high-poverty neighborhoods. Living in high-poverty neighborhoods for multiple generations adds an additional barrier to achievement, and multigenerational segregated poverty characterizes many African American children today. Education policy is constrained by housing policy: it is not possible to desegregate schools without desegregating both low-income and affluent neighborhoods. It has become conventional for policymakers to assert that the residential isolation of low-income black children is now "de facto," the accident of economic circumstance, demographic trends, personal preference, and private discrimination. But the historical record demonstrates that residential segregation is "de jure," resulting from racially motivated and explicit public policy whose effects endure to the present (para. 1).

Source: Rothstein, R. (2014, November 12). Race and Social Problems. Retrieved from http://www.americanbar.org

Those Black businesses that overcome the trifecta of an education gap, housing gap, and wealth gap are resilient and can inspire others to follow in their footsteps while they make contributions to their communities and to the nation as a whole through their entrepreneurship.

Black-Owned Businesses Help Strengthen Local Economies

Black-Owned Businesses Foster Job Creation

Black Inventors and Innovators Help America Remain at the Leading Edge

It has been noted in the case of Black inventors that America's ascent as the preeminent industrialized nation in the world was driven by the "golden age" of innovation and invention during the late nineteenth and early twentieth centuries and that early Black inventors were critical participants in the patent system during this time. Today, against the odds, Black American inventors have developed technologies that not only advance American technology but also continue to save lives. These inventors have improved our health and safety. Collectively, these examples show that we may be down, but we are not out and should never be counted out. These examples of Black inventors mentioned below are just a few of the many who matter and who are making a difference:

- **Marie Van Brittan Brown** invented the first home security system and obtained a patent for it in 1969. She invented the system because police did not respond quickly to emergencies happening in her New York neighborhood. Brown's invention allowed a homeowner to see the person at the door and hear their voice on a television set that was controlled by a wireless radio system. Some iterations of Brown's home security are still being used in the twenty-first century.

- **Dr. Patricia Bath**, an ophthalmologist and academic, received multiple patents related to cataract treatment between 1988 and 2003. The technology she invented, including the Laserphaco Probe, is used around the world to painlessly treat cataracts. Bath used her successes to found the American Institute for the Prevention of Blindness in Washington, D.C. She travels the world on humanitarian missions, restoring sight for those without access to adequate medical treatment.

- **Marian Rogers Croak** currently holds more than 135 patents primarily related to voice-over internet protocol (VoIP) technology, which paved the way for VoIP systems like Skype and Google Hangouts. Croak spent more than 30 years at AT&T, where she managed 2,000+ engineers and led AT&T to replace wired communications with IP. She currently serves as a vice president of engineering at Google, where she is responsible for Google's global expansion of internet access in emerging markets and elsewhere.

■ **Jesse Ernest Wilkins Jr.** was an African American nuclear scientist, mechanical engineer, and mathematician at the University of Chicago. He attended the University of Chicago at the age of 13, becoming its youngest-ever student. Wilkins contributed to the Manhattan Project during the Second World War. He also gained fame working in and conducting nuclear physics research in both academia and industry. His career spanned seven decades and included significant contributions to pure and applied mathematics, civil and nuclear engineering, and optics.

Rays of Hope: Some Black-Owned Businesses Are Thriving Through COVID-19

Though dark clouds loom over many Black-owned businesses, some are no doubt able to survive and even thrive, but they are the exceptions, including the three Black-owned companies that are currently listed on the stock exchange. These companies include Urban One, Inc., the largest Black-owned media company in America; American Shared Hospital Services, founded by a board-certified neurosurgeon, which leases medical equipment to hospitals; and RLJ Lodging, a Black-owned asset company with footprints in investment trusts and full-service hotels that was founded by the founder of Black Entertainment Television.

What has made them exceptional is possessing the right skillset, being in positions to leverage their networks from their universities or work experiences, being able to access financing, and having the right business idea at the right time and the right execution.

Although Black entrepreneurs are less likely to receive venture capital funding and start out their businesses with three times less capital than White-owned businesses, some are getting funded and disrupting the status quo in a variety of industries, according to Stephen (2020). In her article for Crunchbase, "25 Black Entrepreneurs Making Waves," she showcases 25 Black entrepreneurs who have built successful companies in logistics, tech, retail, and more, setting new standards for business. The top 3 in the U.S. in her list in terms of investment capital received are shown below:

Paul Judge, Co-Founder & Executive Director of Pindrop Security

- Total Funding Raised: $212.8M
- Investors Include: Vitruvian Partners, Goldman Sachs, Citi Ventures
- HQ: Atlanta, Georgia

Pindrop helps banks, insurers, and retailers identify their customers by voice, reducing fraud and improving the customer experience. In addition to Pindrop, a voice fraud prevention company, Paul is also the founder of Luma and the TechSquare Labs incubator.

Ryan Williams, Co-Founder & CEO of Cadre

- Total Funding Raised: $133.3M
- Investors Include: Andreessen Horowitz, Ford Foundation, Thrive Capital, Goldman Sachs Investment Partners
- HQ: New York, New York

Before becoming an entrepreneur, Ryan attended Harvard and worked at Goldman Sachs. He leveraged his experience in the financial sector to develop Cadre, an online marketplace connecting real estate investors and operators. Cadre makes it easy for investors to manage their investments and gain liquidity by selling their interests in the secondary market.

Diishan Imira, Founder & CEO of Mayvenn

- Total Funding Raised: $36M
- Investors Include: Essence Ventures, MaC Venture Capital, Impact America Fund, Muse Capital
- HQ: Oakland, California

Diishan graduated from Georgia State School of Business and developed a strong background in international trade logistics. He co-founded Mayvenn in 2012 when he realized that 95% of African American salons did not retail the products their customers wanted. Mayvenn makes the process of selling compatible products in a salon setting easier.

These and the other businesses profiled in the *Crunchbase* article have achieved the American dream, there are also many others such as firms owned by media moguls, entertainers, and athletes that did not follow the traditional venture capital route.

Robert F. Smith, for instance, is the founder, chairman, and CEO of Vista Equity Partners, where he directs Vista's investment strategy and decisions, governance, and investor relations. Vista currently manages equity capital commitments of over $58 billion and oversees a portfolio of more than 60 enterprise software, data, and technology-enabled companies that employ over 70,000 people worldwide. Since Vista's inception, Mr. Smith has supervised over 440 completed transactions representing more than $140 billion in aggregate transaction value.

Can Black-owned firms succeed on a level playing field—*and even on one that's not?* The evidence shows they can, but it's like playing basketball with one hand tied behind one's back. The challenge is to untie their hands to make it easier and fairer so that others can follow in the footsteps of those few who have thrived and won at the game against all odds.

Ecosystems of Failure and Success

It is important to underscore that just as systemic racism created an ecosystem for failure among Blacks, there have been ecosystems of support for the successes of Blacks as well. Those highlighted in the *Crunchbase* (2020) article, and other successful Black-owned businesses, have no doubt been the recipients of some aspects of such support.

The ecosystems of support for Blacks and their businesses have come in many forms from the public and private sectors. In the public sector, support comes from the federal, state, and local governments, and in the private sector, it comes from private foundations and corporations. All such support has mattered and made a difference, but the problems of Black businesses are so deep and multifaceted that they need more help.

Blacks also have a responsibility to help themselves. One important step in this process is to obtain an education that is sufficient to enable them to succeed in business. Failure to do that will help ensure the continued marginalization of Blacks and their businesses.

For those who have done the work of becoming educated and familiarizing themselves with opportunities they "theoretically" can access, there is more hope than not.

For them, the Minority Business Development Agency of the U.S. Department of Commerce stands ready to lend a helping hand, as does the Small Business Administration (SBA), which provides a broad range of small business support. Collectively, these agencies and their counterparts at the state and local levels provide financing, technical assistance, information, and more, but they only provide it to those who seek it out and to those who are qualified and eligible to receive it.

On Being Eligible to Receive Government Business Assistance

Due in part to systemic racism, many Black people and their businesses have had to go around the system and go underground to do their business. This has inadvertently created a culture of "going around" the authorities because when they applied for loans, they

weren't granted them and when they applied for employment, they were passed over. As a result, an ecosystem of a "shadow" economy developed because there was no alternative to it.

Now that COVID-19 has created a greater need than ever for Blacks to work within the system, many are coming up short in terms of being able to provide proof of income, to establish formal bank accounts, to provide proof of tax filings, and to show that they have obtained necessary certifications and licenses and the like. In the absence of these aspects, many are ineligible for the very programs that were designed to help them.

As a new day is dawning for Blacks because of COVID-19, they must adopt a new way of doing business—but this will take time. In the meantime, it is not in society's interest to have most Black businesses fail. Therefore, something must be done in the short, medium, and long terms to help Black businesses and their owners survive.

———

In a nutshell, here we are: The good, the bad, and the ugly are on full display.

The ugly truth is that systemic racism has landed most Black businesses at the lowest rung of the ladder, and, as they are falling, the ground has shifted and might not even be there to brace their fall.

As has been stated over and over, most Blacks just can't catch a break, as the ethical failures ingrained in racism have kept them tied to leaky life rafts.

Though this chapter only skims the surface of the numerous complex challenges and issues that explain and constrain the scope, extent, and activity of Black-owned businesses, it provides a snapshot of the moving picture of how COVID-19 is impacting Black-owned businesses.

The Road to Progress: People, Places, and Things?

While the challenges that Black-owned firms face are magnified during the COVID-19 crisis, they have always been there. Today, however, we have a clearer view of them as a "pandemic" within the pandemic.

In pondering how to tackle these problems, it's important to be reminded that there is no one cause and therefore not one solution to racism; as it is a complex and multifaceted problem of longstanding.

Yet, we must start somewhere. Many private wealthy individuals and big corporations are stepping up to help Black businesses. For instance:

> Singer and philanthropist Beyoncé Knowles-Carter is donating proceeds from her new single, Black Parade, to small, Black-owned businesses. Netflix is donating $5 million to organizations dedicated to creating opportunities for Black creators, Black youth, and Black businesses. Google will spend $175 million on financing Black-owned businesses and supporting Black entrepreneurs. Facebook will spend $200 million to support Black-owned businesses and organizations. And Charter Communications will invest $10 million "to support Black and other minority-owned small businesses in underserved communities."

While these and other philanthropic efforts are very meaningful and important, it is apparent that Black enterprises need much more than grants and charity. They need a new **"New Deal."** Just as the Roosevelt Administration's New Deal was a comprehensive "leave no stone unturned" approach, one is likewise needed to truly help Black-owned businesses.

What Roosevelt knew when his administration created the New Deal was that they were facing their own "pandemic-scale" catastrophe and that nothing short of a New Deal could change the trajectory of the prevailing circumstances. This same thinking and perspective needs to be adopted to address the state of Black-owned business, which is a catastrophe within a pandemic.

Such a "New Deal" would clearly need three prongs: **people, places,** and **things**. Such a framework is required to redress the totality of the multivariate problems that racism created to land Black people and their enterprises in the situation in which they find themselves during this pandemic—and before it as well. This framework acknowledges that there is no one solution to solving the problems; rather, multiple solutions are required on multiple fronts simultaneously.

In "Investing in Black Lives and Livelihood in the Time of COVID-19", Fitzhugh et al. (2020) clarified what's at stake for society as a whole. Acknowledging the scale of the negative impact of COVID-19 on Black people.

> **A trial can also be an opportunity**. Our society can consider how we can respond to the COVID-19 crisis and fallout to fortify black communities' resilience and help them do more than simply recover. Where can we actually rebuild our systems to be more equitable? The economy stands to unlock between $1.0 trillion and $1.5 trillion. Stakeholders in the private, public, and social sectors all have roles to play. Companies can make decisions that reflect and reinforce equity as a value. State and local actions can help ensure that federal interventions find their way to black citizens, businesses, and institutions. The social sector can deploy capital quickly and test innovative solutions to seemingly intractable problems. Our local, national, and global community will eventually move past the COVID-19 crisis, but we don't have to simply survive it. We call on all stakeholders to commit to equity in our collective actions over the near and long term (para. 25).

Demonstrating commitment to equity in our collective actions in the case of supporting Black-owned businesses boils down to taking actions in the three named areas: people, places, and things.

■ PEOPLE: This part of the imagined "New Deal" to support Black-owned businesses would focus on the current and future purposeful education, training, apprenticeship, and mentoring needs of Black business owners.

As Roosevelt said in 1940 when faced with his administration's own pandemic-scale problem: "We cannot always build the future for our youth, but we can build our youth for the future."

The case of Black business owners is more challenging, as many are no longer youths. However, in building up the capacity of Blacks to be successful business owners, it's important to both act in the immediate term to help those who are already in business and capacitate the youth who might one day go into business in the longer term.

Stakeholders must wrestle with the core questions of what, when, where, who, when, and how to imagine and construct viable solutions to tackle the problem of shoring up existing Black-owned businesses and creating a foundation for others to emerge.

These questions are no doubt being discussed throughout society. While it is beyond this chapter to cite the many examples of actions being taken and considerations being discussed, the example cited below points to a direction that is enlightened and could serve as a building block for skills acquisition among Blacks that could lead to future entrepreneurship. The example highlighted below is important because the world is changing, and what Black business are offering and the ways they are offering it must also change. As the world is clearly moving deeper into providing digital solutions, the highlighted example of Apple partnering with HBCUs to build up the capacity of Blacks to learn coding is particularly meaningful and promising in this new world scenario. Brown (2020) provides information on the partnership.

Apple Partners with HBCUs

Apple is expanding its coding partnership with HBCUs as big tech firms face increased scrutiny surrounding diversity and inclusion. The iPhone giant said Thursday that it's adding 10 more HBCUs to its year-old community education program meant to create opportunities for people seeking to learn coding skills. The announcement comes a month after the company launched a racial equality initiative aimed at communities of color.

Under the expansion into more HBCUs, Apple will give an increasing number of people of color "the building blocks of coding," the company said in a press release. Coding is the infrastructure that makes digital technologies operate, and more Black programmers put more Black people in the running for in-demand, high paying tech jobs.

Morehouse College in Georgia, Tougaloo College in Mississippi, Dillard University in Louisiana, and Prairie View A&M University in Texas are among Apple's roster of partnership schools.

Source: Brown, D. (2020). Apple expands coding partnership with Black schools as tech firms grapple with lack of diversity. Retrieved from https://www. usatoday.com

According to Apple CEO, Tim Cook, "Apple is also making a major commitment to help Blacks enter into computer-related fields". Some of its initiatives, according to Cook, include:

- Committing nearly $3 million to help close the racial equity gaps in computer science education and increase Black representation in STEM fields.
- Expanding Apple's CS First Curriculum to 7,000 more teachers who reach 100,000+ Black students.
- Scaling its Applied Digital Skills program to reach 400,000 Black middle and high school students and making a $1 million Google.org grant to the DonorsChoose #SeeMe campaign to help teachers access materials to make their classrooms more inclusive.
- Increasing its Explore CSR to 16 more universities to address racial gaps in CS research & academia.
- Supporting Black in AI with $250,000 to help increase Black representation in the field of AI.
- Build on Apple's other education initiatives, including CodeNext, focused on cultivating the next generation of Black and Latinx tech leaders, and TechExchange, which partners with HBCUs and Hispanic-serving Institutions (HSIs) to bring students to Google's campus for four months to learn about topics from product management to machine learning.

- PLACES: This part of the imagined "New Deal" to support Black-owned businesses would focus on the neighborhoods in which most Black firms operate. It acknowledges that persistent poverty highlights the need for "place-focused targeting" as policymakers continue to support small and new businesses while shielding communities from continued economic hardship. Continuing to ignore metropolitan neighborhoods that haven't benefited from decades of economic growth in the U.S. in the current downturn and through the next recovery would be public policy malpractice.

While it is beyond the scope of this chapter to identify the many initiatives that may be underway to address the need to revitalize the places and communities wherein Black-owned firms operate, a few examples of thought leadership and suggestions in this area are highlighted as examples only. There are no doubt many more. The point is, there is increasing recognition of the need to finally and sincerely revitalize those communities.

Proposal of the NCRC re: The Community Reinvestment Act (CRA)

The National Community Reinvestment Coalition (NCRC) is an association of more than 600 community-based organizations that promote access to basic banking services, affordable housing, entrepreneurship, job creation and vibrant communities for America's working families.

Over the years, the (NCRC) has advocated for the inclusion of race on CRA exams because people of color and communities of color continue to experience a shortage of affordably priced banking products and a disproportionate amount of high-cost and abusive products.

Adding underserved census tracts as criterion on CRA exams would provide a measure of the extent to which investment in minority and working class neighborhoods is happening in accordance with the intention of the CRA. The CRA is an income-based law that was created in 1977 to reverse redlining and disinvestment from minority and working-class neighborhoods. Its implementation entails regulations and exams to evaluate bank lending and investments in and services to low- and moderate-income borrowers and tracts.

As communities of color continue to encounter shortages of loans, adding the underserved census tracts and race questions will provide the necessary evidence that to undergird advocacy for change. According to Mitchell and Silver's (2020) proposal outlined in their article, "Adding Underserved Census Tracts As Criterion On CRA Exams", here is how it works:

> CRA exams indirectly address racial disparities in lending with an accompanying fair lending review that is designed to ensure that banks are not engaging in discrimination based on race or other prohibited classes. The public information in the fair lending review on CRA exams has been cursory and has usually consisted of a few sentences stating that no discrimination was found.
>
> In addition to the fair lending review, exams ensure that there are no "conspicuous gaps" in lending activity. Examiners scrutinize lending data to make sure that groupings of contiguous census tracts that are in the bank's service area are not arbitrarily excluded from a bank's lending activity. If examiners detect gaps and possible redlining, they refer cases to the Department of Justice, which has resulted in redlining settlements over the years (para(s). 2-3).

The bottom line is that according to NCRC's research and data analysis, it would be feasible and desirable to create a classification of census tracts for CRA called "underserved" defined as those with low levels of lending per housing unit and business. The proposal of adding underserved tracts as a criterion on the lending, investment, and service tests would direct needed lending and investment to these underserved communities.

Association for Enterprise Opportunity (AEO) On Opportunity Zones

As part of the Tax Cuts and Jobs Act, investors can direct their money to investments in low-income areas around the country labeled "opportunity zones" and receive tax breaks. Under the program, taxpayers can invest in designated Opportunity Zones around the country and receive deferred or reduced taxation on their gains. In addition, a portion of the gains may even permanently avoid taxation.

The impetus behind the initiative is a desire to help economically distressed communities by incentivizing people to invest in them. Through the Internal Revenue Service (IRS), investors can create a Qualified Opportunity Fund to invest in a designated Opportunity Zone, with the stipulation that 90% of assets in the fund must be held in the Opportunity Zone.

The AEO is advocating to require tracking indicators about the impact of the zones, such as how many jobs are created; how many of those jobs are being given to low-income people in the community; and whether or not minority business owners in the area are being given more business as a result of these projects. Without these types of analytics, it's not possible to determine whether predominantly Black communities are benefitting. The AEO's (2020) article "Data is Essential to Understanding the Impact of Opportunity Zones" provides more detailed information.

Brookings Institution on Sparking the Revaluation of Black Neighborhoods

In addressing how to spark the revaluation of Black neighborhoods, Perry et al. (2020) in a Brookings Institution article, "Five Star Reviews, One Star Profits: The Devaluation of Business in Black Communities", shared gems of wisdom noting, that there are practical things that cities and local governments can do. For example, they note, "they should invest in city infrastructure by providing adequate public transit, roads, parking, streetlights, and park space near highly rated businesses in Black neighborhoods" (para. 20). Perry et al. added that "cities can also come up with creative financing solutions to provide attractive commercial space for businesses in Black neighborhoods to operate." They also suggested that "local governments should partner with businesses, real estate developers, and building owners to incentivize the renovation of business facades and buildings and ensure that unnecessary bureaucratic and zoning restrictions are removed" (para. 20).

It was noted that some cities are moving into the era of enlightenment by making targeted infrastructure investments in Black communities with the intent of forming a more equitable business environment. New Orleans was mentioned as an example," where firms designated as 'disadvantaged business enterprises' (DBEs) have long been underrepresented in contracts with the local government." To address this, Perry explains, that "the regional transit authority chose to invest simultaneously in its infrastructure and minority-owned businesses by pledging that a minimum of 31% of its federally provisioned grants would go to contracts with DBEs throughout the New Orleans metropolitan area". However, Perry et al. caution the following:

> We must do more than allocate municipal funds from existing projects toward Black workers and Black-owned businesses. We must find ways to restore the value of Black neighborhoods themselves, which has been reduced by racism. The economy stands to gain from anti-discrimination, anti-racist policies that increases capital flow to businesses in Black neighborhoods. If we don't extract the racism inherent in housing, financing, and other related systems, that racism will continue to extract wealth from Black communities (para. 20).

The Urban Institute's Reimagining An Antiracist America—Starting with Neighborhoods

Turner's (2020) article, "Reimagining an Antiracist America—Starting with Our Neighborhoods", in the Urban Institute's blog, provides gems of wisdom about how to revitalize the communities in which Black people live and Black firms operate. Turner wrote:

> Every family should be able to live in a neighborhood that supports their well-being and boosts their children's chances to thrive and succeed. But today, Turner notes, "too many families of color live in neighborhoods suffering from disinvestment, deprived of quality services and amenities, and endangered by over-policing. And too many families of color are excluded from neighborhoods that offer safety, effective schools, healthy environments, and access to good jobs (para. 2).

Turner explained that the prevailing situation didn't happen by accident and that it's not the natural result of unconstrained housing choices or freely functioning housing markets." Rather, according to Turner, "over many decades, the United States built separate and unequal neighborhoods through public policy and institutional practices. Families of color have been blocked from areas rich in amenities and opportunities by housing discrimination and exclusionary zoning, while communities of color have been starved of capital and resources" (para. 3).

In answer to the self-posed question of what should be done about these circumstances, Turner (2020) has six recommendations.

Six Things That Can Be Done Now

Turner (2020) is clear: "we should invest in distressed neighborhoods, so they become springboards for their residents."

She explains, "in neighborhoods experiencing revitalization, we should preserve affordable housing and protect against displacement. Moreover, we should expand housing options in opportunity-rich neighborhoods, so families are no longer excluded based on their race or ethnicity, country of origin, or wealth and income".

Organizations across the country, she notes, are already doing important work on all these imperatives, but they rarely work in tandem or across jurisdictional boundaries to achieve real scale. Incremental efforts—neighborhood by neighborhood or family by family—can't achieve lasting impacts when the underlying patterns of segregation, disinvestment, and exclusion persist.

Turner (2020) suggests a six-pronged more holistic approach, as follows:

1. Adopt a regional approach. Focusing on a single neighborhood or even a single city within a metropolitan region can't overcome the larger market dynamics or the effects of policies, such as exclusionary zoning, in surrounding jurisdictions.

2. Pursue "place-conscious" investments and reforms. Interventions should work in concert to restore well-being and opportunity to distressed neighborhoods, prevent displacement from revitalizing neighborhoods, and expand access to opportunity-rich neighborhoods.

3. Support residents' empowerment as leaders. Residents of neighborhoods suffering from disinvestment and distress must play a leading role in designing solutions and engaging their fellow community members.

4. Strengthen effective organizations. Investments should build and capitalize on the capacities of local organizations already working to support justice, equity, and opportunity at the neighborhood, city, or regional scale.

5. Evaluate and refine based on data. Strategies should include data collection and application to support evidence-based decision-making, community engagement, and continuous learning and program improvement.

6. Confront racism. Lasting change can't be achieved without dispelling racist narratives about the inferiority of Black people that drive people's beliefs about who "belongs" in their neighborhood and who "deserves" to be a member of their community (para. 6).

Source: Turner, M.A., & Greene, S. (2020). Reimagining an Antiracist America— Starting with Our Neighborhoods. Retrieved from https://www.urban.org

McKinsey & Co: Recovery, Rebuilding, and Reimagination

Florant et al. (2020) in "Investing in Black Lives and Livelihoods: What Stakeholders Can Do", imagines how to assist Black people, their communities, and their businesses from COVID-19's outsized impact on them. In imagining possible solutions, the pandemic is seen as an opportunity to invest in addressing structural challenges to help Black Americans recover and to build and sustain more equitable communities. Accordingly, Florant et al. put forth the following suggestions:

Investments in public health, digital infrastructure, institutions of public education, and economic development planning should continue long after the COVID-19 pandemic subsides (Florant, et. al, 2020). In particular, stakeholders could consider setting national goals to improve health equity and create plans to meet those goals.

Support for black homeowners and businesses could be a priority to ensure that black families do not lose their assets and resources. That kind of support could include protection from bankruptcy, insolvency, and eviction, all of which will disproportionately affect black Americans as part of the pandemic's fallout. Institutions could also support equity in compensation and career progression. These types of assistance speak less to protection and more to providing the opportunities and stability required to help black families build a resilient economic foundation.

In addition, they suggest that "Community development financial institutions (CDFIs), churches, and nonprofits could help black-owned businesses and residents to access recovery funds. Similarly, new financial products and programs such as community rainy-day funds could fortify the resilience of communities. Corporations could make a point to work with black-owned businesses" (para(s). 16-18).

■ THINGS: Within the framework of the imagined new "New Deal," "things" would represent the firms themselves. The question is what should be done to directly help Black-owned firms to help them survive COVID-19 and beyond? In this regard, it's an all-hands-on-deck undertaking: All levels of government must be involved, and the thought leadership, imagination, and resources of non-profit and for-profit firms are needed as well.

There are many non-mutually exclusive policy proposals, government initiatives, and private sector efforts that are aimed at building up the resiliency of Black-owned businesses. Ideally, they would be part of an ecosystem of connections and support that reinforce one another.

Big Tech Contributions to Directly Support Black-Owned Businesses

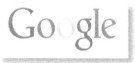

On the philanthropic side, many wealthy individuals, foundations, and big corporations are stepping up to directly lend support to Black-owned businesses. While there are too many of these important efforts to recount, a few include:

Multiple efforts on multiple fronts, including:

- $50 million in financing and grants for small businesses, focused on the Black community and in partnership with Opportunity Finance Network. This commitment builds on our recent $125 million Grow with Google Small Business Fund that is helping underserved minority and women-owned small businesses across the U.S.

- $100 million in funding participation in Black-led capital firms, startups and organizations supporting Black entrepreneurs, including increased investments in Plexo Capital and non-dilutive funding to Black founders in the Google for Startups network.

- $15 million in training, through partners like the National Urban League, to help Black jobseekers grow their skills.

- $10 million+ to help improve the Black community's access to education, equipment, and economic opportunities in our developer ecosystem, and increase equity, representation, and inclusion across our developer platforms, including Android, Chrome, Flutter, Firebase, Google Play and more.

 As part of a broad initiative aimed at bolstering racial justice in the U.S., Microsoft announced investments to bring more Black- and African American-owned partner businesses into its U.S. partner community. The investments include a $50 million partner fund to assist such businesses with access to capital during their startup phase, along with $20 million in financing for supporting cash flow requirements.

 Apple Unveils $100M Racial Equity And Justice Initiative To Focus On 'Unfinished Work'. "The initiative will challenge the systemic barriers to opportunity and dignity that exists for communities of color, and particularly for the black community, with special focus on issues of education, economic equality, and criminal justice reform.

 Created a $10 million fund for empowerment grants to Black-owned businesses impacted by COVID-19 or civil unrest. These grants will provide direct support to business owners to cover expenses related to stabilizing and reopening their businesses. The fund will be managed in partnership with the AEO, a leading national nonprofit expanding economic opportunity for Black entrepreneurs through its Tapestry Project.

Wealthy Blacks Supporting Black-Owned Businesses

At the individual and philanthropic levels, many celebrities are also stepping up to chip in. A few examples include those highlighted, but there are many others. Some, like billionaire Robert F. Smith, are leveraging their connections in the White House and on the Hill to get legislation passed, while others are making direct monetary contributions.

■ **Magic Johnson** is partnering with MBE Capital Partners to offer $100 million in loans to minority-and women-owned companies. The funds will be distributed through the SBA's PPP.

■ **Oprah Winfrey** pledged $10 million toward her COVID-19 relief fund to help communities from cities across the country who have been severely impacted by the viral outbreak. One of the cities was Nashville, Tennessee, which has seen a high rate of COVID-19 cases.

■ **Beyoncé** and **NAACP** partner to help fund Black-owned businesses: Beyoncé and BeyGOOD have partnered with the NAACP to launch the Black-owned Business Impact Fund, which will provide $10,000 grants to Black-owned companies in select cities "to help strengthen small businesses and to ensure economic empowerment for Black businesses. Through her BeyGOOD foundation, she has also partnered with Twitter CEO Jack Dorsey's #startsmall initiative to donate $6 million to community-based organizations in need during COVID-19.

——————

These are just a few of the initiatives being undertaken in support of Black and minority-owned businesses and their communities; there are many others. For instance, the prospect of encouraging more Environmental, Social, and Governance (ESG) sustainability fund investments in minority communities and firms is gaining traction, and recommendations on how to foster more minority firm inclusion in incubators and accelerators, are also being explored.

The bottom line is that there is increasing recognition of the need to support Black-owned businesses, and such support is coming from stakeholders throughout society.

In the meantime, time is of the essence, as more and more Black-owned firms are disappearing while COVID-19 is not.

CHAPTER SEVEN

The Ethics of Empowering and Protecting Women In the Time of COVID-19

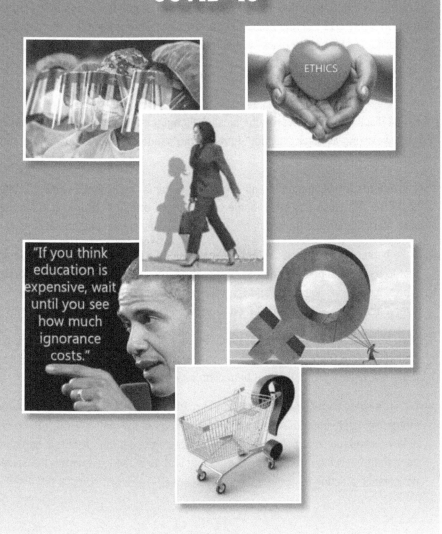

About Chapter Seven: **The Ethics of Empowering and Protecting Women In the Time of COVID-19**

I f women, in general, can be considered the "salt of the earth", in the Black community, they are the salt and the pepper, and are mostly responsible for bringing home the bacon as well. As many Black women are likely to be single heads of households, the erosion of their earnings during this time is disastrous is and robbing their families of essential resources.

Picture a woman carrying a heavy bag on her back, sludging through mile after mile of mud on a dirt road to bring home the bacon. What you are seeing is the picture of the circumstances that many Black women find themselves in during this pandemic.

Of course, this is not so for all Black women, some are thriving, but they are the exceptions.

For all Black women, however, the most challenging pre-existing condition they face is simply existing as Black women. Surviving the pandemic is an additional burden they must bear.

A five-alarm fire is going off in all categories of life for many Black women in the time of COVID-19, which has been kindled by their pre-existing conditions. As is the case with all raging fires, if they are not extinguished, they spread and engulf everything.

This chapter sheds light on the fires that are engulfing many Black women, underscoring that to become empowered and to be protected, they need help. The case is made that ethics, moral consciousness, and the societal contract demand appropriate and timely intervention to relieve the burden on those who are least able to bear it.

Despite the dire circumstances of many Black women, there are rays of hope shining through. Just as there is hope on the vaccine front, there is also hope with the incoming Biden-Harris administration that help is on its way.

But with every step along the way on the road to progress, we must be reminded that ethics is at the heart of the matter and are the heart of the matter. There are no number of laws, regulations, or policies that can be enacted or set forth that that can stick and have their intended result if we, as a society and as individuals within the society, do not commit to acting ethically in our daily actions.

The Ethics of Empowering and Protecting Women In the Time of COVID-19

COVID-19 has colored everything and has shown the true colors of what has been going on in America that has negatively impacted the ability of Black women to be protected and empowered. Little fissures have become craters that are swallowing up Black women, revealing that the most challenging pre-existing condition for Black women is simply existing as Black women.

A five-alarm fire is going off in all categories of life for Black women in the time of COVID-19, which has been kindled by their pre-existing conditions. As is the case with all raging fires, if they are not extinguished, they spread and engulf everything.

Ethics at the heart of the matter. As Federal Reserve Bank Chairman Jerome Powell said in June 2020: "While we are all affected [by COVID-19], the burden has fallen disproportionately on those least able to bear it".

Accordingly, ethics, moral consciousness, and the societal contract demand appropriate and timely intervention to relieve the burden on those who are least able to bear it.

Empowering Women

Before COVID-19, one could imagine that if 50 people on the street were randomly asked whether they thought women were empowered in the United States, perhaps fifty percent of them might say they were. On the other hand, if the same 50 people were asked to define women's empowerment, or better yet, to fill in the blank: "Women are empowered when they [blank...]," one might get 50 different answers.

Some may fill in the blank by describing an end goal, such as "women are empowered when they are wealthy" or "women are empowered when they are the boss." But some would describe more of a process, such as "women are empowered when they have opportunities and choices."

If those same hypothetical 50 random people were asked if they believed that Black women were empowered in America, it's likely that all 50 would say no...with the recent mighty exception of Vice President-Elect, Kamala Harris.

The ethical concern is not whether all women have the same economic outcomes but whether barriers exist that disproportionately prevent some women, especially Black women, from having the opportunities and choices to realize their full economic potential.

The next question is: what opportunities and choices should women have?

And this is where it can get tricky—although there are areas of consensus. For example, most would agree that all women should have equal opportunities and choices in the areas of economic wellbeing, education, and health, but they don't. The extent to which Black American women are afforded such access or not is one of the questions this chapter addresses.

Women and Economic Opportunity in the U.S. During the Time of COVID-19

The big picture is that most women are losing economic ground during the pandemic.

While the economic reality of women before COVID-19 was one thing, it's another today, and while it's generally bad for all women, it's especially bad for Black women. Everything that was left undone and not optimized for women prior to COVID-19 has created a foundation built on sand, and now the houses that women helped build are crumbling and being washed away.

It has been speculated that the COVID-19 crisis could set women back half a decade. In the McKinsey Global Institute article "COVID-19 and Gender Equality: Countering the Regressive Effects," Madgavkar et al. (2020) point to a critical consideration for society as a whole, noting that "what is good for gender equality is good for the economy and society as well" (para. 1). The COVID-19 pandemic puts that truth into stark relief and raises critically important issues.

Yet, "as COVID-19 continues to affect lives and livelihoods around the world," Madgavkar et al. (2020) highlight how "the pandemic and its economic fallout are having a regressive effect on gender equality" (para. 1). By the authors' calculations, women's jobs are 1.8 times more vulnerable to this crisis than those of men. Women make up 39 percent of global employment but account for 54 percent of overall job losses.

One reason for Madgavkar et al. (2020) to claim that there's a greater effect on women is that the virus is significantly increasing the burden of unpaid care, which is disproportionately carried out by women. They explain that "among other factors, [this] means that women's employment is dropping faster than average, even accounting for the fact that women and men work in different sectors" (para 8).

What is at stake if counter measures are not taken to redress the situation? Madgavkar et al. (2020) make it clear that there will be a huge cost to society, and they estimate how much:

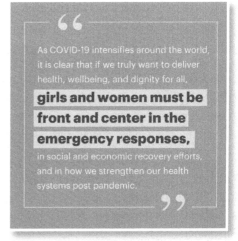

> Given trends we have observed over the past few months, in a gender-regressive scenario in which no action is taken to counter these effects, we estimate that global GDP growth could be $1 trillion lower in 2030 than it would be if women's unemployment simply tracked that of men in each sector (para.2).

Doing nothing to redress the situation does not mean that something won't happen, but it does mean that what will happen will not be good for society as a whole.

As COVID-19 intensifies around the world, it is clear that if we truly want to deliver health, wellbeing, and dignity for all, **girls and women must be front and center in the emergency responses,** in social and economic recovery efforts, and in how we strengthen our health systems post pandemic.

Madgavkar et al. (2020) point out that the impact will be greatest if factors such as increased childcare burdens, attitudinal bias, a slower recovery, or reduced public and private spending on education or childcare force women to leave the labor market permanently.

There Was a Time Before COVID-19 When Black Women Began to Thrive in Business

Black women were beginning to make great strides in business before COVID-19. According to a U.S. Census report in 2016, the number of black/female-owned firms climbed 66.9 percent, from 900,000 in 2007 to 1.5 million in 2012. Additionally, these 1.5 million black/female-owned businesses accounted for 58.9 percent of the nation's 2.6 million black or

African American-owned businesses. By contrast, nationally, women owned just over a third (35.8 percent or 9.9 million) of all firms in 2012.

The positive trend continued from 2014 to 2019. When the number of women-owned businesses grew 21 percent, firms owned by women of color grew at double that rate, according to an annual report on women in business by American Express. But the pandemic blew up the trend.

Yet even under the harshest circumstances that now prevail, some Black women-owned businesses continue to thrive. Those who are thriving, are doing so because they were able to pivot and embrace new technology and to develop new ways of delivering products and services, while summoning their creativity. But they are the lucky ones; they had enough resources, both internally and externally to pivot.

The age-old problem facing most Black women entrepreneurs, as well as established business owners is a lack of access to capital—and a lack of access to other ingredients that would have helped them survive and even thrive in this moment.

Out of the Frying Pan into the Fire for Black Women

As Black women shoulder increasing burdens imposed by the pandemic, in addition to those imposed by the impacts of systemic racism, their abilities to act upon their innate creativity is being thwarted in many cases. It's as if they have existed in a frying pan throughout their lives and must now leap directly into the raging pandemic-induced fire.

In a Society for Research and Child Development article in September 2020 titled, "Addressing Inequities in Education: Considerations for Black Children and Youth in the Era of COVID-19," Gaylord-Harden et al. (2020) paint a picture of the meaning of the phrase "out of the frying pan into the fire" for Black women.

> Due to systemic racism, Black Americans disproportionately face conditions that increase their exposure to COVID-19, and make social distancing challenging, including employment in essential industries, reliance on public transit, overrepresentation in correctional facilities, and crowded, substandard housing. Black Americans are more likely to be underinsured, receive low-quality healthcare, live in food deserts, and be exposed to indoor and outdoor environmental toxins, all of which are linked to underlying health conditions that heighten risk for COVID 19 (para. 1).

As a result, according to the Centers for Disease Control and Prevention, "Black Americans make up 13% of the U.S. population, but represent 33% of COVID-19 hospitalizations and 34% of COVID-19 deaths" (Gaylord-Harden et al., 2020, para. 1).

Another way to visualize the predicament of Black women is to imagine worst-case scenarios of the most negative impact of almost any negative phenomenon in society, look at its impact on Black people, and especially on Black women, and the picture of the worst case will be revealed.

> Think of any issue—such as a concern about job availability or having no job, or the fear associated with having to go into work despite having pre-existing conditions. Then, add to this the fact that a given woman's child has no in-person schooling, no childcare, and the woman has the sole responsibility for taking care of her children and must juggle virtual schooling and going to work. Imagine that she works as an essential worker and is thereby put at greater risk of contracting the virus. Imagine next that she contracts COVID-19 but doesn't have health insurance. Next, imagine that she survives COVID-19, only to learn that because she had it, she now has a pre-existing condition that disqualifies her from accessing affordable health insurance. Next, add in the problem of not having secure housing, and suddenly these factors combined become a tsunami that is sweeping many Black women out to sea without a lifesaving vessel.

This is the reality of the situation that many Black women are in right now, which is why their five-alarm fire requires an urgent response from all available fire engines.

In a paper for the Economic Policy Institute (EPI), Gould et al. (2020) wrote that "Black workers face two of the most lethal preexisting conditions for Coronavirus—racism and economic inequality," and this is without actually contracting COVID-19. Black workers were mostly sick and tired, even before this new virus, due to the other ills they suffered from having experienced a lifetime of systemic racism and economic inequality. Gould et al. (2020) explain this situation as follows:

> Although the current strain of the coronavirus is one that humans have never experienced before, the disparate racial impact of the virus is deeply rooted in historic and ongoing social and economic injustices. Persistent racial disparities in health status, access to health care, wealth, employment, wages, housing, income, and poverty all contribute to greater susceptibility to the virus, both economically and physically (para. 2).

Economic Effects: Devastating Job Losses Are Hitting Black Workers and Their Families Especially Hard

Many institutions are studying the negative economic effects of the pandemic on people of color. Institutions such as the U.S. Census Bureau and other government institutions, thinks tanks, advocacy groups, consulting firms, and many others are providing snapshots from their perspectives of how bad the situation is, and no matter who is taking the snapshot, the picture conveyed is a grim one.

In the view of EPI authors Gould et al. (2020), "there are three main groups of workers in the COVID-19 economy: those who have lost their jobs and face economic insecurity, those who are classified as essential workers and face health insecurity as a result, and those who are able to continue working from the safety of their homes." Unfortunately, Black workers today "are disproportionately found among the essential workers in the economy—continuing to go to their workplaces, risking their health and that of their families because they are unable to sustain adequate social distance from their co-workers and customers" (Gould et al., 2020, para. 4).

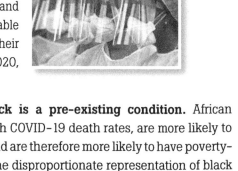

> **Where you live when you are Black is a pre-existing condition.** African Americans have disproportionately high COVID-19 death rates, are more likely to live in areas experiencing outbreaks, and are therefore more likely to have poverty-related underlying conditions. Given the disproportionate representation of black workers in front-line occupations where they face a greater risk of exposure to COVID-19, it is not surprising that illness and deaths are disproportionately found among Black workers and their families (Gould et al., 2020, para. 12).

In the *Forbes* article, "New Research Shows How the Coronavirus Recession Is Disproportionately Affecting Black Working Mothers," Carter (2020) provides a perspective on the impact of the pandemic on Blacks in Louisiana, showing that where Blacks live is a factor that predisposes them to the worse outcomes of Covid-19. Carter's example is particularly noteworthy because Louisiana is one of the places where Blacks have experienced the highest levels of environmental pollution and injustice, such as in "Cancer Alley", and in other districts in Louisiana. Carter discusses some of the "pre-existing" conditions of Blacks in Louisiana that predispose them to the worse outcomes of COVID-19:

Louisiana happens to be one of the top 10 states where Black people live. Black women are 60% more likely to have high blood pressure. The prevalence of high blood pressure in Black people in the U.S. is among the highest in the world. Black people have lung cancer more than any other population group, are 60% more likely than non-Hispanic white adults to have been diagnosed with diabetes, and collectively have the highest death rate and shortest survival of any racial ethnic group in the U.S. for most cancers (para. 2).

In the Brookings Institution article, "Race Gaps in COVID-19 Deaths Are Even Bigger Than They Appear," Ford et al. (2020) make an important point at the outset: "The COVID-19 pandemic has been like the flash of an X-ray, exposing the deep fractures in U.S. society – not least by race" (para. 1). At the heart of the matter is racial injustice; such injustice is not new, but what is new is that everyone can now see what such injustices have caused—they have led to a disproportionally negative impact of the virus on Black people.

If the question is why Black people are so hard hit by COVID-19, the answer is clear: It is because COVID-19 sits atop a mountain of "18" other preceding problems—figuratively speaking—for Black people, which represent their pre-existing conditions. The intersection of vulnerability with COVID-19 and the inequities facing Black people and other Americans of color (but especially Black people) in jobs, housing, education, criminal justice, and health has created a perfect storm that is carrying Black people out to sea.

Black Women and Jobs During COVID-19

It is important to hear what some Federal Reserve Bank governors have said on the matter of the impact of COVID-19 on Black people in their recent speeches, acknowledging the disproportionate impact of the pandemic on people of color.

Federal Reserve Governor Lael Brainard, addressing a meeting on the topic of "Navigating Monetary Policy through the Fog of COVID-19" (July 2020), said that "the pandemic's harm to lives and livelihoods is falling disproportionately on Black and Hispanic families. After finally seeing welcome progress narrowing the gaps in labor market outcomes by race and ethnicity in the late stage of the previous recovery, the COVID-19 shock is inflicting a disproportionate share of job losses on African American and Hispanic workers. According to the Current Population Survey, the number of employed persons fell by 14.2 percent from February to June among African Americans and by 13.4 percent among Hispanics—significantly worse than the 10.4 percent decline for the population overall."

Chair Jerome H. Powell
said:

It is not lost on me that we are meeting on Juneteenth amid a renewed reckoning of racial injustice. The pandemic has again exposed a range of troubling inequalities, most of them of long standing. As the national discussion continues, it is critical to remember that equity includes access to education, work, and economic opportunity. I am reminded that Dr. King delivered his "I Have a Dream" speech, just a few short blocks from the Federal Reserve, at a rally whose full title was the March on Washington for Jobs and Freedom.

We meet today amid the immense hardship and suffering the coronavirus has caused. Lives and livelihoods have been lost, and uncertainty looms large. We are all grateful to our frontline health-care workers who put themselves in harm's way every day and to the essential workers helping us meet our needs. While we are all affected, the burden has fallen disproportionately on those least able to bear it.

In the Center for American Progress article, "On the Frontlines at Work and at Home: The Disproportionate Economic Effects of the Coronavirus Pandemic on Women of Color," Fyre 2020) includes a table, below, that shows the top six occupations held by women of color:

Top 6 occupations held by women of color in the United States, by racial and ethnic group

	Black or African American, non-Hispanic women	Hispanic women	Asian American and Pacific Islander, non-Hispanic women	American Indian or Alaska Native, non-Hispanic women	Other nonwhite single race, non-Hispanic women	Two or more races, non-Hispanic women
❶	Nursing assistants	Maids and housekeeping cleaners	Registered nurses	Cashiers	Maids and housekeeping cleaners	Cashiers
❷	Cashiers	Cashiers	Accountants and auditors	Secretaries and administrative assistants*	Cashiers	Registered nurses
❸	Customer service representatives	Customer service representatives	Cashiers	Maids and housekeeping cleaners	Nursing assistants	Waiters and waitresses
❹	Registered nurses	Secretaries and administrative assistants*	Manicurists and pedicurists	Elementary and middle school teachers	Registered nurses	Elementary and middle school teachers
❺	Personal care aides	Janitors and building cleaners	Personal care aides	Personal care aides	Child care workers	Customer service representatives
❻	Elementary and middle school teachers	Retail salespeople	Retail salespeople	Registered nurses	Retail salespeople	Secretaries and administrative assistants*

Being employed in such professions tends to either put women of color at risk of contracting COVID-19 or at risk of losing their jobs.

As Frye (2020) underscores, women of color often stand at the intersection of multiple barriers, experiencing the combined effects of racial, gender, ethnic, and other forms of bias while navigating systems and institutional structures in which entrenched disparities remain the status quo. Frye draws particular attention to the following facts:

> Early state-level data showing higher rates of COVID-19 contraction and mortality among African Americans only amplify the importance of examining the different biases that could be playing a role in the spread, treatment, and containment of the disease. [T]he inadequate supports for essential frontline workers providing care and critical services—including nursing assistants, home health aides, and grocery store cashiers—demand close scrutiny, as the needs of these workers can no longer be minimized,

> ignored, or devalued. Women of color disproportionately work in many of these jobs where there are unspoken expectations of availability to provide care and services for others; yet there is too little examination of the challenges these women face, their workplace obstacles, and their family needs (para. 3).

COVID-19 Is Undermining the Earnings and Economic Stability of Women of Color

Black female workers who are maids and housekeeping cleaners, nursing assistants, personal care aides, and home health aides, are in the eye of the storm. According to Frye (2020), they represent over half of the workers in those occupations. Specifically, Frye estimates that 60.3 percent of maids and housekeepers, 50.3 percent of nursing assistants, and 45.7 percent of personal care aides are women of color.

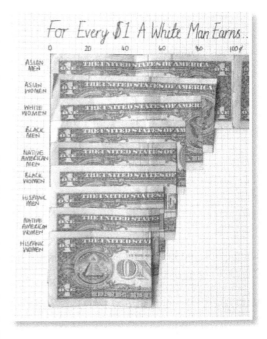

However, no matter their profession, many Black women are likely to be single heads of households; therefore, any erosion of their earnings would be disastrous, worsening instability and robbing families of essential resources (Frye, 2020, para 7).

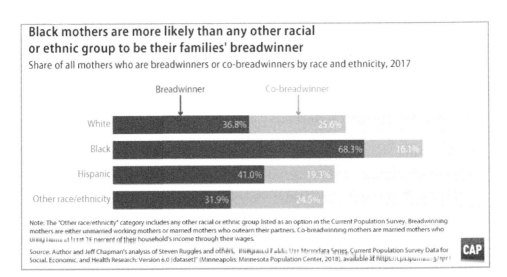

Black mothers are more likely than any other racial or ethnic group to be their families' breadwinner

Share of all mothers who are breadwinners or co-breadwinners by race and ethnicity, 2017

Breadwinner   Co-breadwinner

	Breadwinner	Co-breadwinner
White	36.8%	25.6%
Black	68.3%	16.1%
Hispanic	41.0%	19.3%
Other race/ethnicity	31.9%	24.5%

Note: The "Other race/ethnicity" category includes any other racial or ethnic group listed as an option in the Current Population Survey. Breadwinning mothers are either unmarried working mothers or married mothers who outearn their partners. Co-breadwinning mothers are married mothers who bring home at least 25 percent of their household's income through their wages.

Source: Author and Jeff Chapman's analysis of Steven Ruggles and others, "Integrated Public Use Microdata Series, Current Population Survey Data for Social, Economic, and Health Research: Version 6.0 [dataset]" (Minneapolis: Minnesota Population Center, 2018), available at https://cps.ipums.org/cps/.

CAP

As shown in the previous chart, Glynn (2019), in "Breadwinning Mothers Continue to Be the U.S. Norm," an article for the Center for American Progress, points out that while there is a growing pattern of women throughout the U.S. being the primary breadwinners, Black women are the most likely of any racial group to be in this situation.

In "On the Frontlines at Work and at Home: The Disproportionate Economic Effects of the Coronavirus Pandemic on Women of Color," an article for the Center for American Progress, Frye (2020) explains that "many women of color are less likely to have the wealth and savings necessary to go for an extended period of time without earnings—something that is now necessary on a massive scale as people lose their jobs due to COVID-19" (para. 6). Frye also suggests a number of ways of addressing the problem, which will require the intervention of all levels of government.

> Mitigating the effects of COVID-19 must take into account all of these economic realities for women of color. In order to help all families— especially those that are most vulnerable—stay afloat, state and local policymakers should evaluate any relief strategies to assess their effectiveness in addressing the immediate and long-term challenges associated with gender and racial gaps in wages and wealth. These strategies should include increasing access to income supports, such as paid leave, that provide full wage replacement; making increased pay available for essential workers; requiring increases to the minimum wage; eliminating subminimum wages for tipped workers and workers with disabilities; and bolstering equal pay enforcement (para. 10).

Black People Are Also Undermined in Receiving Unemployment Benefits

Proving that when "you are down you are out" and that many times Black people "can't catch a break," in such cases, they are even disadvantaged with regard to receiving unemployment benefits.

In the *Rand Blog*, Edwards' (2020) article, "The Racial Disparity in Unemployment Benefits," explains that the states with more Black workers have less generous unemployment benefits. So, when we look at this picture on a national level, Black workers are less financially supported in unemployment than White workers simply by virtue of where they live.

Another Bad Aspect of the 1930s New Deal for Black People. That Black workers live in less generous states is not an accident of modern policymaking. The reason unemployment is administered by states at all—unlike Social Security, which is federally operated—dates back to the New Deal in the 1930s.

There were two things going on. A handful of states already had created unemployment programs and did not want a federal program. At the same time, passing the New Deal legislation required a bargain between northern and southern Democrats. The former wanted to expand worker support, and the latter wanted to make sure Black workers in the South did not benefit from that support. Keeping relief programs under state control helped both groups accomplish their aims.

Today's unemployed inherited this system of state policies with racial implications that persist. Southern states today have not only the lowest benefits; they also have the lowest recipiency rates among Black workers. The CARES Act has papered over these troubling inequities by boosting benefits by $600 a week and expanding eligibility, but that add-on ends in July. Soon the miserliness and racial disparity of benefits will become more stark.

For decades there have been calls to reform unemployment insurance; this is one more reason. Economic racial inequality in America cannot be solved through unemployment insurance, but it certainly shouldn't be exacerbated by it.

Source: Edwards, K.A. (2020). The Racial Disparity in Unemployment Benefits. Retrieved from https://www.rand.org/blog

Black Women and Housing During the Time of COVID-19

The big picture is that decades of deep-rooted, structural inequalities in the housing system have set up Black women and other communities of color to bear the brunt of this impending mass eviction crisis. The pandemic's economic fallout has only magnified the existing affordable crisis in this country. Even before the pandemic, nearly eight million renters spent more than half their income on housing. The title of Morris' (2020) article for *The Hill* in July 2020, "A Wave of Mass Evictions Is Inevitable and Black Women Will Be Hit the Hardest," highlights the problem.

As Morris (2020) reported, as of July 2020, "one in three tenants in the U.S. failed to make rent — but that not all renters will experience this housing crisis equally." Black and Brown communities are disproportionately harmed by the pandemic due to racial inequities in health care and employment—and housing is no different: "This country's legacy of housing discrimination and segregation has led to staggering disparities in homeownership and household wealth. Today, 73 percent of White families own their homes, as compared with just 41 percent of Black families and 49 percent of Latinx families" (para. 5).

Adding insult to permanent injury, Morris (2020) explains that not only are Black women twice as likely to be evicted but also, if evicted, the aftermath of eviction could persist for decades. Specifically, "individuals with prior eviction records are indefinitely shut out of future housing opportunities due to unfair tenant screening policies that deny housing to anyone with a prior eviction record" (Morris, 2020, para. 6).

The Impact of COVID-19 on the Role of Black Women in Home Schooling

In highlighting the "Coronavirus Impact On Students and Education Systems" on its website (www.naacp.org), the NAACP underscores that "from individual families to the country as a whole, the pandemic has revealed how crucial early care and learning, educations systems and traditional afterschool supports are to our national wellbeing." Further, it is noted that "the crisis has also laid bare the economic and racial disparities that persist and preclude equal access to these essential public goods."

Yet, the importance of education cannot be overemphasized. President Obama said it best:

Addressing Inequities in Education: Considerations for Black Children and Youth in the Era of COVID-19

Pre-existing disparities with regard to access to adequate internet connections and computer technology are being exacerbated by a shift to remote learning during the pandemic that place Black children at a further disadvantage.

Furthermore, due to decades of underinvestment in Black communities, Black children are more likely to attend schools that have fewer economic resources and less technology to support remote instruction, and the pandemic has strained the limited fiscal resources of these schools as they work to provide remote educational experiences.

There is also an emotional factor that is disruptive to the virtual learning process when children are simultaneously grieving for lost family members.

In an article titled, "How Black Parents Juggle Their Work and Kids' Virtual Schooling During the Pandemic," Habersham (2020) states that Black women are parents, teachers, chefs, and, in the case of the person profiled in the article, also a hairstylist, tech support professional, and nurse.

Habersham (2020) shares the story of a women in Atlanta who explains her situation:

> For some parents, managing the logistics of work and school is the tip of the iceberg. Southeast Atlanta resident Yvonne Clark spent $300 on tablets for her nieces and nephews after she said the DeKalb County School District ran out of Chromebooks to give to students. "With everything going on, I didn't have $300 just lying around," said Clark, who is helping her brother's family after he lost his job in March when the virus forced businesses to close. He's been relying on unemployment until he finds work. "We're just at a point where families have to pull together to have what they need."
>
> The lack of resources for students learning virtually reverberates across metro Atlanta, including in Clayton County where Mitchell lives. She said she had to pay $300 for additional tablets and purchased Wi-Fi hotspots so her children would have adequate access to the Internet (para(s). 2–3).
>
> Source: Habersham, R. (2020). How Black parents juggle their work and kids' virtual schooling during the pandemic. Retrieved from https://www. poynter.org

Another woman profiled by Habersham (2020) provided additional insights to the homeschooling problem, noting that in her case, having a house in which to do home schooling was a problem in itself. The person profiled had to move into her parents' home after she was unable to find an affordable apartment near her child's school. She said: "It's not that I can't afford rent. But when you're a single mom, they want you to make three times whatever the rent is. So, my rent is one thousand dollars. They want you to make three times that, which is not even possible" (para. 27).

In the Economic Policy Institute article, "Why Putting Black Women First May Save Us from Economic Disaster," Opoku-Agyeman (2020) underscores that "Black women are the core of the nation's economy, holding the frontline jobs and running small businesses, and are often the singe heads of households in their communities. If they are elevated through policy, including everything from paid sick leave to stimulus programs targeted directly toward them, the economy at-large will benefit" (para. 4).

Opoku-Agyeman (2020) also points out that if the economy is working for Black women, then the economy is working for everyone. Additionally, "if Black women, who have been among the most disadvantaged by the rules that structure our society can one day thrive in the economy, then it must finally be working for everyone" (Opoku-Agyeman, 2020, para. 6).

But the need for economic empowerment is only half of the story; the other half, which must be addressed, is the need for Black women to be protected.

Protecting Women During and After COVID-19

There are two ways that women need to be protected during the pandemic and afterwards: economically and physically.

What Does Economic Protection Look Like?

Black women need protection in many ways and for many reasons, not just during the pandemic but also afterward.

As Williams (2020) explains in the *Rand Blog* article "Laid Off More, Hired Less: Black Workers in the COVID-19 Recession":

> This COVID-19 recession/recovery is akin to a schoolyard game of kickball. As the economy tries to rebound, companies are adding workers to their team, yet a group is being picked last, Black workers (para.1).

To understand the scope and extent of the economic protections Black women need, one must see the big picture regarding the problems they are facing. Yes, there are many parts to it, but it comes down to the fact that they don't have enough money and nowhere from which to get it. The only solution to the problem of not having money is to get some.

The government can help, corporations can help, and some women can also help themselves when it's possible to do so, given all the tasks they have to juggle simultaneously. On the latter point, one woman featured in the *Washington Post* article by Van Dam and Long (2020), "Moms, Black Americans and Educators Are in Trouble As Economic Recovery Slows", reveals what needs to be juggled:

> **Smith training to become a phlebotomist**. Smith, 31, is a single mother of three kids in school. She lost her restaurant job in Louisiana in March and later learned it was a permanent layoff: the restaurant won't be reopening. Her family is surviving on $93 a week in unemployment. Smith is behind on rent and owes close to $500 in utilities, putting her in danger of losing electricity. In recent weeks, she stopped looking for work. She's struggling to manage her children's classes, and she said she was feeling discouraged by how few jobs are available. Her kids alternate between in-person schooling and virtual learning from home. Smith decided to enroll in an online training course herself to become a phlebotomist (para(s). 8-9).

But Smith is an exception. Many Black women shoulder too many burdens to be able to follow Smith's example.

At the heart of the matter is always a lack of money and what one can do about the shortfall.

An example of what it looks like not to have generational financial safety is provided in an article in the *Business Insider* titled, "As a Young Black Woman, There Is No Such Thing as 'Generational Wealth' − I Am My Family's Safety Net," in which Wallace (2020) profiles the story of a young Black woman that paints the picture:

> Without universal healthcare and an adequate social safety net, young Black people will continue to have difficulty saving. Even if our parents make our lives marginally better, it is at the expense of their own. Later, it becomes our expense because there is insufficient elder support, even as life expectancy increases. In addition to navigating systems designed to benefit white people, we − young Black people − are responsible for our people. Cultural and familial obligations are imperfect, but they are the system we have and the system we trust. Most of us will always risk our own stability for the reward of our family's comfort − a choice we should not have to make (para. 12).

It always comes down to money—no matter how one looks at it. Therefore, solutions to the problem must be on the money trail, one way or another. On that trail is more and better jobs; job diversification; skills development and enhancement; and policies and practices that help Black women be on the trail that finally leads them to the destination—having money.

What Does Physical Protection Look Like?

There are two parts of the story. One part is the need for protection in the home, which is why "defunding the police" is not a solution, especially for Black women. The other part is the need for protection from the ills of society, including systemic racism.

With regard to the first part—the need for protection in the home—it should be noted that Black women experience violence at higher rates than women overall. According to data presented by Susan Green (2017) in an Institute for Women's Policy Research report titled, "Violence Against Black Women – Many Types, Far-Reaching Effects" (2017), the picture as of 2015 was as follows:

- More than four in ten Black women experience physical violence from an intimate partner during their lifetimes. White women, Latinas, and Asian/Pacific Islander women report lower rates.

- Black women also experience significantly higher rates of psychological abuse—including humiliation, insults, name-calling, and coercive control—than do women overall.

- Sexual violence affects Black women at high rates. More than 20 percent of Black women are raped during their lifetimes—a higher share than among women overall.

- Black women face a particularly high risk of being killed at the hands of a man. A 2015 Violence Policy Center study finds that Black women were two and a half times more likely to be murdered by men than their White counterparts. More than nine in ten Black female victims knew their killers.

- Black girls aged 18–19 were four times more likely to be imprisoned than White girls.

- Formerly incarcerated Black women experience long-term economic, political, occupational, educational, and physical consequences.

Even some famous Black women have not been able to escape from this cycle, a case in point being the female rapper Megan Thee Stallion, who was named by *Time Magazine* as a "Pioneer" in its list of "100 Most Influential People of 2020". Yet, she was shot and wrote an essay about it.

Megan Thee Stallion's Op-ed in the *New York Times* on October 13, 2020—"Megan Thee Stallion: Why I Speak Up for Black Women"—was an eye-opener. She told her story plainly:

> **By Megan Thee Stallion**. I was recently the victim of an act of violence by a man. After a party, I was shot twice as I walked away from him. We were not in a relationship. Truthfully, I was shocked that I ended up in that place.
>
> My initial silence about what happened was out of fear for myself and my friends. Even as a victim, I have been met with skepticism and judgment. The way people have publicly questioned and debated whether I played a role in my own violent assault proves that my fears about discussing what happened were, unfortunately, warranted.
>
> After a lot of self-reflection on that incident, I've realized that violence against women is not always connected to being in a relationship. Instead, it happens because too many men treat all women as objects, which helps them to justify inflicting abuse against us when we choose to exercise our own free will.
>
> From the moment we begin to navigate the intricacies of adolescence, we feel the weight of this threat, and the weight of contradictory expectations and misguided preconceptions. Many of us begin to put too much value to how we are seen by others. That's if we are seen at all.
>
> The issue is even more intense for Black women, who struggle against stereotypes and are seen as angry or threatening when we try to stand up for ourselves and our sisters. There's not much room for passionate advocacy if you are a Black woman.
>
> **Source:** *Stallion, M. (2020, Oct 13). Megan Thee Stallion: Why I speak up for Black women. The New York Times. https://www.nytimes.com/2020/10/13/opinion/ megan-thee-stallion-black-women.html*

Where was the mercy of the man who shot her? He had none. Such violence happens too often in the Black community and is one of the reasons many Black communities can't afford to have the police defunded—they need their protection against such merciless criminals in their own communities. But too often, they also need to be protected from the police. Even Megan Thee Stallion didn't immediately report the events to the police because she said she feared being killed by the police.

Black women need to be protected against violence on many fronts, inside their own communities and homes, in the workplace, and generally against sexual abuse and exploitation wherever it may occur.

Delivering on the Promise of Anti-Sexual Harassment in the Workplace

Sexual harassment is illegal. Title VII of the Civil Rights Act of 1964 ("Title VII") makes it illegal for employers to allow anyone to be sexually harassed at work by anyone else, regardless of sex, gender, or sexual orientation. Sexual harassment can happen to anyone. It is about power and not sexual desire. However, in the pursuit of power, it happens all the time.

Anti-sexual harassment is enshrined in law but not necessarily in the hearts of those who do not respect and abide by the law. This is why ethics, compliance, and accountability are important. Together, they are the forces and systems that work toward preventing such harassment. Sometimes they are successful, and sometimes they are not.

Heeding the Lessons of Me Too

The Me Too (or #MeToo) movement, with variations of related local or international names, is a social movement against sexual abuse and sexual harassment, where people publicize allegations of sex crimes committed by powerful and/or prominent men. The phrase "Me Too" was initially used in this context on social media in 2006, on Myspace, by sexual harassment survivor and activist Tarana Burke.

Over the years, the movement has grown, but so too has the number of incidents. In the article, "The Urgency of Now: Corporate Ethics and the #MeToo Movement," Volkov (2019) explained that "the corporate scandal landscape is littered with important examples of governance failures surrounding corporate ethics and mishandling of harassment and sexual assault controversies" (para. 1). Major corporate governance failures surrounding the handling of these issues have occurred in some of the largest corporations in America:

> If there was ever a compelling argument for ethics and compliance professionals to reiterate the importance of a culture of ethics, now is the time. Companies have to recognize that promoting and managing their cultures is one of several important measures to prevent and detect improper sexual harassment and assault incidents from occurring (Volkov, 2019, para. 2).

In addition, "a company has to demonstrate its commitment to its code of conduct by words and by action. Protecting a company's culture cannot be accomplished by avoiding legal and compliance issues – the goal should be set higher: a corporate conduct standard of personal conduct that treats individual employees with respect and dignity" (Volkov, 2019, para. 3).

The bottom line is that ethics must be hardwired into people because if it's not, there are not enough laws and rules in the world to stop them from being bad actors if they seek to be so.

The Road to Progress in Empowering and Protecting Black Women

There are no easy answers or shortcuts to solving the myriad challenges facing Black women—which were problems before the pandemic, during the pandemic, and will surely be exacerbated after the pandemic.

And though a picture can be painted in broad strokes of the challenges facing Black women, the fine strokes portray the fact that the problems facing individual women vary as they are composed of both internally and externally imposed barriers resulting, in part, from systemic racism.

The confluence of these problems has landed Black women in particular places and spaces. One can imagine the situation being akin to a game of musical chairs when the music stops—if you don't have a chair, you're out of luck.

Imagine that there are millions women marching to the music, hoping to get a chair before the music stops, but there are only a few chairs—for those left without a chair, what will they do and where will they turn when they have no money or networks and nothing to hurl them over the massive pile of problems they have? If you are one of these women, you are probably a disadvantaged Black woman in America.

Between January 20, 2020 and December 1, 2020, there have been over 13.6 million confirmed cases in the United States of COVID-19, with over 268,000 deaths, as reported by tho World Ilcalth Oiyaiilzatloii. And while a number of companies are seeking immediate emergency-use authorization for their vaccines, which gives us hope, there are no vaccines to address the larger problems faced by Black women.

There is hope, however.

But it must be underscored that, at best, the government and corporate America can be good partners, but the most important person in the partnership is the Black woman herself. She too must prepare herself to be "at the ready" to take advantage of opportunities and to make the right choices given her circumstances.

Of course, "being able to be at the ready" has been negatively impacted by the realities of systemic racism that have contributed to landing many Black women in a place that makes it difficult even for the long arms of government to reach. In some ways, and for some women, it's a "Catch 22" situation—it is difficult to be helped because they need so much help after so much damage has been done.

But for most, it's not too late to be helped—by themselves and by their own behavior, as well as by the behavior of others and the policies and practices of institutions that impact their lives. It is within this that hope exists.

In closing, the words and reflections of Megan Thee Stallion are fitting as they are both from the heart and about the heart of the matter.

> Wouldn't it be nice if Black girls weren't inundated with negative, sexist comments about Black women? If they were told instead of the many important things that we've achieved? It took a major motion picture, "Hidden Figures," to introduce the world to the NASA research mathematician Katherine Johnson. I wish I'd learned in school about this story as well as more earthly achievements: that Alice H. Parker filed the patent for the first home furnace, or that Marie Van Brittan Brown created the first home security system. Or that Black women, too often in the shadows of such accomplishments, actually powered the civil rights movement.

It's important to note that six of the Little Rock Nine students whose bravery in 1957 led to school integration were Black girls. And that Rosa Parks showed incredible bravery when she refused to move to the "colored section." I wish that every little Black girl was taught that Black Lives Matter was co-founded by Patrisse Cullors, Alicia Garza, and Opal Tometi.

Walking the path paved by such legends as Shirley Chisholm, Loretta Lynch, U.S. Representative Maxine Waters and the first Black woman to be elected to the U.S. Senate, Carol Moseley Braun, my hope is that Kamala Harris's candidacy for vice president will usher in an era where Black women in 2020 are no longer making 'history' for achieving things that should have been accomplished decades ago.

But that will take time, and Black women are not naïve. We know that after the last ballot is cast and the vote is tallied, we are likely to go back to fighting for ourselves. Because at least for now, that's all we have.

Source: Thee Stallion, M. (2020). Megan Thee Stallion: Why I Speak Up for Black Women. Retrieved from https://www.nytimes.com

But hopefully, we do have more than just ourselves to rely on. We now have the hopes and promises of and belief in the new administration that it will follow through on its commitment to create policies and practices that will help protect and empower all women, including Black women.

C H A P T E R   E I G H T

Ethics, Compliance, and Accountability

About Chapter Eight: **Ethics, Compliance, and Accountability**

In a way, this last chapter of the book starts at the beginning to explain what ethics, compliance, and accountability are and how they work in practice.

These systems and functions are the glue that connect and stick the promises of the Constitution to the actions of institutions and people within the society. When they work, they help everybody in the society, and the converse is also true.

When they fail, the impact of their failures is felt most among the Black population because Black people rely on them so heavily for protection and empowerment.

While this chapter explains what ethics means, and how compliance and systems of accountability work, it also clearly shows that no systems, nor any of part of them, are strong enough to force people to act ethically. Ethics, morals, and values must be "hard wired in" to the soul and consciousness of people; when they are, the external systems of laws and regulations and of reward and punishment have a greater chance of achieving their goals of protecting and empowering all people.

Ethics at its heart is about the heart. But just as a heart is one organ in a human body, albeit it an important one, it only beats well when all of the systems of the body are functioning well. If the blood flowing to the heart is tainted, the heart will not beat well.

Ethics seen the lens of the Black American experience entreats readers to comprehend that Black lives matter, not just matter during election time, or when someone puts a knee on our necks and chokes the life out of us; our lives matter because we are human beings. We may be a few shades darker in skin color, but how can that possibly be such a crime? The sentiment of the question being raised is not dissimilar from that raised by Shakespeare in his book, *The Merchant of Venice*. People love that play and understand its words and meaning yet many of those same people don't understand the humanity of their fellow Black American citizens. Shakespeare's play was written in 1598, and here we are 422 years later asking the same questions, but this time about Black people. We are reminded of the famous quote from *The Merchant of Venice*:

> Hath not a Jew hands, organs, dimensions, senses, affections, passions; fed with the same food, hurt with the same weapons, subject to the same diseases, healed by the same means, warmed and cooled by the same winter and summer as a Christian is? **If you prick** us, **do we not bleed**?

Many Black people are bleeding, especially during this time of the pandemic, and we equally matter as human beings.

When the systems of applied ethics, compliance, and accountability work, they are working to protect and empower all of us in society and the future viability and strength of the nation itself.

Ethics, Compliance, and Accountability

I f it can be asserted that the genius of management rests on how well it articulates and facilitates the interconnections of one function to another and that its merits can only be determined when it interacts with other systems, *then wouldn't the same hold true for ethics?*

Accordingly, ethics only matters when it applies to something and influences that to which it applies.

> Ethics, compliance, and accountability are very important topics to Black Americans because these practices, when applied, help **empower** and **protect** Black people, with the converse also being true.

Compliance and accountability are inextricably linked with ethics. Ethics is the internal motivation to do the right thing, and this is where it gets tricky. Ethics has always been easier said than done. The question is how is ethics *being* done—or *undone*—in private and public institutions?

To answer this question, it's important to understand what ethics is *trying* to do in the first place? To understand ethics, it's important to differentiate ethics, morals, and values.

Values, Morals, and Ethics

While these concepts have been studied and debated by great philosophers and scholars over many lifetimes, in practical terms, there is consensus about their basic definitions, as discussed below.

Values: The Foundation of a Person's Ability to Judge Between Right and Wrong

Values include a deep-rooted system of beliefs that have intrinsic worth but are not universally accepted. This system allows individuals to determine what should and should not be. Such fundamental beliefs make up the barometer guiding a person's decisions.

How Does It Work in Practice? For example, if someone's value system is founded upon honesty, they would probably make a proper judgment between cheating on a college entrance exam (wrong) and studying hard to ace a college entrance exam (right). Conversely, if someone valued achievement and success over honesty, that person may opt to cheat on the exam in order to achieve the desired result. This relates to which value is "worth more" to the individual.

Morals Are Formed from Values

Morals are embedded in a system of beliefs that emerges out of a person's core values. Morals are specific and context-driven rules that govern a person's behavior. Because this system of beliefs is individually tailored to a person's life experience, it is subject to opinion.

Amoral vs. Immoral. Sometimes, the words "amoral" and "immoral" are used interchangeably. They are, however, quite different. If someone is amoral, they have no sense of right and wrong and don't have the foundation that comes with a sound set of values. In contrast, if someone is immoral, they are just choosing to do the wrong thing.

A Moral Dilemma. Given the personal nature of morals, someone may deem an action to be "good" even if it's breaking a law. For example, what if a daughter can't afford the life-saving medicine her dying mother needs, but she somehow has access to the storeroom where the medicine is housed? In this instance, her core values may tell her that stealing is wrong, but her morality would tell that her she needs to protect her mother. As such, the daughter may end up doing the wrong thing (stealing, as judged by her *values*) for the right reasons (saving her mother, as judged by her morals).

Ethics Are Morals in Action

Ethics enact the system we have developed in our moral code, against which we determine if someone is behaving ethically or unethically. Admittedly, the line between morals and ethics is so fine that it can be easy to miss—even the *Encyclopedia Britannica* considers "morals" and "ethics" to be interchangeable terms. It is the context in which they are used that provides the critical distinction.

Applying Ethics in the Workplace

Ethics is about the values of an organization as a whole and the organization's actions based on its values. In addition to the rules and laws associated with compliance, ethics adds values, morals, and beliefs into the mix. Ethics includes social, political, technological, religious, and philosophical issues and how they intersect with business, i.e., how they guide a company's conduct and decisions.

Applying ethics or "*doing ethics*" is not easy, however, because ethics attempts to standardize that which cannot be standardized, given the role an individual's values and morals play in determining one's actions and choices. Nevertheless, from an institutional point of view—public or private—it's important for leadership to set the institution's moral compass to the ethical true north and encourage others to march in that direction.

There's a lot at stake when things go wrong. Consider an example from 2014 involving one of the leading financial institutions in America:

The Largest Corporate Settlement in U.S. History. JP Morgan Chase paid the federal government $13 billion in 2019—the largest corporate settlement in U.S. history—to settle charges involving conduct that prosecutors say contributed to the mortgage meltdown. The bank acknowledged that it made serious  misrepresentations to the public about numerous residential mortgage-backed securities. In January 2020, the bank agreed to another $2.6 billion in payments to resolve charges that it failed to adequately warn its clients about Bernard Madoff's multibillion-dollar Ponzi scheme.

There are many examples of high-profile corporate scandals that grab the headlines and damage company reputations and employee morale, such as the millions of fraudulent accounts of Wells Fargo in 2016, the Volkswagen emission scandal of 2017, or the Theranos blood testing scandal of 2017. These examples show that malfeasance can run deep in private enterprises when it is allowed to hide.

There are also many examples of ethical failures that caused the U.S. Government to make improper payments due to fraud, waste, and abuse. According to the U.S. General Accountability Office (GAO), in fiscal year (FY) 2019, agencies across the government made an estimated $175 billion in improper payments—up from about $151 billion for FY 2018. Medicare, Medicaid, and the Earned Income Tax Credit accounted for about 69% of the $175 billion total.

In fact, no institution is immune to ethical failures as *there is no vaccine to cure a corrupted soul.*

When things go wrong, the question is not just *what* went wrong but *why* they went wrong? In the private sector, for instance, a starting place in searching for the answer is understanding how companies view themselves and how they set their moral compasses.

Ethical Leadership

"Executives must demonstrate ethical behavior in their actions"

When the situation needs improvement, Gandhi offers guidance: "You must be the change you wish to see in the world."

Codes of Ethics, Conduct, and Professional Practice in the Private Sector: Setting the Compass to True North

Codes of conduct express how companies set their ethical and moral compasses. Ethical codes are adopted by organizations to assist members in understanding the difference between right and wrong and in applying that understanding to their decisions. An ethical code generally implies documents at three levels: Codes of business ethics, codes of conduct for employees, and codes of professional practice.

In effect, these codes *decode* the culture of the organization and shine a light on the path for doing the right thing. The problem is that not everybody follows this path.

Competing Cultures. The culture of the organization is one thing, but the cultures of individuals working in the companies may be another. Businesses with broad ecosystems that involve buyers, sellers, vendors, and contractors in multiple countries must take respective cultures into account when doing business in those countries in order to understand prevailing norms and how they may impact the decisions of individuals who are influenced by them.

Today, the question of the reconciliation of norms and cultures is both within and between countries. Within the U.S., such a reconciliation is made difficult because the messages we receive in our own bubbles reenforce our own biases. As explained in Chapter One, algorithms know what your biases are based on your daily internet search clicks. "You," in the algorithmic world, are the sum-total of your clicks and other personally identifiable data.

As a result, from our *manipulated* perspectives, it appears that the whole world sees a given matter the same way we see it because our algorithmic personalized curated news feeds choose what we see in order to match with what we want to see. Under such circumstances, what is right and wrong and what we consider the norm is subjective.

Collectively, these considerations are taking society down a road that is difficult for ethics to navigate. It is a road on which everything is relative—where there is no absolute right or wrong and where our moral compasses are pointing in different directions.

In an article for the *Harvard Business Review*, "Why We're Seeing So Many Corporate Scandals," Mukherjee (2016) emphasizes the role of technology in laying the ground for scandals to happen:

Virtually every 21st century business scandal is reducible to a morality tale of a technology that allows us to do things we couldn't before, coupled with major institutional failures that were enabled by failures of omission and commission of corporate leaders (para. 1).

That said, technology doesn't cause ethical failures, people do.

Saying that, technology does play a role in normalizing what otherwise may have been seen as ethical failures. Those with their fingers on the triggers of technology can program algorithmic "workhorses" to run on a track, making 93 trillion calculations per second, that take us to a place of persuasion and manipulation where we don't know where we are when we get there.

In 2016, Mukherjee (2016) could not have known how fast the galloping "workhorses" of the algorithm apocalypse were running, but there were signs of trouble on the road ahead, and he observed the following:

Digital technologies enable individual employees to do much more than they could before. Mid-tier executives, who have serious decision-making power devolved to them (compared to 25 years ago) drive this workflow. These executives lead teams in which globally dispersed people from multiple organizations collaborate on critical tasks. But in most companies, despite the free flow of exchanges, they still lack information they need, can't communicate with team members in real time, or can't foresee the implications of key decisions. Undoubtedly, one of them "pulls the trigger" when something goes wrong – whether it is an inability to design to needed standards at Volkswagen or the opening of unauthorized accounts at Wells Fargo. They are blamed because they can easily be blamed. (More than 5,000 midlevel or junior people were fired at Wells Fargo after the truth came out (para. 4).

Four years ago, Mukherjee (2016) saw the "handwriting on the wall" and suggested that perhaps we need to "rethink how we work in a digital age when work increasingly requires large doses of unseen discretionary effort" (para. 6). When ethical failures happen, institutions allowed them to happen and the leaders sanctioned them. Essentially, the motivating force behind institutional failure is leadership failure.

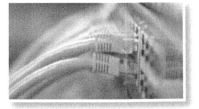

Monkey See, Monkey Do. But what if the monkey can't see what's right or wrong?

Worse, what if the monkey *can* see, but leadership doesn't know what it's seeing or how to interpret the vision? This is the situation that explains Google's shock when it found that its algorithms produced images of gorillas for photo searches of Black people. The sad reality is that the algorithms are in fact seeing things that are there—*which institutions and society thought were hidden*, proving that you can run but you can't hide from the fast galloping algorithms.

It's a mistake, as Mukherjee (2016) opines, "to think 20th century human organizations can thrive amidst 21st century technology—or indeed, to think that mere codes of ethics, conduct, and professional standards provide sufficient guidance to secure desired outcomes" (para. 6).

One point that Mukherjee's (2016) article prompts us to think deeply about is what the acceptable ethical boundaries are for those who must turn those intentions into reality?

What Should We Never Risk? In the highly interconnected digital world, it is very hard to rationally consider the many factors that affect any event. The difficulties are magnified when the factors change unpredictably and with great speed and give rise to precious few "one right answers" and many "no good answers." Given the archaic structures and processes, and without repeated, clear guidance on "what we don't ever risk," is it any surprise that decisions about ambiguous options subsequently turn out to be ethically compromised? (para. 8)

There is no question that we are living in an increasingly complex world that is mediated by digital technologies programmed by mid-tier professionals whose fingers are on the triggers. But if they are programming the algorithms "workhorses," it is the job of leadership to lead them to run on the right tracks. We look to company codes of conduct as an expression of their leadership about the company's ethics and values.

As an example of a large corporation's code of conduct, let's examine JP Morgan Chase' July 2020 Code of Conduct to search for the ethical cues and signals it sends. Our comments are noted beneath the various assertions.

JP Morgan Chase Code of Conduct. **It Begins with Me**.

[Note: *"It Begins with Me" that is the "tone at the top"—taking leadership responsibility*]

JPMorgan Chase has earned the respect of our customers, clients and communities across the globe because of our **strong ethical culture** and dedication to being straightforward and honest in our business dealings. This time-honored commitment defines who we are as a company and has established our firm as one of the world's most respected financial institutions.

[Note: *Emphasizes a strong ethical culture*]

Our Code of Conduct reflects this shared **commitment to operate with the highest level of integrity and ethical conduct**, at all times and wherever we do business — be it in the office, or remotely.

[Note: *Makes it explicit that there is a shared commitment to operating ethically and with integrity*]

We abide by the letter and spirit of the laws and regulations and have **zero tolerance for unethical behavior**. And while we always strive do the right thing, we fully understand it's not always the easiest thing. We believe that fostering an inclusive workplace — one where all employees are treated fairly and respected for their diverse opinions and perspectives — is vital to our success.

[Note: Sends a signal of *zero tolerance for unethical behavior, implying the sanctioning of bad behavior*]

We do not **tolerate inappropriate conduct by, or against**, any colleague, customer, client, vendor, or contractor who does business with our firm.

[Note: *Applies the ethical code to all in the JP Morgan business ecosystem*]

To continually build on our proud heritage, each of us must speak up when we see or experience something that doesn't look or feel right. If you suspect a possible violation of the Code or other improper behavior, know that you can **report it without fear of retaliation**.

[Note: *Empowers all to see something and say something without retaliation*]

The Code of Conduct is here to guide us as we continue to meet our obligations to our constituents — customers, the Board, shareholders, regulators — and ourselves. Remember, preserving our culture of integrity **depends on each of us doing the right thing**.

[Note: *Places responsibility on individuals to do the right thing*]

Source: JP Morgan. (2020). Code of Conduct. Retrieved from website: https://institute.jpmorganchase.com

Given the clear articulation of codes of conduct, how do things continue to go wrong?

Research shows how challenging and complex it is to guide people to be good and do the right thing. Kouchaki et al. (2020), in their article, "Is Your Company's Code of Conduct Encouraging Misconduct?", explore whether the way a code is written makes a difference in its influencing behavior. They found that "it's not just the presence of the code of conduct that matters. It's your culture." The authors further explain the following:

> **Culture is a web of attitudes and practices** that tends to replicate and perpetuate itself beyond the tenure of any individual manager. That culture may instill respect for the law or breed contempt and malfeasance. The organization itself must be held accountable for the culture and the conduct it promotes (para. 5).

Culture inside the organization is important, but so too is the influence of the external cultures that people bring to the organization; these must also be understood as such cultures have a bearing on the values and morals individuals bring with them to the enterprise.

While the influence of codes of conduct can be debated, there is consensus that they *definitely* cannot have an influence if people in the organization are not aware of them.

As codes develop and improve, and as the factors in the digital landscape and the complexity of the global supply chains demand more innovative approaches to persuading people to do the right thing, as long as codes are being relied upon to signal a company's moral compass, two things are important:

- ✔ **Visibility of the Code.** Inadequate employee knowledge of existing codes limit their effectiveness and the ability of employees to use them as a tool for guiding decisions.

- ✔ **Code Violations.** If employees are not encouraged to "see something and say something" when they observe the unethical behavior of coworkers, they can't be part of the solution. In addition, if violations have no consequences, employees may not feel obligated to follow a code of conduct to the letter.

It is underscored that ethics includes social, political, technological, religious, and philosophical issues and how they intersect with business and guide a company's conduct and decisions. With ethics, the process is just as valuable as the outcome. Ethics is about talking and listening, grappling with issues, and seeing different perspectives; it's not about checking boxes. It is a nebulous, moving target that requires gentle guidance and patience.

What Does Doing the Job of the Chief Ethics Officer Look Like?

It may look a little lonely depending on how the function is structured and the industry in which it is being performed. It may look especially lonely and rudderless in Silicon Valley. Underscoring this point, in January 2019, Venture Catalyst's blog "Incorporating Ethics in Silicon Valley and in Startups (Part 1 of 2)", put ethics in the spotlight:

Ethics in the Spotlight. 2018 seemed to be a nonstop news cycle of companies behaving badly. Data/privacy breaches, controversial contracts with law enforcement or government agencies, executive hubris, or mishandling of #MeToo cases by tech companies and/or startups are splashed all over the news. Many companies have a "move fast and deal with consequences later" approach, where profits are the ultimate goal and a sheepish *mea culpa* is offered only if a transgression is caught. In reaction, employees of these companies are starting their own movements to protest their employer's actions. Which leaves people thinking- maybe there should be an ethics officer at these tech companies?

In the 2018 *New York Times* article, "Who Will Teach Silicon Valley to Be Ethical?", Swisher (2018) raises some interesting points that explain the conundrum—it's all about the money, especially for startups that need lots of it. Where does it come from? Suppose the money comes from suspect sources? Swisher gives an example of Saudi funding, for instance. While in the midst of major scandals, the Saudis invested heavily in a number of U.S. startups, including those mentioned by Swisher below.

[In 2018] …Silicon Valley [was] swimming in oceans of money from the Saudi Kingdom's Public Investment Fund. Saudi funding includes hundreds of millions for Magic Leap, and huge investments in hot public companies like Tesla. Most significantly: Saudis have invested about $45 billion in SoftBank's giant Vision Fund, which has in turn doused the tech landscape — $4.4 billion to WeWork, $250 million to Slack, and $300 million to the dog-walking app Wag. In total, Uber has gotten almost $14 billion, either through direct investments from the Public Investment Fund or through the Saudis' funding of the Vision Fund. A billion here, a billion there and it all adds up (para. 5).

The question is: Is it efficacious to create an island that ethics lives on in safety and isolation while the firm swims in shark-infested waters? The "ethics island" is created when *money wins* in the *choice between money and morals.*

In a *Venture Catalyst* article (2019), "Incorporating Ethics in Silicon Valley in Startups" (Part 1 and 2), the reality of what happens when the ethics officer is stuck "over there on an island" is explained in the following way:

While an ethics officer sounds like a good idea on the surface, …others have stated, an ethics officer is often just window dressing, and often without any authority. For example, an ethics officer disagrees with plan X. The chief executive or board will say thank you for your input, perhaps make a few superficial tweaks, then follow through with plan X. They will say that they ran the plan by the ethics officer who gave input (which implies the ethics officer approved plan X). Should plan X go south, then all the fingers point to the ethics officer who will likely be fired (para. 13).

Today, however, the ethical stakes are high, and it shouldn't just be about money. However, for many firms, even when money isn't the question directly, it is a question hovering in the background, as some company executives wonder *how ethics add to the bottom line*—which is ironic because the increasingly influential **E**nvironmental, **S**ocial and **G**overnance (**ESG**) movement is committed to considering factors that go beyond the bottom line.

Ethics in the Public Sector

If preventing ethical failures in the private sector is challenging, imagine how challenging it is to keep the "horses" running on the right track when vast amounts of U.S. Government funding is involved?

There are two aspects of the challenge: One is keeping government workers themselves on the right track, and the other is keeping those who use government funding on the right track. Both are enormous and growing challenges.

The Ethical Compass Guiding Government Workers

As the nation has evolved, so have the ethic policies of the government. From a patchwork of laws and regulations, on October 26, 1978, the Ethics in Government Act established the Office of Government Ethics (OGE) as part of the Office of Personnel Management. Its goal was to bring continuity and uniformity to ethics policies across the executive branch and to establish a system of financial disclosure for senior officials and those in positions with an elevated risk of conflicts of interest. In the ensuing years, changes were made to the OGE and its reporting structure, but its basic mission remained the same.

The OGE leads and oversees the executive branch ethics program, which pertains to 130 agencies. Specifically, the OGE leads and oversees the executive branch ethics program by:

✔ Making and interpreting ethics laws and regulations

✔ Supporting and training executive branch ethics officials

✔ Administering the executive branch financial disclosure systems

✔ Monitoring senior leaders' compliance with ethics commitments

✔Ensuring agencies comply with ethics program requirements

✔Making ethics information available to the public

Yet even this massive structure—with 5,000 ethics practitioners, programs, laws, regulations, training, and guidance—is unable to prevent ethical failures.

The OGE's "Compilation of Ethics Laws" runs to 111 pages, which set forth laws pertaining to 10 major categories in regard to what and what not to do concerning,

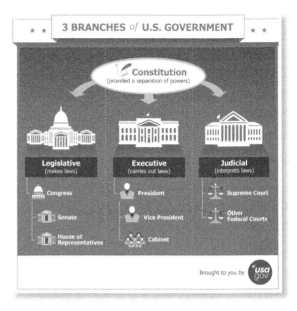

for example, nepotism, conflicts of interest, earning outside income, procurement and contracting restrictions, gifts and travel, political activities, and lobbying. In other words, laws exist that attempt to prevent the instances of ethical failures that can be observed on a daily basis, sometimes from the top down. Such occurrences prove that laws can't prevent ethical failures; it is an individual's moral compass and values that prevent that person from engaging in unethical behavior.

The Ethical Compass Guiding Government Contractors

Multiple efforts—*through laws, regulations, guidance, and sanctions*—have been put forth to try to prevent entities that access U.S. Government funding from engaging in fraud, waste, and abuse, but such unethical conduct is not easily prevented in the private sector because there is often a single bad actor, a series of bad actors, and/or bad companies engaged in bad acts. When there is so much money on the table, there's a lot at stake and a great deal of temptation to access it by hook or by crook. According to Synder's (2019) article for *Insight for Bloomberg Government*, "Federal Contract Spending Trends: Five Years in Five Charts," contract spending has grown by almost 6 percent per year over the past five years as federal agencies have increasingly relied upon government-wide contract vehicles and simplified acquisition procedures. *Bloomberg Government* identified five important spending trends from FY 2014 through 2018.

"Federal spending grew at a rate of about 7.6% annually from fiscal 2015 through 2019, when it rose to $594 billion" (Snyder, 2019, para. 2).

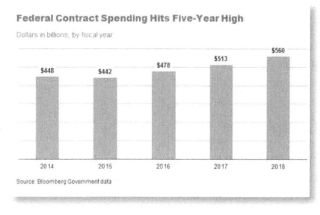

Federal Contract Spending Hits Five-Year High
Dollars in billions, by fiscal year

Source: Bloomberg Government data

Data from *USASpending.gov* shows that as of August 31, 2020, the federal government spent $1.1 trillion in response to COVID-19. As the disease continues to rage on, it is likely that the government will spend more, and it is equally likely that the temptation to engage in fraud, waste, and abuse will be even greater.

When misconduct occurs that involves U.S. Government funding, it occurs because someone had the will and the way to do it. In engaging in misconduct, those who committed it circumvented a body of laws and regulations that were explicit, as contracting with the federal government is a highly regulated process. Unlike commercial contracting, which is generally governed by the Uniform Commercial Code, common law, and civil

torts, federal government contracting is governed by a maze of statutes and regulations. These statutory and regulatory provisions dictate, for example, what method or process an agency must use to solicit a contract; how the agency is required to negotiate or award a contract; and, under certain circumstances, the costs the government will reimburse and how a contractor must account for those costs.

The U.S. Government also imposes a host of socio-economic obligations through its contracts, including requirements related to affirmative action, drug-free workplaces, subcontracting, and minimum employee wages. Although Congress has streamlined the contracting process to reduce the burdens on contractors offering commercial products and services, any entity considering entering into a government contract must tread carefully.

Despite applicable laws and regulations to prevent misconduct, it occurs.

At the end of the day, whether in the private or public sector, codes of ethics and conduct and laws and regulations to encourage ethical conduct are only as strong as the commitment of individuals to abide by them. The responsibility of institutions is to make it as difficult as possible for them to take the low road as opposed to the high road in relation to ethical and moral integrity.

Compliance

While compliance is required legally, unfortunately, ethics is not. Compliance is often the bare minimum; one can be compliant but not ethical. In most cases, being ethical also includes being compliant.

According to Gerry Zack, CEO of the Society for Corporate Compliance and Ethics (SCCE), compliance is a framework for ensuring that an organization complies with the laws and regulations applicable to it and that it minimizes the risk of noncompliance. In contrast, ethics goes beyond what the law requires and involves *doing the right thing* and following both the spirit and the letter of the law.

In the article, "Why Compliance Programs Fail—and How to Fix Them", in *The Harvard Business Review*, Chen et al. (2018) provide a comprehensive overview of the key milestones in the compliance field, from which insights can be gleaned about what and how noncompliance happens in the private sector. In acknowledging that many corporate compliance programs have failed, the authors note:

> The ubiquity of corporate misconduct is especially surprising given the staggering amount firms spend on compliance efforts—the training programs, hotlines, and other systems designed to prevent and detect violations of laws, regulations, and company policies. The average multinational spends several million dollars a year on compliance, while in highly regulated industries—like financial services and defense—the costs can be in the tens or even hundreds of millions. Still, all these assessments deeply underestimate the true costs of compliance, because training and other compliance activities consume thousands of valuable employee hours every year (para. 2).

What Is the Evidence that Compliance Programs Are Not Always Effective?

The Association of Certified Fraud Examiners (ACFE), the world's largest anti-fraud organization, issues an annual report on occupational fraud and abuse. A summary of the key findings from its "2018 Report to Global Nations," which was based on ACFE survey data of fraud examiners from 2016–2017, is presented in Table 1.

Table 1: Key Findings from ACFE's 2018 Report to Global Nations

How many cases were studied?	Value of total losses	Median loss per case	Median duration of the scheme		
2,650 of real fraud	**$7.1 billion**	**$130,000**	**16 months**		
Most common scheme in every country: **Corruption**	Percent of cases that cost +$1 million **22%**	Asset misappropriation scheme most common median loss **$114,000**	Ways discovered		
			40% Tips	**15%** Internal audit	**13%** Mgmt review

Source: *ACFE. 2018 Report to the Nations*

How Did We Get Here?

In an article for the *Harvard Business Review*, "Why Compliance Programs Fail—and How to Fix Them," Chen et al. (2018) explain the evolution of the compliance discipline and shed light on how it has faltered at times along the way. Key milestones include the following:

Milestone #1: Following a stream of corporate scandals in the U.S. in the 1970s and 1980s, industry groups banded together and adopted internal policies and procedures for reporting and trying to prevent misconduct. Such efforts helped assuage legislators, who had sought to regulate and penalize firms more heavily for dishonest practices. Self-policing appealed to business leaders as a way to avoid the cost and disruption of additional regulation, and it also eased the investigative burden on regulators (para. 6).

Milestone #2: Attracted by the perceived benefits, in 1991, the U.S. Sentencing Commission (USSC) amended its guidelines and offered firms substantially reduced fines if they could show that they had an "effective compliance program." A series of memoranda from senior officials at the DOJ soon followed. Other civil regulators, including the Securities and Exchange Commission, the U.S. Department of Health and Human Services, and the Environmental Protection Agency, also adopted this carrot-and-stick approach to compliance (para 7).

Tools in the Toolbox. An industry quickly sprouted to provide compliance training programs, hotlines for whistleblowers, and risk assessments. Not having a compliance program became a liability too significant for any major firm. For many company leaders, compliance programs are protection against worst-case scenarios, akin to an expensive insurance policy. Employees may be asked to sign lengthy codes of conduct attesting that they know their company's polices and to sit through training programs on topics such as privacy, insider trading, and bribery. Yet, individuals often pay only enough attention to these generic classes to pass the 10-question quiz at the end. Even at firms spending millions of dollars annually on their programs, compliance often lacks substance (para.7).

Milestone #3: When the DOJ brought criminal charges against Morgan Stanley employee Garth Peterson in 2012, the prosecution documents noted that Peterson had received seven compliance training sessions and 35 related reminders to eschew the very conduct—bribing a government official—he ultimately engaged in. But those compliance initiatives had little influence on Peterson because he viewed them as pro forma (para. 8).

Milestone #4: The Department of Justice (DOJ) recognized that firms may be spending a lot and creating the components of compliance programs, but their programs may be hollow facades. In its 2008 revision of the "Principles of Federal Prosecution of Business Organizations," the DOJ specifically calls for prosecutors "to determine whether a corporation's compliance program is merely a 'paper program' or whether it was designed, implemented, reviewed, and revised, as appropriate, in an effective manner." In the same year, in a case against Siemens, in which a record-setting $800 million penalty was paid to U.S. authorities, the prosecution repeatedly called out the inadequacies of Siemens's "paper program" (para. 9).

Chen et al. (2018) make the point that "it is often challenging to distinguish substantive programs from those that were merely window dressing, since evaluating a program required considerable time and expertise" (para. 12). The authors also highlight that the DOJ's decision not to prosecute Morgan Stanley in the Peterson case, for example, was seen as validating the firm's approach to ensuring compliance, which included numerous training sessions, in addition to the standard hotline and the usual employee certifications of the firm's code of conduct (para. 12).

Elements of an Effective Compliance Program

Clearly, there is no one cookie-cutter approach that can work in all enterprises across all sectors of business to ensure the best compliance approach or results. But there are some things that have been learned about "how to do compliance" over the years that are taken into account when sentences are contemplated for the punishment of crimes.

The U.S. Sentencing Commission is an independent agency in the judicial branch of government created by the Sentencing Reform Act (SRA) of 1984. Congress enacted the SRA in response to widespread disparity in federal sentencing, ushering in a new era of federal sentencing through the creation of the Commission and the promulgation of federal sentencing guidelines. In determining a sentence for a corporate crime, according to U.S. Sentencing Guidelines,

consideration is given to whether the company had an adequate compliance program. Over the years, what constitutes an adequate compliance program has been operationally defined as one that has the seven key elements outlined in Table 2. The elements discussed in the table are typically used as a road map to establish and maintain compliance and ethics in organizations.

Table 2: Seven Elements of a Compliance Program

Policies and Procedures	**#1** Standards of Conduct, Policies, and Procedures	Put these policies in writing and use them as the foundation for your entire program.
Compliance Officer & Compliance Committee ■ Develop and implement policies, procedures, and practices designed to ensure compliance ■ Adhere to the • Requirements set forth in policy • Requirements of Federal Health Care programs	**#2** Compliance Officer & Committee	Delegate an individual or group with operational responsibility, autonomy, and authority.
	#3 Communication & Education	Create effective ongoing training methods and establish open lines of communication.

	#4 Internal Monitoring & Auditing	Use internal tools to evaluate program effectiveness and detect criminal conduct.
	#05 Reporting & Investigating	Encourage employees to raise concerns and have investigative procedures in place.
	#6 Enforcement & Discipline	Establish appropriate incentives for compliance and disciplinary actions for violations.
	# 7 Response & Prevention	Resolve identified problems promptly and add related issues to monitoring activities.

Source: *Society of Corporate Compliance and Ethics (SCCE)®. Retrieved October 13, 2020 from Corporate Compliance.org*

A Personal Observation: As a former Chief Ethics and Compliance Officer of a for-profit firm that implemented U.S. Agency for International Development projects in developing countries, I have observed firsthand that nothing is more important than the "tone at the top." If the leadership signals the importance of the ethics and compliance function and ensures that the incentives and disincentives align with the prioritization of the function, the probability that the policies, procedures, and systems of the function will work will be greatly increased. (Sharon Freeman)

Yet Things Still Go Wrong—Even in the Non-Profit Sector

Just as the for-profit and public sectors struggle with staying on the right track, so does the non-profit sector. The absence of a profit line item in accounting doesn't mean that there's an absence of malfeasance in the organization—nor does it mean that because the organization was formed for the purpose of doing good, that everything it does is good. A case in point is the Mercy Corps scandal, which showed that in a case of the daughter of the non-profit's founder, it had no mercy. As stated on Mercy Corps' website:

Mercy Corps' roots can be traced back to the Killing Fields of Cambodia when Save the Refugees Fund was launched in November 1979 to alleviate the suffering of Cambodians. Since those early beginnings, Mercy Corps has dedicated itself to helping people facing the toughest challenges survive and move toward a stronger, more resilient future.

But it would appear that Mercy Corps limited its dedication to helping people to survive and face tough challenges who were within the scope of its ongoing paid projects overseas—because for such contracted projects, the rules of its compliance program and ethics are clear. Outside of the realm of specific projects, however, things were not clear. This came to light when the daughter of the founder of Mercy Corps brought charges of sexual abuse against her own father, as reported by The Oregonian (2019).

No Mercy. The investigation by *The Oregonian/OregonLive* detailing heinous sex crimes by Ellsworth Culver, co-founder of Portland-based Mercy Corps, has brought forth renewed anger from the development and humanitarian community. The allegations first brought decades ago by Culver's daughter, Tania Culver Humphrey, are stunning. The dismissive response to them both in 1992 and in 2018, was egregious. It was only when Humphrey told her story publicly, which involved a 10-month media investigation, that Mercy Corps took action. [That led to the 2019 resignation] of Mercy Corps Chief Executive Neal Keny-Guyer — who acknowledged becoming aware of the allegations in 2018 but failed to pursue them.

Source: Huang, C., Raeburn, A. & Midden, K. (2019). Opinion: The Mercy Corps scandal has rocked the aid sector – again. What now? Retrieved from https://www.oregonlive.com

How could an organization that was founded in 1979 as a charitable organization to help those in need fail to come to the rescue of the founder's daughter? How could all the policies, procedures, global experience, and codes of ethics and conduct that Mercy Corps had in place not apply to a problem that involved the leadership of the organization, even if the problem occurred in the home of the then CEO?

As stated on Mercy Corps' website (October 2020), in response to its investigations of what went wrong:

> Mercy Corps' policies addressing sexual exploitation, abuse and misconduct promote leading-edge principles that incorporate and require compliance with guidelines published by the United Nations, USAID, DFID and other major donors. Mercy Corps' policies exceed the requirements of the organization's largest donor—the US Agency for International Development—by taking a survivor centered approach.

> [However] Mercy Corps team members did not consider these policies applicable to the communications with Ms. Culver Humphrey in 2018. Regardless of whether safeguarding policies expressly covered this request, Mercy Corps at least should have drawn upon the values underlying those policies in their response (www.mercycorps.org).

This ethical failure highlights that having many policies, procedures, and systems is not enough to ensure that an organization does the right thing. In fact, they had the opposite effect—because the specific situation was not anticipated, it was apparently deemed that the organization's policies and procedures did not extend to the specific ethical failure that occurred. Common sense was overruled, and the leadership failed to consult its professed moral compass.

The ethical failure here is a failure of the heart. No one who knew about the situation took responsibility for addressing it because it was a domestic problem and not perceived to be a problem for the business. If this was indeed the judgement, then the question is: what business did they think they were in? From its website, one would conclude that they were in the business  of helping people in need. Would that only apply to helping people in foreign countries?

This is why a Chief Ethics and Compliance Officer is needed for such organizations—to help them find their hearts and consult their moral compasses to find the right direction for solving problems. In a sense, compliance is *post facto*—it ensures that laws and regulations that are already in place are complied with—but suppose there is no law or rule for something? This is where having a heart and a moral compass is needed to shine a light on the right direction, and this is where the "tone at the top" matters most.

In the *Venture Catalyst* article (2019), "Incorporating Ethics in Silicon Valley and in Startups (Part 1 of 2)", it is underscored that "there are challenges of combining ethics and compliance into one department, primarily because often the compliance function consumes all the attention to the detriment of ethics. In response, some of these companies are turning to ethics officers as a solution" (para. 9). If the ethics and compliance function was not combined in one position and the ethics officer was separate, what would the ethics officer do? According to the *Venture Catalyst* (2019), the ethics officer would do the following:

> An ethics officer is a person who serves as the company's point person for anything related to the company's ethical culture or code of conduct. An ethics officer would have the authority to develop a code of ethics for the company's culture, investigate possible ethics breaches, issue penalties when appropriate, and protect those who report ethics violations. Responsibilities would include ensuring that ethics are applied in all aspects of the company, reviewing business and strategy decisions for potential conflicts with the company's culture and code of ethics, shaping the company's position on controversial issues such as privacy, data rights, immigration, climate change, private/government partnerships that enable government to infringe on human rights, gender parity, and investors from questionable sources (para 9).

But even if the ethics and compliance functions are consolidated into one function, the issue of accountability remains.

Accountability

The private, public, and non-profit sectors each have an entire ecosystem of accountability. How effectively any of it works is questionable, though no one would suggest "throwing the baby out with the bath water."

Let's first examine the U.S. Government's accountability ecosystem as more often than not, government funding comes into the equation for virtually all sectors and individuals—and wherever U.S. funding is involved, the government has a role in demanding accountability.

At the federal level, the government has many watchdogs in all government agencies. The U.S. Accountability Offices (GAO) is the chief watchdog that looks across agencies to assess accountability. There are also special purpose "watchdogs," such as the Securities and Exchange Commission (SEC), that have their eyes on financial matters, just as there are other issue-specific watchdogs. In short, there is no shortage of government agencies that are "watching"—*but what are they seeing and what do they do about it to hold entities accountable?*

According to *USASpending.gov*, the U.S. Government spent **$4.45 trillion** of taxpayers' hard-earned tax dollars. Of this amount, over $1 trillion was spent improperly. This is the reason that the function of the Offices of the Inspector General (OIG) in federal government agencies is so important—they were created as an important safeguard for protecting federal funds.

> On October 12, 1978, the Inspector General (IG) Act established twelve Federal Offices of Inspector General (OIG), including the Department of Transportation OIG. The Act passed the House of Representatives by a vote of 388 to 6 and was later approved by the Senate by unanimous consent. Two OIGs had previously been established, one in 1976 and another the following year. President Jimmy Carter signed the IG Act into law and described the new statutory IGs as "perhaps the most important new tools in the fight against fraud." The President charged the IGs to always remember that their ultimate responsibility is not to any individual but to the public interest.

The 2019 request for the Office of Inspector General (OIG) was **$387.5 million**, which was an additional $22.8 million above FY 2018.

But there is a problem: the OIGs are not always supported in playing their role. OIGs, it should be noted, fall into two broad categories: (1) OIGs that require the IG to be nominated by the president and confirmed by the Senate; and (2) OIGs that require the agency to nominate the IG. In a word, the problem is politics.

While the IG Act of 1978 requires inspectors general to be selected based upon their qualifications and not political affiliations, presidentially appointed inspectors general are considered political appointees and are often selected, if only in part, because of their political relationships and party affiliations.

How Do Offices of the Inspector General (OIGs) Operate?

The offices employ special agents (criminal investigators, often armed) and auditors. In addition, federal offices of inspectors general employ forensic auditors, or "audigators," evaluators, inspectors, administrative investigators, and a variety of other specialists. Their activities include the detection and prevention of fraud, waste, abuse, and mismanagement of the government programs and operations within their parent organizations. Office investigations are internal, targeting government employees, and external, targeting grant recipients, contractors, or recipients of the various loans and subsidies offered through the thousands of federal domestic and foreign assistance programs. OIGs are essentially watchdogs, but sometimes they are prevented from seeing all and reporting on what they see.

> **War on the Watchdogs**. In April and May 2020, President Trump dismissed the IGs of five cabinet departments in six consecutive weeks. In several cases, the fired IGs had taken an action that Trump disliked, so the dismissals were widely described as "retaliation." In two cases, questions were raised about whether the dismissals related to ongoing IG investigations into the conduct of the cabinet secretary in charge of that department. The cumulative firings were often described as a "purge" or as a "war on watchdogs."

A War On Whistleblowers

In addition to OIGs, an important tool in the toolbox of accountability is whistleblowers. Those who become whistleblowers are people who are guided by their moral compasses to speak up when they witness unethical or non-compliant actions. When they are chastised for doing so, however, it sends a signal that speaking up is not the right thing to do.

There has been an ongoing "war on whistleblowers" in the Trump Administration. As mentioned in Table 1, forty percent of misconduct cases in the private sector were discovered through whistleblowing; in other words, they saw something and they said something. Presumably, many instances of misconduct are also identified by whistleblowers in the public sector, both in regard to the misconduct of public sector employees and the misuse of government funds in the private sector.

Shaub (2020), in his *The Washington Post* article, "Trump's Quest for Revenge Could Mean the End of Whistleblowing", in February 2020, explains what's at stake when the whistles of the blowers are snuffed out. Quite simply, it's tantamount to "killing a crucial tool of democracy." Shaub (2020) further observes that:

> The nation's interests will be harmed if individuals with inside information are afraid to make good-faith reports of suspected wrongdoing. Discouraging whistleblower activity jeopardizes the government's critical efforts to detect corruption, large-scale waste of taxpayer money, and threats to public health and safety (para. 9).

Ethics Seen through the Lens of the Black American Experience: *How Does it Look?*

What we have seen throughout this book is that no systems, nor any of part of them, are strong enough to force people to act ethically. Ethics, morals, and values must be "hard wired in" to the soul and consciousness of people; when they are, the external systems of laws and regulations and of reward and punishment then have a greater chance of achieving their goals of protecting and empowering all people.

We have also seen that the raging pandemic, as devastating as it has been, also offers an opportunity for society to "see" that the historical and present Black experience has positioned Black people to experience the harshest realities of the pandemic and that concrete actions are needed to prevent further devastation. This moment offers an opportunity for society to create and enhance systems that help unleash and unharness the potential of Black people to be a part of future solutions to societal problems, not just for themselves but for society as a whole. Many Black people, no matter what rung they are on the ladder of American society, have the potential to offer solutions to problems because they have a deep understanding of what the problems are. This is why diversity is important. It's not about quotas and proportional representation—it's about tapping into those ingredients that have enabled Black people to survive and sometimes thrive against all the odds.

Ethics applied to Black people is about lowering the odds against them so that they can more easily and broadly contribute their knowledge and perspectives to help make things better not just for themselves but for society as a whole.

This moment creates an urgency, as never before in American history, to level the playing field so that everyone has the potential to hit a home run—because that's how we, as a society, can win the game. But there is work to do in many areas to level the playing field. This book has highlighted just a few of the areas that require urgent attention, such as those reiterated below.

Work to Be Done to Promote Ethics, Compliance, and Accountability in the Area of Algorithm Bias

In the area of algorithm bias, privacy, and accountability, for instance, we have seen that there are three important actors in the ecosystem—the company, consumers, and the U.S. Government— that have an important role to play in prioritizing ethical intentions and actions.

For instance, if a company wants to prioritize removing bias from its algorithms, it can; if it wants to protect the privacy of consumers, it can; and if it chooses to properly reward accountability, it can. But it never will unless the leadership demands it. This is what is meant by the "tone at the top."

Leadership matters, as does the song it is singing and whether it hits the right notes in the song. This applies to all matters within the company, and as the ESG **S-Factors** (social) principles underscore, it matters to employees, sellers, buyers, vendors, contractors, and to the communities that the company serves.

Salesforce is one company that appears to be singing the right tune. It is a cloud-based software company headquartered in San Francisco, California, providing a customer relationship management service and selling enterprise applications focused on customer service, marketing automation, analytics, and application development. It acknowledges that bias comes from the "works instructions" that the "algorithmic workhorses" are given by people, so it is taking action consistent with the **S-Factor** principles of ESG by diversifying its workforce.

In the article "Diversifying Recruitment Methods in Tech Companies to Reduce AI Bias," Yakobovitz (2020) states: "A human-centered approach is required when addressing the bias problem and most organizations disregard logic in their hiring process leading to bad outcomes. Technology solutions such as machine learning and artificial intelligence cannot work alone, and this is where the *human factor* comes in."

A picture is worth a thousand words. Salesforce is addressing bias through their inclusive culture, which attracts diverse talent. Of course, it is not their mere presence that matters but whether their contributions will lead to an absence of bias in the "work instructions" of the algorithms. For this to happen, the programmers must solicit their opinions  *before* and not *after* the fact. In other words, before the "workhorse" algorithms are unbridled, their "work instructions" need to be reviewed by diverse teams to check for biases.

Why does redressing algorithmic bias matter to Black people? It matters because Black people are often the victims of such bias and are powerless to prevent the kind of discrimination that biased algorithms exacerbate; this, in turn, harms the ability of Black people to progress in society, and when they cannot progress, it becomes an uncontainable problem for all of society.

In terms of Big Tech and privacy, as Moss et al. (2019) put forward in their article for the *Harvard Business Review,* "The Ethical Dilemma at the Heart of Big Tech Companies," as the tech industry is trying to establish concrete practices and institutions around tech ethics, hard lessons are being learned about the wide gap between the practices of "doing ethics" and what people think of as 'ethical'" (para. 1). As Mitchell Noordyke (2019) observes in his International Association of Privacy Professionals (IAPP) article, "Big Tech's Shift to Privacy," privacy is top-of-mind for technology companies and their consumers. The IAPP reviewed consumer-facing privacy webpages, prominent publications, public statements by CEOs, and general promotional materials of the tech industry's main consumer-facing players (Google, Facebook, Microsoft, and Apple) to understand what they are doing to protect privacy.

Their findings show that the Big Tech are doing many things in the privacy space, but the jury is still out on its effectiveness as judged by the needs and demands of consumers.

Legislators are doing their part to promote the privacy rights of consumers. For instance, the U.S. Senate's May 2020 Data Privacy Bill is aimed at holding businesses accountable to consumers if they use personal data to fight the COVID-19 pandemic.

Why does data privacy matter to Black people? It matters because many Black people lack the power to prevent—and sometimes even to be aware of—data privacy intrusions that impact their lives; therefore, they rely on the government to protect them against forces bigger than themselves.

Work to be Done to Promote Ethics, Compliance, and Accountability in the Area of Fair Housing and Accountability

There has always been a question of what is right and what is wrong in matters of housing, and the answer has often been: "Ethics is in the eye of the beholder."

In regard to Blacks and other minorities, until the Fair Housing Act of 1964, there was no ethical or moral dilemma; it was clear—simply move them out of the way, by hook or by crook. As noted by Adams (2018) in her *New Yorker* article, "The Unfulfilled Promise of the Fair Housing Act," "…before 1968, it was assumed to be perfectly legal for owners to refuse to sell homes to black families, or for a private bank to deny a potential black homebuyer a loan, or for a broker to lie and say that no homes were available" (para. 6). Then came the Fair Housing Act of 1968. But while the law successfully made certain individual acts of explicit racial discrimination in housing transactions illegal and residential segregation by race decreased, the Fair Housing Act has never fully delivered on its promise to promote and further integration. And it hasn't delivered for many reasons.

To put teeth in the Fair Housing Act, late in President Barack Obama's second term in 2015, Housing and Urban Development (HUD) adopted meaningful regulations to foster integration: "The new rules focused on enhancing access to good schools, jobs, transportation, recreation, and social services. The regulations had strict timelines that held both the local jurisdictions and HUD accountable" (Adams, 2018, para 10). Then came the election of Donald Trump and the rollback of all the Obama-era requirements.

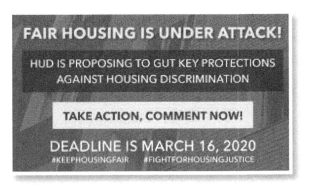

FAIR HOUSING IS UNDER ATTACK!

HUD IS PROPOSING TO GUT KEY PROTECTIONS AGAINST HOUSING DISCRIMINATION

TAKE ACTION, COMMENT NOW!

DEADLINE IS MARCH 16, 2020
#KEEPHOUSINGFAIR   #FIGHTFORHOUSINGJUSTICE

And where are we today at the end of 2020? Not in a good place, but we are hopeful that the incoming administration will provide a good answer that helps and not harms Black people.

As far as environmental injustice is concerned, we have seen in this book and in history that anything having to do with the environment is a story of money and power, and ultimately about the **3Ps—Purse, Policies,** and **Persuasion,** which were discussed in the housing and environmental injustice chapter of this book. So far, with regard to the **3Ps,** the purse is winning.

The Environmental Protection Agency (EPA) is the federal government's agency that focuses on all environmental matters. In FY 2020, it had a budget of over $9 billion and dedicated $4.1 million to a grants program for projects to address multiple needs of "Environmental Justice" (EJ) communities, including the impacts of COVID-19. But is it enough and is the matter of accountability just limited to the accountability of how the grant funds are spent, or does it extend to preventing or stopping the pollution? Black people hope for the latter.

Why do fair housing and environmental justice matter to Black people?

They matter because Black people want to live, and they want to live a life in places and spaces that are healthy and afford them the opportunity to build wealth. If they continue to be **isolated, targeted,** and **destroyed** by the locations they are forced into, they will, at the same time, be forced into poverty in many instances.

FLINT WATER PLANT

Work to be Done to Promote Ethics, Compliance, and Accountability in the Area of Policing and Accountability

A 1988 U.S. Department of Justice, Office of Justice Programs, National Institute of Justice document clearly explains that all organizations have values that are implicit in every action of organizational incumbents. When explicit, statements of values attempt to set forth the beliefs of an organization, the standards that are to be maintained by its members, and the broader mission expected to be achieved through their activities.

Often, the values that undergird routine decisions and practices are so deeply ingrained as to make them automatic. Values, even those we consider positive, can conflict. When police officers decide to close their eyes to the incompetence or corruption of colleagues and draw the "blue curtain" around them, they choose the value of loyalty to peers over other values, such as quality service to the community. In many police departments, other values—some explicit and others implicit—can be identified that shape and drive police performance (p. 3).

According to the DOJ, the responsibility of police managers is to (1) identify values that flow from the law and the Constitution that represent the highest norms of the profession and that are consistent with the ideals of communities and neighborhoods; and (2) enunciate them persuasively and unambiguously.

> **Why does ethical policing matter to Black Americans?** It matters because Black people want to live, and throughout their lives, they don't want to live in fear of being killed or treated unfairly by the police.

Work to be Done to Promote Ethics, Compliance, and Accountability in the Area of ESG and Accountability

There are three outstanding ethical questions about ESG. One is whether ESG is doing what it says it's doing, another is how what it is doing is measured, and the third relates to the risk associated with what it is doing. On the latter point, for instance, Matt Kelly (2020) captured the heart of the current concern about ESG from a compliance perspective in his article, "The New Urgency for ESG Risk Management," noting that "'ESG risk'" is one of those somewhat maddening terms of art in corporate compliance. It's clear enough to understand… but also too imprecise for compliance and risk professionals to have a standard process for dealing with them" (para. 1).

New and unprecedented things are happening in the ESG realm, and it's not always clear whether they are happening within the full context of the policies, procedures, and risk frameworks of the company.

In an article in *Investor Perspectives*—"New Challenges to the Merits of ESG Investing"— Swedroe (2020) notes that there is considerable dispersion in ranking public companies with respect to sustainable attributes. Those inconsistencies lead to inconsistent conclusions about how to construct ESG portfolios. There are also concerns about whether enforcing compliance can be enforced throughout the very long and complex third-party supply chains.

In U.S. corporations, the buck stops with the board of directors. In the area of ESG, and in all matters, to perform their fiduciary duties, the directors typically ask the following questions, and if their answers to these questions are sound, the investments should be as well:

- Is our financial plan consistent with our strategic plan?
- Is our cash flow projected to be adequate?
- Do we have sufficient resources?
- Are any specific expense areas rising faster than their sources of income?
- Are we regularly comparing our financial activity with what we have budgeted?
- Are our expenses appropriate?
- Do we have the appropriate checks and balances to prevent errors, fraud, and abuse?
- Are we meeting guidelines and requirements set by our funders?

Why Does Ethical ESG Investing Matter to Black Americans? It matters because Black people have hope that ESG can be a powerful force for good in society and a powerful movement that supports needs within the Black community. Therefore, it's important for it to work and live up to its ethical commitments and promises. Among those promises, the Black community is particularly hopeful that big corporations will use their ESG investment, and draw on the insights of more diverse executives, to promote and partner with Black businesses and thereby help them overcome decades of harm that the denial of access to capital has caused in their ability to accumulate wealth.

The Road to Progress in Ethics, Compliance, and Accountability

America's history shows that it takes a lot of pushing and pulling to change the status quo; the bigger the issue, the stronger the push and pull must be. What did it take, for instance, to stop allowing people to smoke in public places? It took years and significant stakeholder commitment in society to finally realize the harm that was being done and to commit to changing behavior. What did it take for Black people to push for the Civil Rights Act of 1964 and for President Johnson to pull it into being? It's never easy, but when it happens, it always happens because it was the right and ethical thing to do.

> On a personal note, I once had the opportunity to tour the USS Carl Vinson aircraft carrier in the early 1980s in Hong Kong. At the time, it was America's largest aircraft carrier. The officer in charge of flight and aircraft operations, a Black American man—to my surprise at the time—informed me that it took seven miles to turn that behemoth carrier around, and that everything in those seven miles had to move out of its way. (Sharon Freeman)

Analogously, as we turn our figurative "societal ship" around to move in a different direction that is more fair and just in regard to the treatment of Black people, it's going to take a lot of space and room for maneuver—in our hearts, strategies, and beliefs in and commitment to doing the right and ethical thing toward each other, toward Black people, and on behalf of all people in society.

Afterword

A question is posed in the title of this book, "**Ethics Seen Through the Lens of the Black American Experience: How Does It Look?**"

So, how does it look?

For those of you who have read the many pages in this book, you have seen many images of the picture that has no doubt conveyed two things: COVID-19, added on top of the results of systemic racism, looks like a gathering storm for many Black people, but it also looks like many lifeboats are coming to the rescue in the Biden-Harris Administration.

The conversations that flow through this book feel like one many of us dread having. You know the kind, where your parents, teachers, spouse, or others might have with you that start off with those ominous nine words, "*I would like to have a talk with you*". What typically comes next is never easy to swallow. Still, they are important conversations, which help us to grow in our understanding of things.

The conversations in this book are like that, in many regards. They are tough, enlightening, and necessary. Hopefully, they have allowed you to "walk a mile in someone else's shoes", specifically in the shoes of Black people. Moreover, there is hope that they have implored you to have empathy and imparted a deeper understanding of the Black American experience and of the facts that have shaped such experiences.

This book comes at a momentous time in American history, when the killing of George Floyd, particularly how he was killed, caused many Americans to stand back on their heels and question what had happened and where had things gone wrong?

As we reflect on the answer to this question, we recall the words of Rodney King, who was nearly being beaten to death in a similarly shocking case of police brutality. On May 1, 1992 in answer to the question, "What do you have to say?", King replied, "**Can we all just get along?**" It shocked the nation and has been considered to be the quote of the decade because he showed a level of humanity in his response that many of us knew we could not summon if the shoe had been on the other foot.

By contrast, on January 22, 2017, Kellyanne Conway, (then Counselor to the President), said in an interview about the number of supporters in attendance at Donald Trump's presidential inauguration, that there are "**alternative facts**".

These two equally powerful statements that, in their own way, captured our imaginations represent two different world views expressed thirty years apart. Rodney King's represented a view that many of us want to *run toward* to uncover the best in ourselves. The other, Conway's, represents a view that we, who care about humanity, seek to *run away from* for fear that it would unleash the worst in ourselves and in society. Sadly, Conway's view is the one that defines the moment we are in, one that has torn us apart as a nation.

In writing this book, we associate ourselves with the spirit of King's statement, which we believe moves us toward the light and away from the darkness of "alternative facts".

There are no "alternative facts" in the experience of ethics, as seen through the lens of the Black American experience. In many cases, ethics have not been applied to the treatment of Black people in society. Sadly, in many instances, ethics are more easily said than done and continue to be in the eye of the beholder.

What we hope to have accomplished in this book is to have shone a light on the historical and present circumstances of Black people. We want to encourage society to stop and consider what action can be taken going forward to make the world a better place for us all once again. In such a better world, the promises of the 14th Amendment to the U.S. Constitution will be realized, as follows:

> ...No State shall make or enforce any law which shall abridge the privileges or immunities of citizens of the United States; nor shall any State deprive any person of life, liberty, or property, without due process of law; nor deny to any person within its jurisdiction the equal protection of the laws.

Living up to these words and the ethical principles on which they are based, is not only good for Black people in America; it is good for all people and presents an opportunity for America, at this critical time, to regain its place in the world as a beacon lighting a path toward righteousness.

In conclusion, the one thing we know for sure is that no one can solve a problem that is not understood. We are hopeful that this book helps readers better understand how systemic racism works through the policies, actions, institutions, and sentiments of people that perpetuate it. But beyond merely promoting an understanding of it, it is our hope that through understanding it, more of us will stake a claim in confronting and changing it. Many are already on this "road to progress", as shown in this book. We believe that many more will march on that road to a better place.

Let's keep the conversion going.
Contact us at the Gemini Ethics Movement (GEM Foundation)
(www.theethicsmovement.org)

P.S. (Post-Script): January 6, 2021 Seen Through the Lens of the Black American Experience

H old the press! This book was on its way to the printer when January 6, 2021 happened. On that day, supporters of President Trump, egged on by him, attempted a coup by storming the U.S. Capitol to overturn the lawful and democratic U.S. election. Though much has been said in the 100,000 words of this book, the subject of **permission** and the role it plays in justifying unethical actions has been implied by not expressly stated. It's importance, however, has now been made clear.

When children and adults obtain **permission** from those in charge—their parents, bosses, or leaders—to take actions that otherwise may have been considered unethical or immoral, it changes the calculus and direction of "true north." What is then determined to be fair and just, by virtue of the **permission** granted, is recalculated to be ethical. Such recalculated **permission** structures are what some police officers have drawn on to treat Black people the way they have.

The rage in the hearts, minds, and actions of the domestic terrorists who stormed Capitol Hill is a result of White people *feeling* that they are being treated in the manner in which Black people have always been treated.

Feeling that one is being treated in such a manner is one thing but having evidence of having been treated that way for hundreds of years, is another. This book provides a small sample of the unfair, unjust, and unequal treatment of Blacks in America for hundreds of years. Yet, Black people never stormed the U.S. Capitol Hill, and despite all that has happened to them, they still adhere to and abide by the rules of the law of the land.

Take one moment to imagine if President Barack Obama had incited Black people to storm the U.S. Capitol? Then imagine how he himself, and all of his followers in such a scenario would have been treated? We don't have to express it here, you know it.

Some ardent supporters of Trump, legislators among them, have commented that the actions of the domestic terrorists on Capitol Hill were equivalent to the peaceful protests of Black people and their supporters in reaction to the killing of George Floyd and other unfair killings of Black people by the police—noting that there were some instances of looting of stores. **Is the value of a life of a human being equivalent to the value of a store window?**

Are our ethics and morals so fungible that, seemingly in an instant, we can turn on our fellow man, turn our backs on the founding principles of democracy in America, and seek to do harm to our public servants? The answer is usually "no" but the "no" can turn into a "yes" within the period of four years when the nation's leader continually blares from his megaphone that "we" are not "us"; "we" are White, and everyone who isn't, and who is not for our agenda, is the enemy.

In America, most go through K-12 education, many go to church, and all are born to parents. Along the way from our childhood to adulthood, we have many opportunities to set our moral compasses and beliefs about ethics and morality. But it appears almost half of the voters in America subscribe to Donald Trump's vision of a divided America and of a divided world. So, approximately in less than 25 percent of time that it took us to become eligible to vote, many have been persuaded to adopt a set of beliefs that is 180 degrees different from the majority of Americans.

The truth is that while morals and ethics are normally "**hard-wired**" into people, *all wires can be tripped.* When the leader of the nation is the one tripping the wires, his supporters got **re-wired** and believed they were morally justified in their actions. The question of how to address and reconcile our differences is a matter for the best minds in the nation to determine in the days ahead.

For now, what we know and what we can do is to use three levers of power described in this book, the **3Ps** of the **P**urse, **P**olitics, and **P**ersuasion, to hold terrorists accountable for the insurrection.

As a capitalist nation, perhaps the strongest lever among the **3Ps of power** is the **purse**, so now, the *purse strings* are being pulled. We have explained what the **systems of systemic racism** are in this book and from those explanations, it is clear that many critical systems of them have to do with money and how it is controlled. These systems are now being used to bring Donald Trump and his supporters to heel and to make them accountable. Such systems include, for instance, banks (now, Trump's bankers are ceasing to do business with him); campaign donations (now being held back by many for all political donations); Stripe credit card processing for campaign contributions to Trump (being denied); holding events at Trump-branded commercial properties (pulled back); the ability to sell goods on Spotify (denied); being able to attract investment capital from venture capitalists and Wall Street (curtailed); doing business with the City of New York (denied); resumes of his staff looking for jobs on Wall Street (rejected); putting insurrectionist participants on the "No Fly" list (enacted), and so forth. One could say that Trump, and the insurrectionists are, being "**Black-listed**." *How does it feel?*

If this picture looks grim, imagine that it is a picture that conveys many of the pathways of systemic racism that have blocked many Black people throughout their history in America—they are pathways that led to a series of rejections and denials that Black people have had to continually endure.

The **persuasion** lever in the **3Ps** power equation has been firmly held by social media platforms throughout the Trump presidency. Now, this lever is being pulled to block him, for the first time. Facebook, Instagram, Twitter, and the platforms used by his followers, such as Parler, are being denied. In the case of the Parler App that was used as a platform to plan the insurrection, Google, Apple, Microsoft, and Amazon have each stepped in to block all access to it. In addition, the ability of Trump to post content on YouTube has been suspended for the remainder of his term in office.

It's also noteworthy, and alarming, that the wife of Supreme Court Justice Clarence Thomas, Ginni Thomas, paid for 70 buses used to transport armed rioters to the Capitol Hill rally. Now, her Facebook page has been shut down. When the spouse of a Supreme Court Justice is involved, Black people feel that the system is rigged—not the fake notion of something being rigged that Trump has espoused but rigging for real.

Then there is a **political** lever of the **3Ps** of power to pull to make Trump accountable. As of January 13, 2021, one picture is worth a thousand words. Trump was impeached for the second time.

Holding people accountable is the key to making sure ethics matters. In another landmark case, as of January 14, 2021, ten years after the crime, the former Governor of Michigan is finally also being held accountable after taking unethical actions in switching the water sources in Flint, Michigan from a safe one to a dangerous source that flowed through lead filled pipes that killed and harmed many people.

This shows that the systems of power can work *for* or *against* citizens. Sadly, for many Black Americans throughout much of their history, the systems have worked against them. The blockage of pathways that is occurring shows how surgically such systems can be shut off to change the course and trajectory of future actions that are unwanted and undesirable. Through this current lesson, Black people are hopeful that such skillful interventions will be applied to addressing their disadvantaged position to finally enable them to receive fair, just, and equal treatment.

In closing, we underscore that leadership can have two faces: good and evil. Those who study leadership tend to focus on its positive attributes and the pathways through which it works, but there is an urgent need to better understand the evil side of leadership and its pathways as well. The reactions to the attempted coup on the U.S. Capitol Hill against our legislators and public servants are now showing us the pathways for blocking evil leadership through leveraging the **3Ps**.

We are also observing how **Wall Street**, **Silicon Valley**, and the **Hill**, can work in lockstep to quickly block the main arteries that are the lifeline of undesirable movements.

We also note that when we spoke about **ESG** (**E**nvironment, **S**ocial, and **G**overnance) in this book and appealing to the better angels and *soul* of corporations, it was an important conversation because the corporate response is weighted as heavily as the legislative and political response in leveraging the **3Ps** to cause change.

When we spoke of algorithms in the first chapter of this book, it too was an important conversation because we learned about their ability to calculate 93 trillion calculations per second. With such computing capacity, if they are given the "work instructions" to help discern the good from the evil, they can do it!

Finally, we have observed that indeed, there are certain problems in the policing ecosystem that are not only harmful to policing Black people but that can also be harmful in their failure to protect others in society, including our public servants.

Despite this, we have the power to make a better future for all of "us" in America; now, the real work begins!

REFERENCES

Chapter One: **Algorithm Bias, Data Privacy, and Ethics**

Alake, R. (2020, July 13). Are There Black People in AI? Retrieved from https://towardsdatascience.com/are-there-black-people-in-ai-fb6928166d73

Balboa, L. (2020, May 27). Embedding fairness into algorithmic decision-making. Retrieved from https://lisabalboa.com/2019/05/27/embedding-fairness-into-algorithmic-decision-making/

Brookings Institution. (2020, January 14). The Ethical Algorithm: A Conversation with Authors Michael Kearns and Aaron Roth. Retrieved from https://www.brookings.edu/events/the-ethical-algorithm/

Congressional Research Service. (2020). Deep Fakes and National Security. Washington, DC.

Data Privacy Manager. (2020, August 20). 100 Data Privacy and Data Security Statistics for 2020. Retrieved from https://dataprivacymanager.net/100-data-privacy-and-data-security-statistics-for-2020/

Forbes Insight Team. (2019, March 27). Managing The Ethics of Algorithms. Retrieved from https://www.forbes.com/sites/insights-intelai/2019/03/27/managing-the-ethics-of-algorithms/?sh=43c303623481

Foucek, C. (2020, June 24). Is Data Privacy A Privilege? The Racial Implications Of Technology Based Tools In Government. Retrieved from https://www.techdirt.com/articles/20200622/07255444756/is-data-privacy-privilege-racial-implications-technology-based-tools-government.shtml

Hao, K. & Stray, J. (2019, October 17). Can You Make AI Fairer Than a Judge? Play Our Courtroom Algorithm Game. Retrieved from https://www.technologyreview.com/2019/10/17/75285/ai-fairer-than-judge-criminal-risk-assessment-algorithm/

Hill, K. (2020, June 24). Wrongfully Accused by an Algorithm. Retrieved from https://www.nytimes.com/2020/06/24/technology/facial-recognition-arrest.html

Holst, A. (2002, March 2). Big data market size revenue forecast worldwide from 2011 to 2027. Retrieved from https://www.statista.com/statistics/254266/global-big-data-market-forecast/#:~:text=The%20global%20big%20data%20market,data%20market%20segment%20by%202027.

Jamison, D. (2020, June 23). How Much is Our Personal Data Worth? Retrieved from https://gvwire.com/2020/06/23/how-much-is-our-personal-data-worth/

Kearns, M., & Roth, A. (2019, November 14). To Improve Algorithms, Embed Human Principles Into Code. Retrieved from https://medium.com/penn-engineering/to-improve-algorithms-embed-human-principles-into-code-25b01a0faf12

Kleinman, Z. (2018, March 21). Cambridge Analytica: The story so far. Retrieved from https://www.bbc.com/news/technology-43465968

MacCarthy, M. (2019). Fairness in Algorithmic Decisionmaking. Retrieved from https://www.brookings.edu/research/fairness-in-algorithmic-decision-making/

Metz, C. (2020, March 23). There is a Racial Divide in Speech-Recognition Systems, Researchers Say. Retrieved from https://www.nytimes.com/2020/03/23/technology/speech-recognition-bias-apple-amazon-google.html

Petersen, L., & Dinkins, S. (2020, January 16). What Atlanta Can Teach Tech About Cultivating Black Talent. Retrieved from https://www.wired.com/story/what-atlanta-can-teach-tech-about-cultivating-black-talent/

Panch, T., Mattie, H., & Atun, R. (2019, December 9). Artificial Intelligence and Algorithmic Bias: Implications for Health Systems. Retrieved from https://pubmed.ncbi.nlm.nih.gov/31788229

Popovich, N, Albeck-Ripka, L., & Pierre-Louis (2020, November 10). The Trump Administration Is Reversing More Than 100 Environmental Rules. Here's the Full List. Retrieved from https://www.nytimes.com/interactive/2020/climate/trump-environment-rollbacks-list.html

Praharji, K. (2020, June 27). Bias In AI Algorithms. Retrieved from https://towardsdatascience.com/how-are-algorithms-biased-8449406aaa83

Quach, K. (2020, April 13). Google Cloud's AI Recognition Code Biased Against Black People. Retrieved from https://www.theregister.com/2020/04/13/ai_roundup/

Shead, S. (2020, May 13). Elon Musk has a complex relationship with the A.I. community. Retrieved from https://www.cnbc.com/2020/05/13/elon-musk-has-a-complex-relationship-with-the-ai-community.html

Silberg, J. & Manyika, J., (2019). Tackling Bias in Artificial Intelligence (and in Humans). Retrieved from https://www.mckinsey.com/featured-insights/artificial-intelligence/tackling-bias-in-artificial-intelligence-and-in-humans

Teichmann, J. (2019, October 13). Bias and Algorithmic Fairness. Retrieved from httpo://towardsdatascience.com/bias-and-algorithmic-fairness-10f0805edc2b

Tellado, M. (2020, July 29). Biased Big Tech Algorithms Limit Our Lives and Choices. Stop the Online Discrimination. Retrieved from https://www.usatoday.com/story/opinion/2020/07/29/big-tech-abuses-consumers-stop-online-discrimination-column/5525703002/

Turner-Lee, N., Resnick, P., & Barton, G. (2019, May 22). Algorithmic Bias Detection and Mitigation: Best Practices and Policies to Reduce Consumer Harms. Retrieved from https://www.brookings.edu/research/algorithmic-bias-detection-and-mitigation-best-practices-and-policies-to-reduce-consumer-harms/

Yin, L., & Sankin, A. (2020, July 23). Bias Against Black Girls: Google Ad Portal Equated 'Black Girls' with Porn. Retrieved from https://themarkup.org/google-the-giant/2020/07/23/google-advertising-keywords-black-girls

Chapter Two: **Unfair Housing, Environmental Injustice, COVID-19, and Ethics**

Baradaran, M. (2017). *The Color of Money: Black Banks and the Racial Wealth Gap*. Harvard University Press.

Baurick, T. (2019, October 30). Welcome to "Cancer Alley," Where Toxic Air Is About to Get Worse. Retrieved from https://www.propublica.org/article/welcome-to-cancer-alley-where-toxic-air-is-about-to-get-worse#:~:text=Series%3A%20Polluter's%20Paradise-,Welcome%20to%20%E2%80%9CCancer%20Alley%2C%E2%80%9D%20Where%20Toxic%20Air%20Is%20About,predominantly%20black%20and%20poor%20communities

Berkovitz, C. (2010, May 19). Environmental Racism Has Left Black Communities Especially Vulnerable to COVID-19. Retrieved from https://tcf.org/content/commentary/environmental-racism-left-black-communities-especially-vulnerable-covid-19/?agreed=1

Bousquin, J. (2018, July 20). Socially Responsible Investing Accelerates in U.S. Multifamily Space. Retrieved from https://www.multifamilyexecutive.com/business-finance/socially-responsible-investing-accelerates-in-u-s-multifamily-space_o

Caffrey, M. (2017, August 8). Princeton Study: Being Black Doesn't Cause Asthma; the Neighborhood Does. Retrieved from https://www.ajmc.com/view/princeton-study-being-black-doesnt-cause-asthma-the-neighborhood-does

Ellen, I., Graves, E., & O'Regan et al. (2020, June 8). Strategies for increasing affordable housing amid the COVID-19 economic crisis. Retrieved from https://www.brookings.edu/research/strategies-for-increasing-affordable-housing-amid-the-covid-19-economic-crisis/

Federal Register. (2015, July 15). Affirmatively Furthering Fair Housing. Retrieved from https://www.federalregister.gov/documents/2015/07/16/2015-17032/affirmatively-furthering-fair-housing

Hanks, A., Solomon, D., & Weller, C. (2018, February 21). Systematic Inequality: How America's Structural Racism Helped Create the Black-White Wealth Gap. Retrieved from https://www.americanprogress.org/issues/race/reports/2018/02/21/447051/systematic-inequality/

Kapfidze, T. (2020, July 7). LendingTree Study: Black Homebuyers More Likely to Be Denied Mortgages Than Other Homebuyers. Retrieved from https://www.lendingtree.com/home/mortgage/lendingtree-study-black-homebuyers-more-likely-to-be-denied-mortgages-than-other-homebuyers/#:~:text=LendingTree%20Study%3A%20Black%20Homebuyers%20More,Denied%20Mortgages%20Than%20Other%20Homebuyers&text=For%20both%20purchase%20and%20refinance,the%20overall%20population%20of%20homebuyers.

Kim, T. (2016). Stuck in the Ghetto. Retrieved from https://www.thenation.com/article/archive/stuck-in-ghetto/

Kummer, F. (2020, September 18). N.J. Gov. Murphy signs environmental justice law designed to protect minority communities. Retrieved from https://www.inquirer.com/science/climate/new-jersey-governor-phil-murphy-environmental-justice-law-20200918.html

Lerner, M. (2020, August 3). The Washington Post: One Home, a Lifetime of Impact, featuring Andrew Fellows. Retrieved from https://ischool.umd.edu/news/washington-post-one-home-lifetime-impact-featuring-andrew-fellows

Manhertz, T. (2020, January 16). Recovery Riches: The U.S. Housing Market Gained $11 Trillion in Value in the 2010s. Retrieved from https://www.zillow.com/research/us-total-housing-value-2019-26369/

McKinsey & Co. (2020, May 8). Black Americans face disproportionate share of disruption from coronavirus. Retrieved from https://www.mckinsey.com/featured-insights/coronavirus-leading-through-the-crisis/charting-the-path-to-the-next-normal/black-americans-face-disproportionate-share-of-disruption-from-coronavirus

National Association of Realtors. (2018). A Snapshot of Race & Home Buying in America. Retrieved from https://www.nar.realtor/research-and-statistics/research-reports/a-snapshot-of-race-and-homebuying-in-america

Patronella, A., & Griffin, S. (2020, February 27). Communities of Color Bear the Brunt of Trump's Anti-Environmental Agenda. Retrieved from https://www.americanprogress.org/issues/green/news/2020/02/27/480820/communities-color-boar-brunt-trumps-anti-environmental-agenda/

Popovich, N., Albeck-Ripka, l., & Pierre-Louis, K. (2020, November 10). The Trump Administration Is Reversing More Than 100 Environmental Rules. Here's the Full List. Retrieved from https://www.nytimes.com/interactive/2020/climate/trump-environment-rollbacks-list.html

Rothstein, R. (2017). A 'Forgotten History' of How The U.S. Government Segregated America. Liverlight Publishing Corporation.

Science News. (2019, March 11). US Black and Hispanic minorities bear disproportionate burden from air pollution. Retrieved from https://www.sciencedaily.com/releases/2019/03/190311152735.htm

Solomon, D., Maxwell, C., & Castro, A. (2019, August 7). Systemic Inequality: Displacement, Exclusion, and Segregation: How America's Housing System Undermines Wealth Building in Communities of Color. Retrieved from https://www.americanprogress.org/issues/race/reports/2019/08/07/472617/systemic-inequality-displacement-exclusion-segregation/

Stanford Encyclopedia of Philosophy. (2017, September 13). W.E.B. Du Bois. Retrieved from https://plato.stanford.edu/entries/dubois/

U.S. Census Bureau. (2017). State and County Maps. Retrieved from https://www.census.gov/library/visualizations/2018/demo/2017-state-county-maps.html

U.S. Census Bureau. (2018). State and County Maps. Retrieved from https://www.census.gov/library/visualizations/2019/demo/2018-state-county-maps.html

University of Minnesota. (2019). US black and Hispanic minorities bear disproportionate burden from air pollution. Retrieved from https://twin-cities.umn.edu/news-events/black-and-hispanic-minorities-us-bear-disproportionate-burden-air-pollution

Wallace, E. (2020, January 16). Addressing Racial Inequality by Investigating Mortgage Denials. Retrieved from https://www.policymap.com/2020/01/addressing-racial-inequality-by-investigating-mortgage-denials/

Weber-Davis. (2015, October 19). How A 1900s Black Detroit Community Was Razed For A Freeway. Retrieved from https://wdet.org/posts/2015/10/19/81771-curiosid-how-a-1900s-black-detroit-community-was-razed-for-a-freeway/

Zephyrin, L., Radley, D., & Getachew, et al. (2020, April 23). COVID-19 More Prevalent, Deadlier in U.S. Counties with Higher Black Populations. Retrieved from https://www.commonwealthfund.org/blog/2020/covid-19-more-prevalent-deadlier-us-counties-higher-black-populations

Chapter Three: **Policing and Ethics**

Aufrichtig, A., Beckett, L., & Lartey, J. (2017, January 9). Want to fix gun violence in America? Go local. Retrieved from https://www.theguardian.com/us-news/ng-interactive/2017/jan/09/special-report-fixing-gun-violence-in-america

Brune, T. (2020, June 22). What does qualified immunity for police officers mean? Retrieved from https://www.newsday.com/news/nation/qualified-immunity-congress-police-floyd-1.45899746#:~:text=The%20doctrine%2C%20called%20qualified%20immunity,bar%20for%20plaintiffs%20to%20overcome.

Cornell University's Legal Information Institute. Qualified Immunity. Retrieved from https://www.law.cornell.edu/wex/qualified_immunity#:~:text=Qualified%20immunity%20is%20a%20type%20of%20legal%20immunity.&text=Specifically%2C%20qualified%20immunity%20protects%20a,established%E2%80%9D%20statutory%20or%20constitutional%20right.

Desilver, D., Lipka, M., & Fahmy, D. (2020, June 3). 10 things we know about race and policing. Retrieved from https://www.pewresearch.org/fact-tank/2020/06/03/10-things-we-know-about-race-and-policing-in-the-u-s/

Haberman, M. (2020, September 4). Trump Moves to Cancel Contracts for Government Sensitivity Training. Retrieved from https://www.nytimes.com/2020/09/04/us/politics/trump-race-sensitivity-training.html

Le Claire, M. (2016, October 19) The Use Of The Term "Superpredator": History And Application. Retrieved from https://www.huffpost.com/entry/the-use-of-the-term-super_b_12526462

Los Angeles Times (Editorial Board). (2020, June 4). A Very Abbreviated History of Police Officers Killing Black People. Retrieved from https://www.latimes.com/opinion/story/2020-06-04/police-killings-black-victims

Miller, B. (2019, May 24). The Militarization of America's Police: A Brief History. Retrieved from https://fee.org/articles/the-militarization-of-americas-police-a-brief-history/

National Institute of Justice. (2009, August 3). The Use-of-Force Continuum. Retrieved from https://nij.ojp.gov/topics/articles/use-force-continuum

Pumphrey, J. (2016). Turning Ethical Theory into Practice in Policing. (URL no longer available).

Ray, R. (2020, August 25). How can we enhance police accountability in the United States? Retrieved from https://www.brookings.edu/policy2020/votervital/how-can-we-enhance-police-accountability-in-the-united-states/

Reamer, F. G. (2017). Teaching Ethics in the Training Academy: A State-of-the-Art Approach. Retrieved from https://www.policechiefmagazine.org/teaching-ethics-in-the-training-academy/

Rodriguez, A. (2020, September 10). Lower Courts Agree — It's Time to End Qualified Immunity. Retrieved from https://www.aclu.org/news/criminal-law-reform/lower-courts-agree-its-time-to-end-qualified-immunity/

Sibilla, N. (2020, June 11). Court Rejects Qualified Immunity For Cops Who Shot A "Motionless" Black Man 22 Times. Retrieved from https://www.forbes.com/sites/nicksibilla/2020/06/11/court-rejects-qualified-immunity-for-cops-who-shot-a-motionless-black-man-22-times/?sh=3fd446139d29

White House. (2002, September 22). Executive Order on Combating Race and Sex Stereotyping. Retrieved from https://www.whitehouse.gov/presidential-actions/executive-order-combating-race-sex-stereotyping/

Chapter Four: Switching the Light On: The Ethical Example of the Harlem Children's Zone® (HCZ®)

Boyd-Pates, T., & Canada, G. (2020, August 20). Tyree Boyd-Pates In Conversation With Geoffrey Canada: 'America's Future Is Predicated on Knowing the Full History. Retrieved from https://time.com/5880936/rethinking-education-race/

Fagan, J., West, V., & Holland, J. (2004). *Neighborhood, Crime, and Incarceration in New York City*. Colombia Law School, 36 COLUM. HUM. RTS. L. REV. 71

Harlem Children's Zone. https:///www.hcz.org

Harlem Children's Zone. (2014). Whatever It Takes: A White Paper on the Harlem Children's Zone. Retrieved from https://www.sccgov.org/sites/bhd/AboutUs/MHSA/PEI/Documents/Harlem-Children%27s-Zone.pdf

Mabli, J., Bleeker, M., & Fox, M.K. (2017, September 1). *The Impact of Healthy Harlem on the Prevalence of Child Overweight and Obesity and Contributing Factors: Final Report*. Mathematica Policy Research.

Mustain, G. (2017, August 14). When the crack scourge swept New York City. Retrieved from https://www.nydailynews.com/new-york/crack-scourge-swept-new-york-city-article-1.813844

National Advisory Commission on Civil Disorders. (1967). Retrieved from https://www.history.com/this-day-in-history/kerner-commission-report-released

Shipp, E. (1991, July 31). Harlem Battles Over Development Project. Retrieved from https://www.nytimes.com/1991/07/31/nyregion/harlem-battles-over-development-project.html

U.S. General Accountability Office. (2014, May 5). *Education Grants Promise Neighborhoods Promotes Collaboration but Needs National Evaluation Plan.* Retrieved from https://www.gao.gov/products/GAO-14-432

Chapter Five: **Ethical Environmental, SOCIAL, and Governance (ESG) Investing**

Armstrong, R. (2019, December 29). Warren Buffett on why companies cannot be moral arbiters. Retrieved from https://www.ft.com/content/ebbc9b46-1754-11ea-9ee4-11f260415385

CFA Institute. (2019, January 10). Positions on Environmental, Social, and Governance Integration. Retrieved from https://www.cfainstitute.org/en/advocacy/policy-positions/positions-on-environmental-social-governance-integration

CFA Institute. (2015, October). Environmental, Social, and Governance Issues in Investing: A Guide for Investment Professionals. Retrieved from https://www.cfainstitute.org/en/advocacy/policy-positions/environmental-social-and-governance-issues-in-investing-a-guide-for-investment-professionals

Chen, J. (2020, September 8). Morningstar Sustainability Rating. Retrieved from https://www.investopedia.com/terms/m/morningstar-sustainability-rating.asp

Coleman, J. S. (1988). Social Capital in the Creation of Human Capital. *The American Journal of Sociology* (94), S95-S120

Eaves, P. (2020, September 15). Diversity Push Barely Budges Corporate Boards to 12.5%, Survey Finds. Retrieved from https://www.nytimes.com/2020/09/15/business/economy/corporate-boards-black-hispanic-directors.html

Fleischmann, A. (2020, June 11). Turning 'ESG' into 'ESGD': How investors can support diversity with their dollars. Retrieved from https://fortune.com/2020/06/11/diversity-inclusion-investing-esg-esgd/

Gelles, D. (2018, February 19). The C.E.O. Who Stood Up to President Trump: Ken Frazier Speaks Out. Retrieved from https://www.nytimes.com/2018/02/19/business/merck-ceo-ken-frazier-trump.html

Gelles, D. (2018, March 9). Merck C.E.O. Ken Frazier on Death Row Cases and the Corporate Soul. Retrieved from https://www.nytimes.com/2018/03/09/business/merck-ceo-ken-frazier-on-death-row-cases-and-the-corporate-soul.html

Hale, J. (2020, March 30). The Number of Funds Considering ESG Explodes in 2019. Retrieved from https://www.morningstar.com/articles/973432/the-number-of-funds-considering-esg-explodes-in-2019

Harvard Law School. (2020, January 18). 2020 Global and Regional Corporate Governance Trends. Retrieved from https://corpgov.law.harvard. edu/2020/01/18/2020-global-and-regional-corporate-governance-trends/

Henderson, T. (2019, December 19). Poverty Grew in One-Third of Counties Despite Strong National Economy. Retrieved from https://www. pewtrusts.org/en/research-and-analysis/blogs/stateline/2019/12/19/ poverty-grew-in-one-third-of-counties-despite-strong-national- economy#:~:text=Poverty%20Grew%20in%20One-Third%20of%20 Counties%20Despite%20Strong%20National%20Economy,-Stateline%20 Article%20December&text=Despite%20an%20economic%20recovery%20 that,state%20between%202016%20and%202018.

Kenton, W. (2020, August 17). Ethical Investing. Retrieved from https://www. investopedia.com/terms/e/ethical-investing.asp

Kochhar, R. (2020, June 11). Unemployment rose higher in three months of COVID-19 than it did in two years of the Great Recession. Retrieved from https://www.pewresearch.org/fact-tank/2020/06/11/unemployment-rose- higher-in-three-months-of-covid-19-than-it-did-in-two-years-of-the-great- recession/

Hecker, J., & Dubourg. (2020, July 1). Why COVID-19 Could Prove to Be a Major Turning Point for ESG Investing. Retrieved from https://www.jpmorgan.com/ insights/research/covid-19-esg-investing

Lefkovitz, D. (2020, July 20). ESG at a Tipping Point. Retrieved from https://blogs. cfainstitute.org/investor/2020/07/20/esg-at-a-tipping-point/

Morath, E., Francis, T., & Baer, J. (2020, October 5). The Covid Economy Carves Deep Divide Between Haves and Have-Nots. Retrieved from https://www. wsj.com/articles/the-covid-economy-carves-deep-divide-between-haves- and-have-nots-11601910595

Reynolds, F. (2020, October 10). Big investors, we can't fight poverty or protect the planet without you. Retrieved from https://fortune.com/2020/07/10/ investing-esg-sustainable-development/

Woods, H. (2020, October 30). How billionaires saw their net worth increase by half a trillion dollars during the pandemic. Retrieved from https:// www.businessinsider.com/billionaires-net-worth-increases-coronavirus- pandemic-2020-7

Chapter Six: **Imperiled Black-Owned Businesses, COVID-19, and Ethics**

Asare., J.G. (2020, March 22). 13 Entrepreneurs Of Color Share How COVID-19 Has Impacted Their Business. Retrieved from https://www.forbes.com/sites/ janicegassam/2020/03/22/13-entrepreneurs-of-color-share-how-covid-19- has-impacted-their-business/?sh=5b33009272dd

Association for Enterprise Opportunity. (2020). Data is Essential to Understanding the Impact of Opportunity Zones. Retrieved from https://aeoworks.org/data-is-essential-to-understanding-the-impact-of-opportunity-zones/

Berkon, A. (2020, April 27). After Six Decades, Ben's Chili Bowl Faces Its Greatest Challenge Yet: Coronavirus. Retrieved from https://wamu.org/story/20/04/27/after-six-decades-bens-chili-bowl-faces-its-greatest-challenge-yet-coronavirus/

Brooks, R. (2020, July 17). More than half of Black-owned businesses may not survive COVID-19. Retrieved from https://www.nationalgeographic.com/history/2020/07/black-owned-businesses-may-not-survive-covid-19/

Brown, D. (2020, July 16). Apple expands coding partnership with Black schools as tech firms grapple with lack of diversity. Retrieved from https://www.usatoday.com/story/tech/2020/07/16/apple-expands-hbcu-partnership-tech-grapples-lack-diversity/5449823002/

Economy League. (2020, July 29). The Impact of COVID-19 on Greater Philadelphia's Black-Owned Businesses. Retrieved from http://economyleague.org/providing-insight/leadingindicators/2020/07/29/covid19blackbusinesses

Federal Reserve Bank of New York. (2020, August 20). Double Jeopardy: COVID-19's Concentrated Health and Wealth Effects in Black Communities. Retrieved from https://www.newyorkfed.org/medialibrary/media/smallbusiness/DoubleJeopardy_COVID19andBlackOwnedBusinesses

Florant, A., & Noel, N. (2020, April 18). COVID-19: Investing in Black Lives and Livelihoods. Retrieved from https://www.mckinsey.com/industries/public-and-social-sector/our-insights/covid-19-investing-in-black-lives-and-livelihoods

Mitchell, B., & Silver, J. (2020, January 14). Adding Underserved Census Tracts As Criterion On CRA Exams. Retrieved from https://ncrc.org/adding-underserved-census-tracts-as-criterion-on-cra-exams/

O'Brien, T. L. (2020, June 15). PPP Isn't Enough for Black-Owned Businesses. Retrieved from https://www.bloomberg.com/opinion/articles/2020-06-15/coronavirus-ppp-isn-t-enough-for-black-owned-businesses

Perry, A. (2020, February 19). Five-star reviews, one-star profits: The devaluation of businesses in Black communities. Retrieved from https://www.brookings.edu/events/five-star-reviews-one-star-profits-the-devaluation-of-businesses-in-black-communities/#:~:text=The%20report%2C%20titled%20%E2%80%9CFive%2D,businesses%20in%20otherwise%20similar%20neighborhoods.

Pew Trusts. (2019). State of the City: Philadelphia Research and Policy Initiative. Retrieved from https://www.pewtrusts.org/en/projects/philadelphia-research-and-policy-initiative/state-of-the-city

Rothstein, R. (2014, November 12). Race and Social Problems. Retrieved from http://www.americanbar.org/publications/

Schermerhorn, C. (2019, June 19). Why the racial wealth gap persists, more than 150 years after emancipation. Retrieved from https://www.washingtonpost.com/outlook/2019/06/19/why-racial-wealth-gap-persists-more-than-years-after-emancipation/

Stephan, D. (2020, February 10). 25 Black Entrepreneurs Making Waves. Retrieved from https://about.crunchbase.com/blog/25-black-entrepreneurs-making-waves/

Turner, M.A., & Greene, S. (2020, June 19). Reimagining an Antiracist America—Starting with Our Neighborhoods. Retrieved from https://www.urban.org/urban-wire/reimagining-antiracist-america-starting-our-neighborhoods

U.S. Census Bureau. Annual Business Survey (2018). Retrieved from https://www.census.gov/programs-surveys/abs.html?

U.S. Bureau of Labor Statistics. (2019, July). Supplemental data measuring the effects of the coronavirus (COVID-19) pandemic on the labor market. Retrieved from https://www.bls.gov/cps/effects-of-the-coronavirus-covid-19-pandemic.htm

U.S. Bureau of Labor Statistics. (2019, October). Labor force characteristics by race and ethnicity, 2018. Retrieved from https://www.bls.gov/opub/reports/race-and-ethnicity/2018/home.htm#:~:text=The%20employment%E2%80%93population%20ratio%20was,and%2063.2%20percent%20for%20Hispanics.

Chapter Seven: **The Ethics of Empowering and Protecting Women in the Time of COVID-19**

Board of Governors of the Federal Reserve System. (2020, June 19). Introductory Remarks, Chair Jerome Powell. Retrieved from https://www.federalreserve.gov/newsevents/speech/powell20200619a.htm

Carter, C.M. (2020, May 19). New Research Shows How The Coronavirus Recession Is Disproportionately Affecting Black Working Mothers. Retrieved from https://www.forbes.com/sites/christinecarter/2020/05/19/new-research-shows-how-the-coronavirus-recession-is-disproportionately-affecting-black-working-mothers/?sh=3e68489c1a5f

Edwards, K.A. (2020, July 15). The Racial Disparity in Unemployment Benefits. Retrieved from https://www.rand.org/blog/2020/07/the-racial-disparity-in-unemployment-benefits.html#:~:text=Previous%20(%20PDF%20)%20 research%20(%20PDF,an%20accident%20of%20modern%20policymaking.

Ford, T., Reber, S., & Reeves, R. (2020, June 16). Race gaps in COVID-19 deaths are even bigger than they appear. Retrieved from https://www.brookings. edu/blog/up-front/2020/06/16/race-gaps-in-covid-19-deaths-are-even-bigger-than-they-appear/

Frye, J. (2020, April 23). On the Frontlines at Work and at Home: The Disproportionate Economic Effects of the Coronavirus Pandemic on Women of Color. Retrieved from https://www.americanprogress.org/issues/women/ reports/2020/04/23/483846/frontlines-work-home/#:~:text=And%20a%20 separate%20household%20survey,options%20to%20make%20ends%20 meet.

Gaylord-Harden, N., Adams-Bass, V., & Bogan, E. (2020, September 9). Addressing Inequities in Education: Considerations for Black Children and Youth in the Era of COVID-19. Retrieved from https://www.srcd.org/ research/addressing-inequities-education-considerations-black-children-and-youth-era-covid-19

Glynn, S.J. (2019, May 10). Breadwinning Mothers Continue To Be the U.S. Norm. Retrieved from https://www.americanprogress.org/issues/women/ reports/2019/05/10/469739/breadwinning-mothers-continue-u-s-norm/

Gould, E., & Wilson, V. (2020, June 1). Black workers face two of the most lethal preexisting conditions for coronavirus—racism and economic inequality. Retrieved from https://www.epi.org/publication/black-workers-covid/

Green, S. (2017, 13). Violence Against Black Women – Many Types, Far-reaching Effects. Retrieved from https://iwpr.org/iwpr-issues/race-ethnicity-gender-and-economy/violence-against-black-women-many-types-far-reaching-effects/

Habersham, R. (2020, September 4). How Black parents juggle their work and kids' virtual schooling during the pandemic. Retrieved from https://www. poynter.org/ethics-trust/2020/how-black-parents-juggle-their-work-and-kids-virtual-schooling-during-the-pandemic/

Madgavkar, A., White, O., Krishnan, M., & Mahajan, D. (2020, July 15). COVID-19 and gender equality: Countering the regressive effects. Retrieved from https://www.mckinsey.com/featured-insights/future-of-work/covid-19-and-gender-equality-countering-the-regressive-effects

Thee Stallion, M. (2020, October 13). Megan Thee Stallion: Why I Speak Up for Black Women. Retrieved from https://www.nytimes.com/2020/10/13/ opinion/megan-thee-stallion-black-women.html

Morris, L. (2020, July 24). A wave of mass evictions is inevitable, and Black women will be hit the hardest. Retrieved from https://thehill.com/blogs/congress-blog/politics/508897-a-wave-of-mass-evictions-is-inevitable-and-black-women-will-be

NAACP. Coronavirus Impact On Students and Education Systems. Retrieved from https://www.naacp.org/coronavirus/coronavirus-impact-on-students-and-education-systems/

Opoku-Agyeman, A.N. (2020, June 25). Why putting Black women first may save us from economic disaster. Retrieved from https://www.epi.org/blog/black-women-best-why-putting-black-women-first-may-save-us-from-economic-disaster/

U.S. Census. (2016, February 26). Women Are Leading the Rise of Black-Owned Businesses. Retrieved from https://www.census.gov/newsroom/blogs/random-samplings/2016/02/women-are-leading-the-rise-of-black-owned-businesses.html

Van Dam, A., & Long, H. (2020, October 2). Moms, Black Americans and Educators Are in Trouble As Economic Recovery Slows. Retrieved from https://www.washingtonpost.com/business/2020/10/02/september-jobs-inequality/

Volkov, M. (2019, February 12). The Urgency of Now: Corporate Ethics and the #MeToo Movement. Retrieved from https://www.jdsupra.com/legalnews/the-urgency-of-now-corporate-ethics-and-29599/

Wallace, A. (2020, June 23). As a young Black woman, there is no such thing as 'generational wealth' — I am my family's safety net. Retrieved from https://www.businessinsider.com/personal-finance/young-black-woman-my-money-is-familys-safety-net-2020-6

Williams, J. (2020, September 29). Laid Off More, Hired Less: Black Workers in the COVID-19 Recession. Retrieved from https://www.rand.org/blog/2020/09/laid-off-more-hired-less-black-workers-in-the-covid.html

Chapter Eight: **Ethics, Compliance, and Accountability**

ACFE. (2018). Report to the Nations: 2018 Global Study On Occupational Fraud and Abuse. Retrieved from https://www.acfe.com/report-to-the-nations/2018/default.aspx

Adams, M. (2018, April 11). The Unfulfilled Promise of Fair Housing. Retrieved from https://www.newyorker.com/news/news-desk/the-unfulfilled-promise-of-the-fair-housing-act

Chen, H., & Soltes, E. (2018, March-April). Why Compliance Programs Fail—and How to Fix Them. Retrieved from https://hbr.org/2018/03/why-compliance-programs-fail

Huang, C., Raeburn, A., & Midden, K. (2019, October 14). Opinion: The Mercy Corps scandal has rocked the aid sector – again. What now? Retrieved from https://www.oregonlive.com/opinion/2019/10/opinion-the-mercy-corps-scandal-has-rocked-the-aid-sector-again-what-now.html

JP Morgan. (2020). Code of Conduct. Retrieved from https://www.jpmorganchase.com/about/governance/code-of-conduct

Kellogg Insight. (2020, March 6). Is Your Company's Code of Conduct Encouraging Misconduct? Retrieved from https://www.industryweek.com/leadership/article/21125565/is-your-companys-code-of-conduct-encouraging-misconduct

Kelly, M. (2020, January 22). The New Urgency for ESG Risk Management. Retrieved from https://www.navexglobal.com/blog/article/the-new-urgency-for-esg-risk-management/

Moss, E., & Metcalf, J. (2019, November 14). The Ethical Dilemma at the Heart of Big Tech Companies. Retrieved from https://hbr.org/2019/11/the-ethical-dilemma-at-the-heart-of-big-tech-companies

Mukherjee, A. (2016, December 28). Why We're Seeing So Many Corporate Scandals. Retrieved from https://hbr.org/2016/12/why-were-seeing-so-many-corporate-scandals

Noordyke, M. (2019). Big Tech's Shift to Privacy. Retrieved from https://iapp.org/resources/article/big-techs-shift-to-privacy-2/#:~:text=Big%20Tech's%20Shift%20to%20Privacy&text=Understand%20Europe's%20framework%20of%20laws,policies%2C%20most%20significantly%20the%20GDPR.&text=Steer%20a%20course%20through%20the,laws%20governing%20U.S.%20data%20privacy.&text=Develop%20the%20skills%20to%20design,a%20comprehensive%20data%20protection%20program.

Shaub, W.M. (2020, February 7). Trump's Quest for Revenge Could Mean the End of Whistleblowing. Retrieved from https://www.washingtonpost.com/outlook/trumps-quest-for-revenge-could-mean-the-end-of-whistleblowing/2020/02/07/a576b860-4918-11ea-9164-d3154ad8a5cd_story.html

Snyder, D. (2020, January 6). Federal Contract Spending: Five Trends in Five Charts. Retrieved from https://about.bgov.com/news/federal-contract-spending-five-trends-in-five-charts/

Swedroe, L. (2020, August 31). New Challenges to the Merits of ESG Investing. Retrieved from https://www.advisorperspectives.com/articles/2020/08/31/new-challenges-to-the-merits-of-esg-investing

Swisher, K. (2018, October 21). Who Will Teach Silicon Valley to Be Ethical? Retrieved from https://www.nytimes.com/2018/10/21/opinion/who-will-teach-silicon-valley-to-be-ethical.html

U.S. Department of Justice. (1988). *Police Accountability and Community Policing.* Retrieved from https://www.ncjrs.gov/pdffiles1/nij/114211.pdf

U.S. General Accountability Office. (2019). Performance and Accountability Report Fiscal Year 2019. (*GAO-20-ISP*). Retrieved from https://www.gao.gov/products/GAO-20-1SP

U.S. Office of Government Ethics. (2019, January 1). Compilation of Federal Ethics Laws. Retrieved from https://www.oge.gov/Web/oge.nsf/Resources/Compilation+of+Federal+Ethics+Laws

Venture Catalyst. (2019, January 5). Incorporating Ethics in Silicon Valley and in Startups (Part 1 of 2). Retrieved from http://www.venturecatalyst.nyc/blog/2019/1/5/incorporating-ethics-in-silicon-valley-and-in-startups-part-1-of-2

Yakobovitch, D. (2020, September 26). Diversifying Recruitment methods in Tech Companies to reduce AI bias Recruitment Trends and Bias. Retrieved from https://medium.com/towards-artificial-intelligence/diversifying-recruitment-methods-in-tech-companies-to-reduce-ai-bias-1785e7fc350d

Made in the USA
Middletown, DE
12 February 2021